PHENOMENOLOGY IN AMERICA

PHENOMENOLOGY

STUDIES IN THE

EDITED WITH AN INTRODUCTION BY

Chicago

IN AMERICA

PHILOSOPHY OF EXPERIENCE

James M. Edie

Quadrangle Books 1967

CONTENTS

INTRODUCTION

There is good reason to believe that in future surveys or histories of twentieth-century American philosophy the 1960's will be recognized as the period when the phenomenological movement finally took root in our philosophical soil and became an active and creative force in its own right. For the first time we are beginning to have available to us in reliable English translations the major works of European phenomenologists—though much more work, particularly on the texts of Husserl and Heidegger, remains to be done. More importantly, phenomenology in this country is passing from the stage of repetition, commentary, and critical analysis of what has been achieved in Europe to the stage of producing new kinds and genres of phenomenological investigations of a surprising originality and variety. Since most of these studies are being undertaken by younger philosophers who came to maturity during or after the Second World War, it is still too early to assess the fecundating and transformative effect they may eventually have in American philosophy. Philosophy, unlike mathematics and music, has never produced "child prodigies," and the very serious difficulties—the psychological, academic, and cultural obstacles that divide contemporary "continentals" from "Anglo-Saxons"—which have retarded the "domestication" of German and French phenomenology in our intellectual climate, have likewise delayed the production of American contributions to this style of thought.

The essays in this book represent some of the best and most recent work undertaken under the aegis of phenomenology in this country. They are the most important of the studies presented at the last three annual meetings of the Society for Phenomenology and Existential Philosophy,[1] and form a worthy sequel to the first volume of such studies published in 1965 under the title *An Invitation to Phenomenology*. Nearly all of these essays have been revised and sometimes extensively rewritten for this volume (and thus are not simply a record of the proceedings of the society), and many of them are serving as the basis for books to appear in the future. While they do not and cannot give a completely comprehensive and systematic picture of a unified phenomenological philosophy making statements on and contributions to every single branch of philosophy, symmetrically arranged, they do give us a good picture and a partial map of the area covered by contemporary American "phenomenologists."

It is well to keep this title, "phenomenologist," in quotation marks. Many of the contributors to this book would hesitate to apply it to themselves in any form, and none would do so without qualification. There is, in this book, almost no phenomenological flag-waving, almost no trace of any desire to show how these studies are based on earlier European sources. There is rather the obvious intent to get on with the work, to come to grips with the universal philosophical issues, and to test the phenomenological approach by attempting to see what it comes to in concrete research. There is an unspoken but clearly evident aban-

---

1. The third, fourth, and fifth annual meetings of the Society for Phenomenology and Existential Philosophy were held at Yale University, October 22-24, 1964, at the University of Wisconsin, October 28-30, 1965, and at the Pennsylvania State University, October 20-22, 1966, respectively.

donment of the intricacies of technical jargon when this is not specifically helpful or necessary to the argument. Many of these papers are concerned with what Husserl and Schutz would have termed the "phenomenology of the natural attitude," the study of intra-mundane structures of experience without explicit reference to transcendental constituting consciousness. The transcendental dimension is certainly not denied, but I think it would be fair to say that it is bracketed and rendered somewhat implicit in these essays, which center more on working out the broader implications of a descriptive and phenomenological approach to the data and problems of philosophy than in defending its methodological purity.

This is not, therefore, a systematic treatise on phenomenology as a whole. It is a book which selects and traces certain salient themes—perhaps the most living and vital incursions of phenomenology into contemporary American thought. As editor of this collection, I have had to arrange the papers in some order and divide them into categories which, without doing violence to the intent of the authors, would at the same time make their work more easily approachable by the interested reader. I have no desire or intent in this introduction to speak in the name of the authors; this they do very well for themselves. Nor do I conceive my task as editor to be that of parading the individual contributions before the reader in critical review; it would be a most ungrateful editor who would use his position to mete out praise or blame, with particular judgments on the intentions and accomplishments of the several contributors. I shall not, finally, attempt to summarize the content of each paper or comment in detail on each, nor force them into some systematic framework or a series of dialectical oppositions which the authors could not have anticipated or intended.

The following introductory remarks thus do not pretend to be complete or in any way exhaustive of the rich variety of the papers which follow. I may sometimes refer to aspects of an author's work which are not necessarily the only or even the most central concerns he may have had in writing it. I have arranged the papers to illustrate *some of the current tasks and problems of phenomenological research* in the light of their philosophical importance in contemporary philosophy. My introduction is limited, therefore, to calling to the attention of the interested reader a few of the "grander" themes with which these papers deal, and thus of initiating the reader somewhat into the more general problematic which underlies them.

I

The studies in Part One, though frequently directed to specific concerns, clearly pose methodological, historical, even ontological problems of very wide scope; those in Part Two are more closely focused on epistemological, anthropological, and ethical problems which nevertheless touch on almost every aspect of value theory, including aesthetics and the philosophy of religion.

Thinking and the Emergence of Sense

Taking them in a perspective unintended by their authors, the first two papers, by Hubert Dreyfus and Zygmunt Adamczewski, present a complementary argument. In opening his paper with the observation that phenomenologists have up to now held aloof from the controversies over thinking machines which have begun to assume a large place in meetings of the American Philosophical Association and similar bodies, Dreyfus touches on one of the elusive, unexamined, but extremely important philosophical factors that continue to distinguish the intellectual climate of Western Europe from that of England and America. The disciples of Heidegger take it as nearly axiomatic that the algebraizing of thought accomplished in modern symbolic logic is not only symptomatic of the totalitarianism of modern technology and technological methods (even in the realm of the "sciences of the spirit") but that it is the very root and cause of the breakdown of modern philosophy. They trace the hold which this "technique" has progressively gained on the Western mind from the time of Plato and Aristotle through Descartes and Kant up to the "nihilism" of Nietzsche and the subsequent disappearance of all truly philosophical thought in technology. Because Heideggerian thought is wholly turned toward overcoming the identification of thought with the techniques of formal logic, and because it culminates in an extremely negative critique of "technological consciousness" in general, it clearly does not provide a climate in which thinking machines (not to mention "time machines") are taken with much seriousness. To Heideggerian philosophers, the suggestion that machines "think" is either a gross category mistake or, at the very least, in the language of the scholastics, an analogy of improper proportion.

In our own environment, however, no such inhibition exists, and British and American philosophers generally are willing to treat any range of robots and "mechanical brains" as exhibiting the behaviors of genuine thought, behaviors which presumably would fulfill the scholastic requirements of an analogy of proper proportion between what we call thinking in a human sense and what is called thinking in a mechanical sense. This is, therefore, in itself, a good phenomenological problem, and phenomenologists have been dilatory in inquiring, from their own perspective, whether or not and, if so, how and to what extent such an analogy may mask a profound conceptual confusion.

Dreyfus is the first American philosopher to attempt a full-fledged examination of the claims of artificial intelligence from a phenomenological point of view. The results published here are only a small part of a larger study. There would be many ways of characterizing his arguments, but we would not be wrong if we were to see in at least some of his reflections the influence of Merleau-Ponty, the "philosopher of ambiguity" and the author of *Sense and Non-Sense*.[2] Digital computers are, Drey-

2. Dreyfus himself translated and introduced this work to the American philosophical public (Northwestern University Press, 1964).

fus argues, utterly intolerant of "ambiguity"; they are necessarily and in principle completely devoid of the horizonal consciousness which is the very definition of human awareness, whether subconscious or fully conscious. They are, in a way, models of what human consciousness would be if it were *nothing but* a series of processes of completely formalized logical thought operating on completely determined and discrete bits of information. But any phenomenology of human thought must recognize as its most essential characteristic the ability of consciousness to see and organize meanings (and relationships) in a field of ambiguity, to live in what does "not yet have sense," and to assist at the emergence of sense from non-sense, by "zeroing in," as Dreyfus expresses it, on those elements of a given and ambiguous field of awareness which, in terms of its present interest, enable consciousness to restructure that given field in a newly meaningful way.

Husserl established, in his phenomenology of perception, the essentially perspectival character of the perception of material objects and, on this basis, distinguished perceiving from such other modes of consciousness as imagining, thinking, feeling, etc. But he showed not nearly so well that thinking itself is "perspectival" in its own distinctive way, and it is on this aspect of thinking which Dreyfus and Zygmunt Adamczewski concentrate in these essays. Either thinking is "information processing in terms of the searching for and combining of determinate bits of information" (associationism), or it involves a "horizonal" awareness whose structures precede and condition such "processing." Such non-associationist structures of consciousness become particularly evident when we focus our attention on the understanding of language and linguistic contexts. Such contexts include, but are not limited to, sub-understood and pre-understood linguistic "rules" which remain unformulated both in the ordinary human learning of a natural language and in its ordinary use. Since digital computers cannot "get the sense" or style of any language whose grammatical and syntactical rules are not completely and exhaustively formulated for it beforehand, it is extremely doubtful that such machines will ever be able to learn or speak any natural language (even if we leave aside the subjective experience of meaning, which is, no doubt, a constitutive element of understanding and thought). In his paper Dreyfus concentrates on this restricted sense of "context" to argue that a complete disambiguation of the contexts of linguistic behaviors is impossible *in principle*.

Adamczewski takes the context of language in a larger sense and turns to the behavioral and existential "background" from which meaning originates. For the expression of meaning is not limited to linguistic utterances but is to be found in more fundamental and inchoate experiences, such as the moods, affections, sentiments, and levels of experience which former, rationalistic philosophy had uncritically consigned to the realm of the "irrational." When we see that the "perspectives"—through which meanings are formulated in language, and thus are "thought"—ultimately extend to the whole concrete, historical experience of human existence in the world, we realize ever more clearly that such human perspectives cannot be completely described, "not only because there are too many but because others are always latent." It becomes more and more evident as we proceed from "the most precise and refined keys" of language to the "master keys," writes Adamczewski, from the fully explicit univocal terms which "open but one door," to such "gloriously vague" terms as "God," "act," "know," "right," "home," that words function in many free contexts whose rules cannot be fully fixed or foreseen beforehand. Adamczewski suggests that the most vague and englobing of all terms, "being," is not for that reason the least but perhaps the most meaningful of all, since it expresses our experience of the ground of all meaning.

At any rate, it is evident that human thought is able and is constrained to think the world through categories whose contextual morphology can never be rendered fully explicit. Such words do not cause us the same embarrassments they cause machines; we easily and almost effortlessly operate in natural language in realms of meaningful vagueness. Heidegger has said that *the* characteristic feature of human consciousness is that it is characterized by a primordial understanding of being (*Seinsverständnis*), of an ultimate context in terms of which all else makes sense. This primordial context of all human thought and the subsequent necessity for man to think "perspectively," in terms of meanings which emerge from a ground of sub-understood relationships, seems to indicate that the primary and most generic categories of human thought are not to be derived as progressive degenerations from an original distinctness and clarity, but that it is the other way around, that we proceed from the universal to the particular, from the vague and abstract to the concrete, and that the understanding of "being" is the precondition for the emergence of any particular sense.

The Challenge of Existentialism

One of the embarrassments of contemporary phenomenology is that it is inextricably bound up with the much broader cultural movement called "existentialism." This historical fact has introduced a certain drama into the existence of such organizations as the Society for Phenomenology and Existential Philosophy in this country, and the shades of opinion on the proper interrelationships which obtain or ought to obtain, whether *de facto* or *de jure,* between phenomenology and existentialism are enormously varied. On one extreme there are those who would claim that phenomenology is a rigorous philosophical method, utterly independent of existentialism, to which existentialism owes *per accidens* whatever genuine "philosophy" it may contain, and which ought to preserve its purity by avoiding the contamination of any "existentialist" ontology at all. At the opposite extreme there are, suitably, those who see phenomenology as a necessary first step, a methodological propaedeutic to existential philosophy, but who would consider any phenomenology which did not

develop into an existential ontology (of concrete, personal existence) as abortive. There are, of course, variations on these extreme positions and any number of intermediate compromises.
The question is complicated by the undeniable historical convergence of these two movements and by their concrete co-
existence in the thought of such major philosophers as Heidegger,
Scheler, Sartre, Merleau-Ponty.

No doubt most philosophers would agree, however, that the
mere description of this historical convergence, whether accidental or not, is not a sufficient answer to the problem. In his
essay entitled "Ontological Autobiography," William Earle poses
the question *de jure* and in so doing takes an extremist position
from the side of existentialism. He recognizes the "freshness" and
validity of Husserl's phenomenological method understood in its
most radical and transcendental sense, in its aspect of "strict
science," but he argues that this very perspective necessarily
leaves aside "existence," historical and contingent "human life,"
as a phenomenologically irreducible residue. The search for the
essential and the necessary, the "eidetic" meaning-structures of
experience, necessarily brackets all that is "autobiographical"
in experience.

Many phenomenologists would readily grant this much of
Earle's contention.They would agree that experience is not the
science or the philosophy of that experience. But they would not
grant that any analysis of the necessary structures of human experience must be directed only or even primarily to one's own
experience, or that such an analysis radically and irredeemably
betrays the thinker's own existence. But ontology in the existentialist sense, writes Earle, aims at what is "ontologically richest,"
namely at the fleeting, singular, free, perishable, individual consciousness itself. In this sense ontology is *necessarily* autobiographical and must remain so under pain of falsification. Anything more than this, any giving in to the traditional aspiration
of philosophy toward the universal, any incorporation of the
structures of my individual consciousness within the structures

of consciousness *as such*, even the attempt of "existential psycho-analysis" to grasp the "fundamental project" of an individual existence, is, Earle argues, "highly delusive." Can and does phenomenology have any value as a method for the elucidation of the structures of an individual life? Or, does it, in making such an attempt, necessarily dissolve into autobiography? Earle challenges phenomenology to recognize its impotence to clarify the meaning of any individual human life whatsoever. Here, then, the issue is joined.

Phenomenology and Science

There are many contemporary philosophers who view phenomenology as either anti-scientific or, at the very least, as completely uninterested in the problems of the physical sciences. This view is as unfortunate as it is historically incorrect. While it is true that, apart from Husserl, phenomenologists have made few contributions to the philosophy of the physical sciences, this has been due in large part to historical circumstances, one of them being the fact that phenomenology has, up to now, been practiced mainly in Western Europe and not in England or America. When the phenomenological method began to develop it was seen almost immediately that this method and the philosophical conclusions it supported were of great importance and value to the "human" sciences, and it was thus very quickly embraced by European sociologists, historians, anthropologists, psychologists, psychotherapists, and others. This immediate efflorescence in so many non-philosophical realms seems to have had its effect in directing and determining the interests and energies of phenomenologists themselves, and it led to their relative neglect of the physical sciences.

In fact, the paper included here by John J. Compton is one of the few contributions on this subject—and perhaps the first of any length by an American philosopher. As such, it is meant to be only an introduction to an area of interrelated problems in the philosophy of science which have been almost wholly neglected in contemporary philosophy. It is an attempt to analyze the phenomenological claim of the ontological primacy of the perceived world as it relates to physics and other natural sciences. Compton attempts to make clear, in order to reassure the timid and the hesitant, just what such a claim amounts to in terms of former philosophical approaches and in terms of the actual working scientist who, however much he might desire to do so, can never escape some "ontological" view of his endeavors. Compton claims that the phenomenological thesis of the "primacy of perception" offers a more complete and exact "ontological" basis for scientific theorizing than other alternatives. In so doing, he is extending the thesis first clearly enunciated by Merleau-Ponty far beyond anything Merleau-Ponty himself (whose scientific interest was bounded by psychology) achieved.

Realism versus Idealism: The Question of the A Priori

The three remaining essays in Part One have at least this in common: they pose in new—and complementary though sometimes conflicting—ways a fundamental ontological-epistemological question which has exercised philosophers from the time of Plato and Aristotle, and which presided over the birth of phenomenology as a current of contemporary philosophy. It is the problem of "realism" versus "idealism." Phenomenologists like Husserl and Merleau-Ponty claimed to have overcome this perennial dichotomy of Western philosophy and to have inaugurated a style of thought which is neither realistic nor idealistic, but it does not seem that their claim has been fully justified or fully understood. In the Tenth Book of the *Laws*, Plato argued that all forms of physical motion, and therefore all intelligible structure in *this* world, are due to the existence of "soul" (we might say *subjectivity*) in the world; Aristotle followed him in the *Metaphysics* by showing that, ultimately, Anaxagoras was correct, and that all order and structure in reality are due to a nonphysical, immaterial reality called "mind" or *nous*. This "mind" was not understood to be the human mind as such but a divine consciousness in which individual human minds somehow participated (or by which they were activated) and through which they could come to understand the established, teleological order of nature. The Neo-Platonists and the Augustinians showed a clearer sensitivity to how the ultimate ontological structure of reality was to be discovered by a "turning within" to an analysis of the human thought in and to which Being *is given*. Thus, even in the most objectivistic age of Greek metaphysics, when meaning, value, and structure were found to be "in things," utterly independent of human consciousness as such, we find a recognition that, ultimately, such meaning, value, and structure come not from nature but from consciousness.

It is not possible today, of course, to pose the question in this pre-Kantian fashion, but if we are to understand the contributions of Heidegger, for instance, to the problem of being and meaning, we must not forget even the most primitive Greek statement of a problem which philosophy clearly has not yet and may never overcome. Thomas Langan argues that realism and idealism are ultimate metaphysical positions or choices, neither of which can be "proved" against the other, though he attempts to show that the "realistic" position (understood in a pre-Kantian sense) is more plausible than its idealistic alternative. William Richardson concludes that Heidegger's own (definitely post- but non-Kantian) solution to the problem is more in accord with Brentano and Aristotle than with Kant.

Perhaps it is possible to elucidate at least one of the concerns of these three papers by referring to the problem of the *a priori*. There are at least two senses of the *a priori* discussed in these papers which are only implicitly distinguished. In the first sense it would be taken to designate knowledge which is not derived from but presupposed by experience, the realm of necessary and universal truths which empirical experience cannot itself account for, even though their only application may be within the realm of such contingent experience. The second sense, which seems to be that primarily intended by Langan, involves the post-Augustinian and more particularly the post-Kantian argument that such *a priori* truths find their source in the very structure of (human) consciousness and not in the world as it is in itself independently of consciousness.

J. N. Findlay approaches the question in the most general way, first through the experience of "the necessary," and then through the experience of "the probable" in such a way as to compare and contrast the approach of Plato and Husserl to the problem with that of Wittgenstein and his followers. He brings the Plato of the *VIIth Epistle* together with the Husserl of the *Ideas* to show that there is no experience of contingent fact which is not also the experience of a necessary "essence." There is, in short, no purely factual, contingent, empirical experience possible for human consciousness which is devoid of all eidetic necessity. A fact is not an essence and an example is not a definition, as Socrates and Plato show us in dialogue after dialogue, but every time a fact is *understood*, and every time an example is given as an instance or an example of an essential definition, the essence is always implicitly contained in the factual instance as that *of which* it is the instantiation. The "essential" is thus what the human mind understands when it understands something in the flux of experience; what the mind adds to the world of fact is "the necessary" or "the essential." "The necessary," writes Findlay, "is what you cannot get away from, no matter what you may do, and no matter what may be the case: it presupposes a variable field of alternatives, in respect of which . . . it remains invariant." It is not this *a priori* element in knowledge, he says, which is "strange," or in need of explanation so much as *a posteriori* experience itself; radical contingency is much more unintelligible and necessary to explain than the manner in which we understand and specify experience through generic categories. The understanding of a generic *a priori* is the necessary condition for any detailed instantial experience, and it occurs whenever we see something before us as the embodiment of an *eidos*.

But Findlay's main purpose, similar to Husserl's in the first chapter of *Ideas*, is to show that "fact" and "essence" are strictly correlative, that the relation of the mind to the world is not "external and fortuitous," that our understanding of the *a priori* is not the imposition of categories conceived elsewhere and independently of the facts of which they are the essences. He invokes to this purpose Plato's *Timaeus*, the one dialogue in which Plato comes to grips with the realm of "the probable," the "doxic," in human experience. The *a prioris* which characterize human reason are strictly correlative to the field of factual encounters; they cannot be "necessary" in some intemporal, non-mundane sense, and thus Findlay, like Husserl and like Plato (but like a Husserl and a Plato we seldom refer to), argues that "the real domain of reason is in the field of the inherently plausible and the analogically coherent, not in the barren, interstitial play of dirempted possibilities."

Findlay's argument thus tends to show that the discovery and description of presumptive or probable essences will give us a more adequate solution of the problem of the relationship between ideal necessity and factual contingency in experience. It is a solution which will—though he does not deal explicitly with this—enable us to reach a phenomenological approach to the *a priori* which will fall into the impasses of neither idealism nor realism.

Langan and Richardson present, by contrast, much less ambitious programs. Langan, in particular, believes that the problem is ultimately insoluble and limits himself to giving evidence which would tend to account for the emergence of the universal and the necessary in experience in an Aristotelian manner, and which would require, at the limit, that such "structures" or "meanings" exist in the "things themselves" (whether due to the activity of nature or of a divine mind is unclear), utterly independently of human consciousness.

The *status quaestionis* on this subject presented in Richardson's paper is necessarily and quite properly restricted to Heidegger, for it deals with Heidegger's historical relation to Kant. Such Heideggerian questions as "What does it mean to be a thing?" and "What is it that makes human knowledge and human science possible at all?" clearly suppose a post-Kantian approach to the problem of *a priori* knowledge. But it would be going beyond Richardson's own intentions and would be a hazardous thing to give a final interpretation to the orphic opacity of Heidegger's own conclusion, namely, that *aletheia*, self-concealing revealment, is the (cosmic? human?) *e-vent* out of which Being "is given," and Time "is given," as unfathomable gift to thought. When, earlier, Heidegger had centered his philosophy on an analysis of *Dasein* as *understanding*, as the necessary condition of the possibility of truth and the very structure of the meaning of Being, it was possible to interpret him in a Kantian (and even a Husserlian) sense. But the later Heidegger clearly has a much more "objectivistic" view of truth and if, as Richardson argues so persuasively, Kant's influence on Heidegger was "extrinsic" from the beginning to the end, then Heidegger may have to be taken, in spite of himself, to represent the contemporary apotheosis not of German romanticism but of Greek metaphysics.

II

It is properly distinctive of the phenomenological approach to philosophy that its discussions of ontological and epistemological problems do not rely exclusively or even primarily on the techniques of conceptual analysis but involve a return to experience, a going to see, a marshalling of new empirical and experiential evidence. Thus it would not be correct to view the papers brought together in Part Two of this volume as merely the concrete applications of more general theories, such as those discussed in Part One. They represent, rather, attempts to establish distinctions and map out new and unexplored terrain in the expectation that further theoretical conclusions and more general conceptual constructs will result from this immersion in experience.

To establish a general framework within which these variegated studies can be presented as a unity is, thus, an even more hazardous undertaking, if that is possible, than the arranging of the more theoretical papers in Part One. But certain themes recur, and there is a unity in diversity among the first four which distinguishes them from the last four. We could say that the first four papers are concerned with the analysis of certain structures of individual consciousness, whereas the last four are primarily concerned with questions of intersubjective or social awareness. The first belong primarily to the realm of epistemology; the last are concerned with value theory and social philosophy.

Embodied Consciousness

The problem of the embodiment of consciousness and of the relationships between body and mind is another of the most ancient paradoxes of Western philosophy. A certain dualism, at least on the level of the way in which we speak about body and mind, seems almost inescapable. Many philosophers have attempted to overcome this dualism only at the cost of virtually eliminating one element or the other and thus falling into the extremes of spiritualism on the one hand or materialism on the other. Clearly, the phenomenological approach to this problem requires that we give full weight to the evidence for either a dualistic or a monistic explanation of human reality. Descartes, Sartre, Edith Stein, even Husserl have established certain characteristics of consciousness which seem to require that we look on consciousness as at least functionally distinct from the body since it "constitutes" its own body as an object for itself. One could, on such evidence, argue that consciousness is the true self and the body is only the envelope or material instrument of the spirit within. But there is another strain of phenomenological evidence, in Scheler, in Merleau-Ponty, in existential psychoanalysis, which discloses the phenomena of embodiment, the bodily expression of meaning through gesture, the indissoluble unity of such body-mind functions as affection and perception, and so on. Such evidence would lead toward the conclusion that the one self which is the subject of experience is not a pure consciousness but a completely unified body-mind whole.

This metaphysical conundrum cannot be solved here, and none of the contributors to this volume has undertaken its solution; it is even questionable whether phenomenological evidence alone could provide us with an ultimate solution. But it would seem quite exact to say that the evidence relevant to this question which is given in the papers by Gerald Myers and Frank Tillman tends in the direction of Merleau-Ponty's monistic thesis, though both of them begin from a point of departure independent of anything Merleau-Ponty has undertaken. Myers argues that the experience of the body is not a perception like others, that the body is experienced "as a unit," and that this perception of oneself is conditioned by the total personal psycho-dynamics of the individual. His discussion would seem to add weight to the argument—though this is tangential to the main point of his paper—that the manner in which one's body is constituted as an object to oneself is quite distinct from the manner in which other objects are constituted, and this precisely because the body is itself incorporated into the perspective of the subject, the center of life from which everything else is experienced.

Tillman's argument, taken in this perspective, presents a parallel tendency, this time directed not to the experience of self but to the experience of others. He attempts to show that such "mental" states as anger or pain can be "perceived," that they emerge as forms of action in bodily behavior, and that our recognition of them does not require a complex system of purely mental inferences to the interior life of other persons. Though he does not say so, his argument would seem to parallel Merleau-Ponty's questioning of whether it is proper or possible to speak of an "interior" or "mental" life independent of the incarnation of sense and intentionality in bodily behavior, in bodily gestures and language. Any theory which would deny that we bodily "perceive" other persons must then logically postulate some kind of non-bodily reality to be "inferred" purely by the mind as the independent substratum of behavior. Tillman, like Merleau-Ponty but without reference to him, argues in the opposite direction.

These first four papers in Part Two have two things in common: negatively, they argue against a Humean view of perception and the perceiving (or experiencing) self, and, positively, they are concerned with the phenomenological import and meaning of some kinds of first-person statements, descriptions of experienced meanings as approached from the standpoint of the subject of such experience. Fernando Molina, through a reflection upon and an extension of the doctrines of Hume and James on belief, presents a theory of belief as an all-pervasive attitude of consciousness in the face of reality, one might almost say the source and foundation of a "reality principle" which, like perception, functions "passively" rather than "actively" (in the Husserlian sense of these terms) and which is the noetic correlate of the real world. Frederick Crosson's juxtaposition of Ryle's concept of mind and Husserl's concept of consciousness is an instructive reminder of the ambiguities involved in all talk about consciousness and its embodiment in behavior, and of the fateful antinomies which separate the traditional British and Continental approaches to this question.

Eidetic Analysis of Social Relationships

The studies which are grouped together as the concluding items in this collection are of wider scope and usher us into larger vistas than those in the earlier part of the volume. To the reader unacquainted with phenomenology or the claims of the phenomenological method it may seem, at first, that such studies of ethics, of the source of tragedy, of the experience of the holy are rather informal essays without any evident common direction or pretension. In what, one might ask, does such phenomenology differ from literary criticism or even sociology? Of all these papers Maurice Natanson's is the only one which concerns itself explicitly with the question of methodology, but it seems evident that what he says can be extended implicitly to the others. What these and similar phenomenological studies have in common, and must have in common under pain of lapsing into mere, undirected empirical description and fact-finding, is the phenomenological aim to elucidate eidetic structures, certain structural conditions of human (social) experience. Concrete and well-chosen paradigm cases and examples are found, as in a Platonic dialogue, which will illustrate the range of eidetic possibilities of a given modality of experience. But such concrete examples and descriptions are only the means of access to the underlying *a prioris* of experience which ultimately account for them. It is these *a prioris* or eidetic structures of experience which a phenomenological investigation attempts to thematize. This "transcendental" aspect of phenomenological research, so explicitly and so well illustrated by Natanson in his eidetics of role-taking, is what specifies phenomenological descriptions and gives them their philosophical import.

Of the several phenomenological investigations given here, John Silber's study of "Being and Doing" is a particularly good illustrative case because of its more comprehensive and highly articulated development. It is the longest single study in this volume and has been several times revised by the author prior to publication. There is no need for me to recapitulate in this introduction what can be read in Silber's own text, but I would like to point out the manner in which a philosophical argument—in this case, one of great importance for the history of philosophy—emerges from a phenomenological description of moral responsibility.

It has been taken as almost axiomatic in moral and legal philosophy since the time of Kant (and the triumph of the "Lutheran" conscience in the West) that the individual can be held responsible only for those fully intentional actions whose immediate consequences he could reasonably and explicitly foresee. This doctrine has been the gradual and hard-earned conquest of Western morality. We are not likely to give it up easily or return to an ancient Roman conception of "objective" guilt which could be incurred through no personal fault; we no longer execute pigs for having caused the death of a child, nor do we destroy buildings *in damnationem loci* because of the evil thoughts they may have harbored. But we may nevertheless ask with Silber whether there is not an ontological ground of moral guilt and whether a man has any moral responsibility for what he is and what he has become, whether his "ontological matrix" is not part of his person as well as his voluntary and limited present acts.

Such moralists as Dostoevsky and Sartre have already said that everybody is responsible for everybody else, but they have not presented much phenomenological evidence for such ethical assertions. In his essay Silber undertakes a large-scale investigation of such concepts as moral intentionality (and the experiential behaviors they thematize) to rid them of the "simplistic voluntarism" of their post-Kantian formulations. When intention is ultimately situated with respect to its subconscious and pre-conscious manifestations, when it is integrated into the life projects of the human organism as a whole, when it is examined as a highly complex continuum which ranges from the "organic intentionality" of the biological organism to fully deliberative acts of reflexive judgment, having traversed all the more or less dim intermediate stages, we see more clearly how and why our concept of moral responsibility must be "reshaped" to bring it into conformity with actual human reality. Silber, in effect, argues that there is a phenomenological basis for speaking of "ontological guilt" and for claiming that in some cases and within certain limits a man may be responsible not only for what he does but for what he is.

In conclusion, I would like to thank the editors of the *Journal of Existentialism* for permission to reprint "The Concept of Mind and the Concept of Consciousness" by Frederick Crosson, "Natural Science and the Experience of Nature" by John Compton, and "Being and Sense" by Zygmunt Adamczewski; I likewise wish to thank the editors of *Social Research* for permission to reprint "Alienation and Social Role" by Maurice Natanson. All the other essays in this book appear here in print for the first time. "Being and Doing" by John R. Silber will also appear in the proceedings of the Study Group on the Foundations of Cultural Unity, edited by Marjorie Grene.

JAMES M. EDIE

Northwestern University

PART ONE

SOME CURRENT PROGRAMS OF
PHENOMENOLOGICAL RESEARCH:
THE TASKS AND LIMITS OF
PHENOMENOLOGY

Hubert L. Dreyfus

PHENOMENOLOGY AND ARTIFICIAL INTELLIGENCE

Research dedicated to the construction of intelligent artifacts has, from its inception, intrigued philosophers, but thus far their discussions have been remarkably out of touch with the work actually being done. Analytic philosophers, such as Putnam, Scriven, and Ziff, use the present interest in "mechanical brains" to recast the conceptual issues dividing behaviorists from Cartesians. Following unquestioned philosophical assumptions reinforced by what they assume has already been accomplished, they are persuaded that robots will eventually be built whose behavior will be indistinguishable from that of human beings, and they ask under what conditions we would be justified in saying that such an artifact was thinking. On the other hand, moralists and theologians evoke certain highly sophisticated forms of behavior—moral choice, love, creative abstractions, and so on—which they claim are beyond the powers of any

Research for this paper was sponsored by the RAND Corporation. A more detailed analysis of the problems discussed, as well as those in the fields of problem solving, theorem proving, and pattern recognition, can be found in the author's *Alchemy and Artificial Intelligence,* RAND paper, P 3244.

machine. Neither side tries to show that in principle a specific sort of machine can or cannot exhibit the behavior in question.

Phenomenologists have thus far held aloof from these controversies, probably because they, like the parties involved in the debate, credulously assume that highly intelligent artifacts have already been developed. Indeed, if such artifacts exist or are about to be built, they are evidence for the truth of traditional empiricism in psychology and some sort of logical atomism in metaphysics. Such machines would certainly be acutely embarrassing to phenomenologists and existentialists. But before we panic and bury our heads in the sand, we had better first determine what, if anything, has actually been accomplished.

It is fitting to begin with a statement made in 1957 by H. A. Simon, one of the originators of the field of artificial intelligence:

It is not my aim to surprise or shock you. . . . But the simplest

> way I can summarize is to say that there are now in the world machines that think, that learn and that create. Moreover, their ability to do these things is going to increase rapidly until—in a visible future—the range of problems they can handle will be co-extensive with the range to which the human mind has been applied.[1]

The speaker predicts:

(1) That within ten years a digital computer will be the world's chess champion.

(2) That within ten years a digital computer will discover and prove an important mathematical theorem.

We do not have time to go into the deliberate confusions surrounding the supposed proof of an important theorem. Suffice it to say that to date no important or even original theorem has been proved. We will, however, follow the chess-playing story in some detail, for it might serve as a model for the production of intellectual smog in this area. In 1958, a year after his pre-

---

1. H. A. Simon and Allen Newell, "Heuristic Problem Solving: The Next Advance in Operations Research," *Operations Research*, VI (January-February 1958), 7 and 8.

diction, Simon presented an elaborate chess-playing program. As described in his classic paper, "Chess Playing and the Problem of Complexity," his program was "not yet fully debugged," so that one "cannot say very much about the behavior of the program." Still, it is clearly "good in the opening." [2] This is the last detailed published report on the program. In the same year, however, Simon announced: "We have written a program that plays chess." [3]

In fact, in its few recorded games the Simon program played poor but legal chess, and in its last bout (October 1960) was beaten in thirty-five moves by a ten-year-old novice. Fact, however, had ceased to be relevant. Simon's claims concerning his still bugged program had launched the chess machine into the realm of scientific mythology. In 1959 Norbert Wiener, whose optimism was strengthened by the claim that the program was "good in the opening," informed the N.Y.U. Institute of Philosophy that "chess-playing machines as of now will counter the moves of a master game with the moves recognized as right in the text books, up to some point in the middle game." [4] In the same symposium, Michael Scriven moved from the ambiguous claim that machines play chess to the claim that "machines are already capable of a good game." [5]

While his program was losing its five or six poor games—and his mythical machine was holding its own against masters in the middle game—Simon kept silent. When he spoke again, three years later, he did not report his difficulties and disappointments; rather, as if to take up where the myth had left off, Simon published an article in *Behavioral Science* announcing a program

2. Allen Newell, J. C. Shaw, and H. A. Simon, "Chess-Playing Programs and the Problem of Complexity," in Edward A. Feigenbaum and Julian Feldman, eds., *Computers and Thought*, New York, 1963, p. 60.

3. Allen Newell, J. C. Shaw, and H. A. Simon, *The Processes of Creative Thinking*, RAND Corporation, P 1320, 1958, p. 6.

4. Norbert Wiener, "The Brain and the Machine," in Sidney Hook, ed., *Dimensions of Mind*, New York, 1960, p. 110.

5. Michael Scriven, "The Compleat Robot: A Prolegomena to Androidology," in Hook, ed., *Dimensions of Mind*, p. 128.

which would play "highly creative" chess end games involving "combinations as difficult as any that have been recorded in chess history." [6] That the program restricts these end games to dependence on continuing checks, so that the number of relevant moves is greatly reduced, is mentioned but not emphasized. On the contrary, Simon misleadingly implies that similar simple procedures would account for master play even in the middle game.

Thus the article gives the impression that the chess prediction is almost realized, and indeed, with such progress the chess championship may be *claimed* at any moment. This production of confusion makes one think of a French mythical beast which is supposed to secrete the fog necessary for its own respiration.

Equally unjustified claims have been made in the areas of problem solving and pattern recognition, but we do not have space to examine them here. For our discussion it will be more instructive to concentrate on the area that had the earliest success, the most publicity, the most extensive and expensive research, and the most unequivocal failure: the field of language translation.

It was clear from the start that a mechanical dictionary could easily be constructed in which linguistic items, whether parts of words, whole words, or groups of words, could be processed independently and converted one after another into corresponding items in another language. This was soon accomplished. This initial success and the subsequent disillusionment provides a sort of paradigm for the field. It is aptly described by Yehoshua Bar-Hillel in his report on "The Present Status of Automatic Translation of Languages."

> During the first year of the research in machine translation, a considerable amount of progress was made. . . . It created among many of the workers actively engaged in this field the strong feel-

6. H. A. Simon and Peter A. Simon, "Trial and Error Search in Solving Difficult Problems: Evidence from the Game of Chess," *Behavioral Science*, VII (October 1962), 429.

ing that a working system was just around the corner. Though it is understandable that such an illusion should have been formed at the time, it was an illusion. It was created . . . by the fact that a large number of problems were rather readily solved. . . It was not sufficiently realized that the gap between such output . . . and high quality translation proper was still enormous, and that the problems solved until then were indeed many but just the simplest ones, whereas the "few" remaining problems were the harder ones—very hard indeed.[7]

During the ten years since the development of a mechanical dictionary, five government agencies have spent about $16 million on mechanical translation research. In spite of journalistic claims at various moments that machine translation was at last operational, this research has produced primarily a much deeper knowledge of the unsuspected complexity of syntax and semantics. As Anthony Oettinger of the Harvard Computation Laboratory remarks, "The major problem of selecting an appropriate target-correspondent for a source-word on the basis of context remains unsolved, as does the related one of establishing a unique syntactic structure for a sentence that human readers find unambiguous." Oettinger concludes: "The outlook is grim for those who still cherish hopes for fully automatic, high-quality mechanical translation." [8]

Once we cease to be intimidated by false claims of computer triumphs, we can recover some of our common-sense skepticism and our philosophical doubts. We can even begin to see the early success and later failure characteristic of work in the field of artificial intelligence as just what phenomenologists and existentialists should have expected. We shall now consider in more detail the ease and difficulties encountered in trying to develop chess playing and language translating programs, and draw out their psychological and metaphysical implications. I shall try to

7. Yehoshua Bar-Hillel, "The Present Status of Automatic Translation of Languages," in *Advances in Computers,* I, New York, 1960, p. 94.

8. Anthony G. Oettinger, "The State of the Art of Automatic Language Translation: An Appraisal," *Beitraege zur Sprachkünde und Information Verarbeitung,* I, Heft 2 (Munich, 1963), p. 27.

show first that the attempt to make a chess playing program can be understood as an attempt to make a working model of the mind as it is conceived by associationist psychology, and that its difficulties demonstrate the limits of such a theory. Secondly, I shall argue that the attempt to make a language translating program involves the metaphysical assumption (I am using "metaphysical" in Heidegger's sense) that everything that is can be treated as a determinate object; and that its failure suggests that information about *the world,* as opposed to objects *in* it, is not the sort of information that can be fed into a computer.

It is necessary first to say a word about computers. I am not trying to argue in this paper that *no* computer could produce intelligent behavior. It seems obvious to common sense that at least one information processing device, viz. the brain, does produce such behavior. What I am trying to argue here is that such behavior cannot be exhibited by a certain kind of computer: the digital computer, which is the only high-speed, all-purpose, information processing device that we know how to design or even conceive at present, and therefore the device on which all work in artificial intelligence has been and must be done. The fundamental characteristic of the digital computer which concerns us here is that all information with which it operates must be represented in binary digits, i.e., in terms of a series of yes's or no's, of switches being open or closed. The significance of this condition will become apparent in what follows.

I. *The Chess Program: Horizonal Consciousness vs. Heuristically Guided Search*

It is common knowledge that a certain class of games is decidable on present-day computers with present-day techniques —games like nim and tic-tac-toe can be programed so that the machine will win or draw every time. But other games cannot be decided in this way on present-day computers and yet have been successfully programed. In checkers, for example, because only two kinds of moves are possible, the captures forced, and pieces block each other, one can explore all possibilities to a depth of as many as twenty moves, which proves sufficient for playing a good game.

Chess too is in principle decidable, but chess presents the problem inevitably connected with very large choice mazes: exponential growth. We cannot run through all the branching possibilities far enough even to form a reliable judgment as to whether a given branch is sufficiently promising to merit further exploration. The right heuristics are supposed to limit the number of branches explored while retraining the most promising alternatives. But no successful heuristics have as yet been found. All current heuristics either exclude some possibly good moves or leave open the risk of exponential growth.

Simon is nonetheless convinced that minds work like digital computers, and since people find chess moves in a reasonably short time they must be using rules of thumb or heuristics to pick out the most promising paths. He is confident that if we listen to the reports of chess masters, follow their eye movements, perhaps question them under bright lights, we will eventually be able to discover these heuristics and build them into our program—thereby pruning the exponential tree. But let us examine more closely the evidence that chess playing is governed by the use of heuristics.

Consider the following report quoted by Simon, noting especially how it begins rather than how it ends. The player says, "Again I notice that one of his pieces is not defended, the Rook, and there must be ways of taking advantage of this. Suppose now, if I push the pawn up at Bishop four, if the Bishop retreats I have a Queen check and I can pick up the Rook. If, etc., etc." [9] At the end we have an example of what I shall call "counting out"—thinking through the various possibilities by

9. Allen Newell and H. A. Simon, "Computer Simulation of Human Thinking," *Science*, CXXXIV (December 22, 1961), 15.

brute-force enumeration. We have all engaged in this process, which, guided by suitable heuristics, is supposed to account for the performances of chess masters. But how did our subject notice the opponent's Rook was undefended? Did he examine each of his opponent's pieces and their possible defenders sequentially (or simultaneously) until he stumbled on the vulnerable Rook?

We need not appeal to introspection to discover what a player in fact does before he begins to count out; the report itself indicates it: the subject "zeroes in" on the promising situation. Only *after* the player has zeroed in on an area does he begin to count out, to test what he can do from there.

The player is not aware of having explicitly considered or explicitly excluded from consideration any of the hundreds of possibilities that would have had to be enumerated in order to have arrived at this particular area by counting out. Still, the specific portion of the board that finally attracts the subject's attention depends on the overall configuration. This phenomenon has been systematically studied by Husserl in his account of perceptual horizons.

Michael Polanyi aptly describes this horizon:

> Seen thus from the corner of our eyes, or remembered at the back of our mind, this area compellingly affects the way we see the object on which we are focusing. We may indeed go so far as to say that we are aware of this subsidiarily noticed area mainly in the appearance of the object to which we are attending.[10]

If information, once it has been explicitly considered, or perhaps without ever being explicitly considered, can remain on the fringes of consciousness and be implicitly taken into account through its effect on the appearance of the objects on which our attention is focused, then there is no reason to suppose that, in order to discover an undefended Rook, our subject must have counted out rapidly and unconsciously until he arrived at the

10. Michael Polanyi, "Experience and the Perception of Pattern," in Kenneth M. Sayer and Frederick J. Crosson, eds., *The Modeling of Mind*, Notre Dame, 1963, p. 214.

area in which he began consciously counting out. Moreover, there are good reasons to reject this assumption, because it raises more difficulties than it resolves.

If the subject has been unconsciously counting out thousands of alternatives with brilliant heuristics to get to the point where he focuses on that Rook, why doesn't he carry on with this unconscious process all the way to the end, until the best move just pops into his consciousness? Why, if the *unconscious* counting is rapid and accurate, does he resort at the particular point where he spots the Rook to a cumbersome method of slowly, awkwardly, and consciously counting things out? Or if, on the other hand, the unconscious counting is *inadequate,* what is the advantage of switching to a conscious version of the same process? This sort of teleological consideration—while not a proof that unconscious processing is not digital—does put the burden of proof on those who claim that it is or must be.

Moreover, even if he does unconsciously count out, using unconscious heuristics—which there is no reason to suppose and good reason to doubt—what kind of program could convert this unconscious counting into the kind of fringe-influenced awareness of the centers of interest, which is the way zeroing-in presents itself in our experience? Of course, there could be a cruder process which could leave out steps and make cruder evaluations, but these would be equally determinate. How can a determinate process give rise to the experienced indeterminacy? It seems that "unconsciously" the subject must be engaged in a sort of information processing which differs from counting out, and that conscious counting begins when he has to refine this global process in order to deal with details.

Following Merleau-Ponty, I shall call any psychological theory that attempts to analyze human information processing in terms of the searching for and combining of determinate bits of information, associationism. It is not important for these considerations whether these determinate elements are associated by habits or by rules connecting their representations in consciousness. Thus, from the phenomenological point of view, Hume, Kant, and Artificial Intelligence theorists are all associationists, and all, for this reason, find it impossible to account for horizonal consciousness and the kind of information processing it makes possible.

In the case of game playing, this distinction between associationist and gestaltist forms of information processing underlies the distinction between counting out and zeroing in, and explains the early success and later failure in this area of artificial intelligence. In all game playing programs, early success is achieved by working on those games or parts of games in which counting out is feasible; failure occurs when global awareness is necessary to avoid exponential growth.

The difficulties of artificial intelligence thus call our attention to the necessity for a non-associationist function of consciousness —a non-digital form of information processing—precisely the horizonal awareness which phenomenologists and gestalt psychologists have claimed is essential to human intelligence.

II. *Language Translation: Situational Disambiguation vs. Context-free Formalization*

Thus far we have restricted ourselves to the implications of work in artificial intelligence for the philosophy of mind. We have considered a case where the information to be given the computer is of the discrete and determinate kind which can be punched on cards and stored in computer memories, and we have concentrated on the computer's inability to process such information. But in order to count as humanly intelligent, computers would not only have to play chess but would also have to deal with situations in the world in which we ordinarily perceive and live. Here the ambition of the workers in artificial intelligence takes on ontological or metaphysical dimensions, for such a claim not only asserts that the *way* we process information can be formalized and represented in a series of discrete

PHENOMENOLOGY AND ARTIFICIAL INTELLIGENCE

steps, so as to be simulated on a digital computer, but further that the *information itself* can be made exhaustively explicit and determinate so that it can be fed into a digital machine.[11] Merleau-Ponty calls this assumption that whatever is can be treated as a set of atomic facts, the *préjugé du monde*. Heidegger calls it *"rechnende Denken,"* calculating thought, and views it as the goal of philosophy, inevitably culminating in technology. Thus, for Heidegger, technology, with its insistence on the "thoroughgoing calculability of objects," is the inevitable culmination of metaphysics, the concern with beings to the exclusion of Being. In *Der Satz vom Grund* Heidegger remarks that "the determination of language as information originally supplies the sufficient reason for the construction of thinking machines, and for the construction of large-scale computer installations," and that "information theory is, as pronouncement, already the arrangement whereby all objects are put in such form as to assure man's domination over the entire earth and even the planets." [12] It is thus less sensational but more appropriate that in his recent UNESCO address Heidegger cites cybernetics (no longer the atomic bomb) as the culmination of philosophy.[13]

Heidegger also claims that "the only fruitful way [to get beyond metaphysics] must lead through modern axiomatizing representation and its hidden ground." [14] If this be so, workers in artificial intelligence are the most sensitive prophets of what Heidegger calls our metaphysical destiny, and their work may be leading us to see the limits of this particular understanding

11. Just as associationism can be thought of as Humean, this ontological assumption can be considered Cartesian, for it claims that all that can be known can be analyzed in terms of clear and distinct ideas.

12. Martin Heidegger, *Der Satz vom Grund*, Pfullingen, 1957, p. 203. My translation.

13. Martin Heidegger, "La fin de la philosophie et la tâche de la pensée," in *Kierkegaard Vivant*, Paris, 1966. "Philosophy has come to an end in the present epoch. It has found its place in the scientific view . . . The fundamental characteristic of this scientific determination is that it is cybernetic, i.e., technological" (pp. 178, 179).

14. Heidegger, *Der Satz vom Grund*, p. 42.

of Being. A study of the difficulties encountered in work on automatic language translation, then, is a confrontation with the limits of metaphysics.

We have seen that Bar-Hillel and Oettinger, two of the most respected and most informed workers in the field of automatic language translation, have each been led to pessimistic conclusions about the possibility of further progress in the field. They have each discovered that the order of the words in a sentence does not provide enough information to enable a machine to determine which of several possible phrasings is the appropriate one, nor does the context of a word indicate which of several possible readings the author had in mind.

As Oettinger puts it:

> [Work] to date has revealed a far higher degree of legitimate *syntactic* ambiguity in English and in Russian than has been anticipated. This, and a related fuzziness of the boundary between the grammatical and the non-grammatical, raises serious questions about the possibility of effective, fully automatic manipulation of English or Russian for any purposes of translation or information retrieval.[15]

Instead of claiming, on the basis of his early partial successes with a mechanical dictionary, that, in spite of a few exceptions and difficulties, the mystery surrounding human understanding is beginning to dissolve—a frequent Simon claim—Oettinger draws attention to the "very mysterious semantic processes that enable most reasonable people to interpret most reasonable sentences univocally most of the time. . . ."[16]

Here is another example of the fringe effect. Obviously, the user of a natural language is not aware of many of the cues he responds to in determining the intended syntax and meaning. But here the fundamental difficulty is not that machines, lacking fringe consciousness, cannot deal with formal complexities, but rather that what has to be dealt with may not be formalizable.

15. Oettinger, *op. cit.*, p. 26.
16. Oettinger, *op. cit.*, p. 26.

The cues in question may not be the sort of determinate data which *could be* taken up and considered by a sequential or even parallel list-searching program.

To understand this difficulty in its purest form we must distinguish between the *generation* of grammatical and meaningful sentences, and the *understanding* of such sentences in actual instances of their use. For the sake of the argument we shall grant that linguists will succeed in formulating rules for generating any sentences that native speakers recognize as grammatical and meaningful and excluding all sentences that native speakers reject as ungrammatical or meaningless. The remaining difficulty can then be stated as follows: In an instance of linguistic usage, a native speaker is able to interpret univocally a sentence that, according to the rules, could have been generated in several different ways, and therefore could have several different grammatical structures and several legitimate meanings. (A famous example is the sentence: "Time flies like an arrow." A computer would read it as a statement that a certain kind of fly likes to eat arrows, and a command to rush out and clock flies, as well as a statement about the passage of time.)

In narrowing this legitimate ambiguity, the native speaker may appeal to either specific information about the world (as, for example, when we recognize that the sentence "The book is in the pen" means that the book is in a playpen or pig pen, not in a fountain pen), or to a sense of the situation (as when a person hears his friend say, "Stand by me," and interprets it differently depending on whether his friend is on trial or on parade).

The appeal to context, moreover, is more fundamental than the appeal to facts, for the context determines the *significance* of the facts. Thus, in spite of our *general* knowledge about the relative size of pens and books, we would interpret "The book is in the pen" when whispered in a James Bond movie, as meaning just the opposite of what it means at home or on the farm.

A natural language is used by people involved *in situations* in which they are pursuing certain goals. These extra-linguistic goals, which are not themselves precisely stated and do not seem to be precisely statable, provide the cues which reduce the ambiguity of expressions as much as necessary for the task at hand. The practical context, or more broadly the world, which enables us to use languages as precisely as necessary and yet in a non-rulelike way, is not given as a determinate object or set of objects which can be handled by information theory.

Pascal, the inventor of the calculator, noted that the *esprit de finesse* functions "tacitly, naturally, and without technical rules." Wittgenstein has spelled out this insight in the case of language: "In general we don't *use* language according to strict rules—it hasn't been taught us by means of strict rules either." [17]

But to refute the metaphysical assumption that all ambiguity can be overcome in advance, that, in the case of language, the rules governing the disambiguation of actual utterances can in principle be completely formalized, it is not enough to point out that thus far no adequate language translation system has been developed, or that our language is used in flexible and apparently non-rulelike ways. The formalizer can always retort that our inability to feed information describing the *Lebenswelt* sufficient to disambiguate into a digital computer shows only that we have not fully understood (analyzed) the rules governing the use of natural language.

This rejoinder might at first sight seem to be similar to the heuristic programer's assurance that he will someday find the heuristics that will enable a machine to play chess, even if he has not yet found them. But there is an important difference. The heuristic programer's confidence is based on a misconception of the way the mind processes information, while the formalist's claim is based on a correct understanding of the nature of scientific explanation. To the extent that we have not specified our behavior in terms of unique and precisely definable

17. Ludwig Wittgenstein, *The Blue and Brown Books*, Oxford, 1960, p. 25.

reactions to precisely definable situations, we have not understood that behavior in the only sense of "understanding" appropriate to science.

We must be more specific in our critique of the metaphysical presupposition of artificial intelligence in order to show in what sense the attempt to formalize is misguided. A machine can always revise its program each time it makes a mistake and fails to disambiguate as a human would, but it would have to fail first and then revise its rules to take account of the new case. Humans, however, are able to adapt as they go along and then reflect on and formalize the revision they have already made. In trying to program a computer to use natural language, any specific uses of words, once they have occurred, can be added to the rules, even if the rules become more and more complicated. What can't be accounted for, however, is the open texture of language, our ability to use words in ever new situations and still be understood.

This is not a problem for science, because science is always done from the point of view of an objective observer, and, as Kierkegaard pointed out in the *Postscript,* the objective thinker treats all experience as if it were already in the past. We have seen that a general theory of syntax and semantics can be scientific—because it is a timeless formalism which makes no claim to formalize the use of language in specific situations. We have seen the contradictions that arise when one demands a comparable formalism for linguistic *use.*

The originality, the importance, and the misery of artificial intelligence is that it tries to push the scientific attitude one step further and to use its formalization to cope with real life situations *as they occur.* Thus the believer in mechanical translation is not merely laboring under a misconception of the way consciousness functions, but a misconception of the relation between theoretical and practical understanding. He supposes that one can understand the practical world of an involved active individual in the same terms in which one can understand the objective universe of science, that is, he supposes that the world or situation can be understood as an object. This, in Heidegger's terms, is just another way of saying that the champion of artificial intelligence is the ultimate metaphysician, and his failure is the failure of metaphysics.

Conclusion

Descartes, the first to have conceived the possibility of robots, was also the first to grasp the essential inadequacy of digital computers. He remarks in the *Discourse* that

> . . . although such machines could do many things as well as, or perhaps even better than, men, they would infallibly fail in certain others. . . . For while reason is a universal instrument which can be used in all sorts of situations, the organs of a machine have to be arranged in a particular way for each particular action. From this it follows that it is morally impossible that there should be enough different devices in a machine to make it behave in all the occurrences of life as our reason makes us behave. (LLA, p. 36)

Thus, although not aware of the difference between the world and things in the world, Descartes already saw that the mind can cope with an indefinite number of acts or situations, whereas a machine has only a limited set of on/off states and so will eventually reveal itself by its failure to respond appropriately. This intrinsic limitation of mechanism, Descartes claims, shows the necessity of presupposing an immaterial soul.

Of all the workers in artificial intelligence, only C. E. Shannon, the inventor of information theory, seems to be aware of this important incapacity of the digital computer. In a discussion of "What Computers Should Be Doing," he observes:

> . . . Efficient machines for such problems as pattern recognition, language translation, and so on, may require a different type of computer than any we have today. It is my feeling that this will

be a computer whose natural operation is in terms of patterns, concepts, and vague similarities, rather than sequential operations on ten-digit numbers.[18]

Such a brain-like machine would not be mechanical in Descartes' narrow and precise sense, and, not being limited to a definite number of states, might be able to respond to an indefinite number of specific situations. It would thus, on Descartes' view, be indistinguishable from a human, destroying his argument that intelligent behavior is possible only if the mechanism behaving is somehow attached to a non-material soul. But one can raise a new objection, in some ways the exact opposite of Descartes', to this robot. If the arguments developed by S. J. Todes [19] are correct, a brain in a bottle or a non-digital computer would still not be able to respond to new sorts of situations because our ability to cope with the open texture of the *Lebenswelt,* i.e., to be in-a-situation, depends not just on the flexibility of our nervous system but rather upon our ability to engage in practical activity. If such a Shannon-type computer is ever built, it might become apparent that what distinguishes persons from machines, no matter how cleverly constructed, is not a universal immaterial soul but a self-moving material body. Existential phenomenologists could then turn to the artificial intelligence experts and say, as the transcendental phenomenologists already have, "We could have told you so."

18. C. E. Shannon, *Computers and the World of the Future,* Cambridge, Mass., 1962, pp. 309-310.

19. S. J. Todes, *The Natural Philosophy of the Human Body,* forthcoming, Evanston, Ill., Northwestern University Press.

Zygmunt Adamczewski

BEING AND SENSE

Philosophy in the twentieth century has advanced well into what
Brentano conceived as a stage of dispersal. To become whole
and grow again it requires radical, embracing thought. Such is
the thought of being. It may not be the only reviving thought,
but it reaches toward its own deepest sources. Therefore the
word "being" will be sounded here, now and again, not as a note
of judgment but of appeal, not as a magic term of explanation
but as a clue to confirmation of man's thought with man's life,
not to straiten but to point to the origin of sense. Because philosophy today needs very badly to make sense for men once more.

What has and what makes sense? What, in a wider reach, is
sense?
To begin with ease, it can be said: there is sense in words of
human speech. It is easy to observe about words that to have
sense they must consist of an appreciable order of sounds, and
beyond that they must belong to a larger order of a language;
only that determines which sounds may yield words. This observation offers a hint to be kept in mind: it is less easily seen
that words are there in a scattered availability. Languages gen-

erally have words as names—so-called "proper" ones—for singular things, as titles or descriptive references for grouping entities together, and as phrases to provide links among the former two kinds of words. But all of these kinds are incomplete in that sometimes words are given for what is encountered and sometimes not. It is tempting to say that the availability of words is arbitrary; although in individual situations we can account for particular words but not others. It would seem that the presence of any word is somehow demanded, yet the source of such demands may not be clear. Human speech is like a mesh structure spread over what there is. The net may be tightened, its gaps filled; a mesh is still a mesh.

This view of sense in words needs elucidation by examples of the three kinds of words mentioned. Of the first, words as names, the least needs to be said, since it is easily granted that fewer entities are individually named than are not. Men have names, so do their habitations, the waters they sail and the mountains they climb. Familiar living beings are named—household animals or pets—though not all: dogs and horses always are, but chickens or goldfish not always, and plants hardly ever. Some inanimate pets have names—dolls, cars, weapons—but many do not. Very few temporal spans have singular names as does the day of victory in 1945 or that of the birth of Jesus. As for spatial localities, they are often named vaguely: a stretch of coast or mountains is called Lovers' Cove or Dead Man's Gulch, but the stretch next to it is not called anything, nor is it settled just how far the cove or the gulch extends. It appears that names must be in some way deserved by entities, even that such deserving often involves some sort of intimacy. But this notion cannot be pursued here, especially as someone may wonder about the point of these observations. The point is this: there is more in heaven and earth than is ever named. Of course, what has no singular name may yet be described or circumscribed by means of other words. These will now be considered.

In the second and most numerous class of words are those

which name or speak of a plurality of entities. Even what has a singular or "proper" name can contain several entities: the head, arms, and legs of Julius Caesar are entities; so are the cells of his body. That suggests the difficult question: what is an entity? This is of serious relevance to any ontology, but here it must be answered only abruptly: an entity is what does or can have a name. A singular name conceals or disregards plurality, holding together whatever it names into unity. But a word of the second kind renounces the claim to strict "property" in its naming and openly refers to many and varied entities, every one of which could have a name of its own. Such a word then need not be "nomen" (name or noun); it can be verb, adverb, or adjective, though as the Latin indicates, naming may have a wider scope which the ancients accepted at least for nouns. Thus more widely the word "name" is used here.

While singular words screen pluralities, more common words cover discrepancies because they embrace entities similar in just one respect. This stress on similarity, with which Plato hypnotized men, has conveniently helped to build patterns of the world. And thus it is demanded. Nonetheless, the groupings are selected by similarities in class-forming properties. Dissimilarities fall beyond them, unspoken. For example, think of everything subsumed under the title "blue": in respect of color these many entities are akin; they could possibly be ordered as more or less alike, and their blue order could conceivably be measured. But their wide dissimilarities apart from color are not conceived, not ordered, least of all measured. It would not make sense to put them into words. And so they remain "unworded."

Someone might object that whatever is unspoken in a word group of entities, such as in the above example, can be said by means of other words, other groupings. But in every case, i.e., every word, the grouping is aimed at what is gathered within, not what is left without; every collection undertaken on its own disregards possible others; thus the residuum is not likely to be exhausted. It is as though some place were independently searched by a detective, a uranium prospector, a philatelist, an archaeologist, and many others like them; they would hardly empty it altogether. Nor are there any vacuum cleaners in human speech.

A few brief illustrations of the selective naming in ordinary words: to measure length it has been thought useful to rely on human feet, but the obvious discrepancy in sizes necessitated today's word "foot," meaning twelve inches. But there are no words to specify the length of hands, thighs, or big toes. Perhaps there need not be—at any rate there are none in English—though the average foot is in no way more real than the average thigh. Again, there is a verb to describe erect posture, grave if benign facial expression, with the right hand making the sign of a cross—tradition calls this "blessing"; but there is no verb to summarize a bend with a grin, a hip wriggle and a left-foot tapping—unless a dancer dignifies it with a name. Then there are silly collections usually without a covering title, sometimes mentioned by philosophers, such as the class containing, i.a., the blue of the water in Capri's Grotta Azzurra, Hitler's moustache, Birgit Nilsson's "Ho-yo-to-ho," the air on certain stretches of the New Jersey Turnpike, and the evening walk on the Champs Élysées. A name could be introduced for this grouping which has none. Although such a collection appears silly, there could be a method in this silliness: the above class could accommodate the most delightful and the nastiest of entities. Introducing a novel grasp of what there is—the privilege of genius—may also deserve a new word, because available words do not say everything. Yet word selectiveness has never shown its obtrusive power more than today, when of proliferating books on related subjects everyone produces its own jargon.

The third kind of words serve as tying devices to supplement the others: speech particles, prepositions, conjunctions. Their sense is not appreciated apart from statements. But their presence and scope, as it may occur, depends more on the structure of particular languages. This confirms the view that there is always "more" where any words come from. To illustrate: no word might seem to cover a more natural, simple, and homogeneous scope than the conjunction "and"; yet in the Polish language its role is performed by two quite distinguishable words. Again, English has no word equivalent to the German "Da," which oscillates between "here" and "there." On the other hand, many languages do not render the difference in using "between" and "amongst"; for that matter, English could generate other such words as "bethreen," "befoureen," and so on. This wealth may be contrasted with the poor clumsiness of "for its own sake," where the need for four words is unclear and nobody knows what a "sake" could be or how exclusively "owned" by "it." Further, there could be single words to abbreviate such circumscriptions as "not less than half but not more than two thirds" or "on top of but to the left or right at the angle of forty-five degrees." It would not be advisable to object here that these lengthy phrases say, after all, what has to be said; because quite often how something is said decides whether anything has been said—as will be granted by anyone who ever rushed to obtain street directions in an unfamiliar town. And if someone requested explanation of a word saying what could not be said at all by means of other words no matter how many, the request clearly could not be complied with.

This brief survey of words available as the handiest instances of sense was meant to clarify the thought already given: that human speech disposes words with variable doses of sense. Among them are left unworded gaps; the question whether what "there is" in such gaps makes sense or not, may not be settled unless the gaps are filled by more words. But this suggests what need not be true—that sense is posed only in word expression—because no more has been discussed thus far. Certainly more must be considered, e.g., how particular words belong together, which they must do to be words. No word in isolation ever makes proper sense. The word "proper" indicates that words are owned by their context. The context is often taken to consist only of other words, but this may not suffice. It can be debated whether some verbal context itself is or is not proper. Such debates take place notably with reference to the context of the word "nothing," which names no entity. Still, to attend for the moment to this context of other words, it is easily seen that the popular trend toward making words more precise is contextually limited. To aim at precision beyond some context would be to expropriate the word. And precision as such is virtuous only in a few contexts, such as scientific terminology.

Men take comfort and preoccupy themselves with the non-precision of words: consider the delights and excitements in local disputes about whether a certain place is really in the mountain region, whether its inhabitants are genuine mountain folk—how dreary would be a bureaucratic decree on this, how apt to be disregarded by the people involved! And yet contempt is sometimes voiced for imprecise ordinary language, although everyone knows that precision is an artifice fitting artificial linguistic systems. Its full worth pertains to the context of specific communications, not to communication as such. Also, the paramount import of communication for men is hardly questioned today, as it well could be, because the order of speech exceeds communication. If words be keys, the most precise and refined key will open but one door; the least shaped, least specialized are the master keys. There are words of glorious vagueness, in which communication may be deceived but without which speech could not do; they resist futile attempts at sharpening and enjoy the freedom of many contexts. Such are the words: "God," "act," "know," "right," "home." Such must remain the word "being."

All words there are, and words there could be, belong to the extensible order of speech. To extend itself, speech relies on a background beyond whatever makes sense in words, beyond whatever is said. Of course, more could be said, more words introduced. This is the finite spread of speech at the hands of finite men; an ideal language of an infinite speaker would not be human. But the sense of any words, old or new, their wide naming power, lies in calling together entities from an unworded background and holding them forth for future thought. "There is" ever more than words say. And if entities are grouped available to thought by means of words, what about the background from which entities come forth? It stays vaguely covered rather than named by a word unlike any other: "being." That is the word of wording as such. It may not make sense in some contexts, especially the precise ones; but it can be responsible for sense.

Words are drawn from a background that yields, perhaps demands, them. To be proper words, however, they must be properly arranged. This means that a word must be given a range of sense when ranged alongside others within a stand or status. Such an arrangement is a statement. The word "statement" is used here to bypass a controversial opposition: on one side physically given but only "grammatical" sentences, on the other more "logical" but dubiously given propositions; yet the former must be understood and the latter available. Neutral to this conflict, statements make sense for men no less immediately than words, whether they inform, command, or question; their modal variations will thus be disregarded for brevity.

How do statements make sense? A direct answer may not be provided to this question. In the preceding section it has been accepted that ordinary words such as "blue" make sense, but no direct observations have been offered as to what actually happens in the moment of hearing the word. This momentary phenomenon may be as little accessible to verbal analysis as the moment of waking up or being hit by a bullet. Instead of such evanescence, it has been queried what is involved in the sense of individual words. Similarly, instead of analyzing the event in hearing, "The sky is blue"—though speculative attempts at this have been made—it will be more to the present point to explore what is involved in the sense of such word arrangements: how that sense enters into man's life, how it is secured and fitting.

As it is with words, so with statements: criteria for the availability of their sense are selectively picked, heterogeneous, and thus inadequate for showing any kind of completeness. In other words, new modes of word arrangement may always be demanded, with other sense-making capacities. To claim a positively exhausting system of statement sense is to provide evidence of short sight. The main criteria available today for affirming the sense of statements are these: verification in terms of certain experiences and actions, coherence with a definite context of other statements, and significance because of a subjectively striking effect. These will have to be considered one by one, but it is well to reiterate that these are consequences flowing from sense, ways of securing or proving sense already grasped. For example, verification cannot be equivalent to sense which is its precondition. The grasping of spoken sense is acceptance of an order and direction in words. A specialized complex of symbolic arrangements, such as the language of contemporary logic, cannot be constructed without specifying the admissible well-formed formulas or statements; to specify these, it must begin with other modes of speech. But to have sense all speech must be, though less unequivocally, well-formed. If it is a universal human privilege, then every man must in time cope with its directed order. From this all-human source, individual paths divide: some speak one language and some another, some read books of a certain kind and some none at all, some tinker with science and some compose poetry. Yet all are empowered with speech. Its many modes tie with divergent ways of life, discordant thoughts, and dissimilar steps in acquiring and proving sense.

One of these, verification, has been much discussed lately, threatening for a while to monopolize the concern with sense as meaning. This is only to be expected in a time possessed by technological, experimental conquests. Verification is a proper way of responding to many statements. Among them could be such as these: "It snows outside," "The stream of electrons has been interrupted," "There are not enough epicycles in this orbit." These simple examples should make clear that such statements have sense for some but certainly not for all people, and that their sense is temporally limited. Conditions vary as to who may grasp such sense and when. Where such statements do make sense, it can be confirmed by undertaking certain actions or exposing oneself to specified experiences. At this stage they may be proved true or false, or in other words verified. But the sense of the statement is not the same as, rather antecedent to, what may be taken as the "sense" of the verifying activity: the latter may be entirely in doubt, or someone may be sure that there is a verifying procedure without being able to specify which. To doubt, to seek, to describe its verification, however, presupposes that the statement has sense. Further, the stress on verification overshadows the fact that in innumerable situations the securing of sense is not pursued at all but is taken for granted: a man wishing to verify all verifiable statements would find his life too short and brutish. But what does this mean?

This indicates that statements are no more independent than words in their sense: not only must they be well arranged internally, but this arrangement depends on every statement's fitting externally into what may be called a "perspective." And it is not simply a perspective of thought. Anyone who listens to a given statement, while he grasps its sense, relies already on a perspective: to assign the statement to a non-arbitrary context, to decide whether it can be verified and how, to act upon it or not, and if to act then to possess the adequate skill, acuity, strength. The perspective of sense is not just intellectual; into it enter a man's past experiences and future tendencies, his mood, attentiveness, agility, and choice—briefly, how he exists. Statements make proper sense perspectivally, i.e., they are proper to or owned by a perspective. How? Here gives help the fact that verification is an act, and one that is more often than not omitted. The proper sense of statements means that in their perspectives men act as well as think, and they can neglect to act because they already move therein with secure familiarity, indeed they belong there. Any such perspective is then by no means verbal, for man does not live by words alone. The perspective includes entities and reaches toward their unworded background.

Brief consideration may now be given to another group of statements, such as these: "The unknown equals the square root of minus one," "There must be three parts to constitute the soul of man," "It is possible to reconcile harmoniously causality through freedom and universal necessity." It would not be common to hear of verification for such statements. Nevertheless, their sense may not be entirely unlike the sense of statements usually taken as verifiable. Thus it would be hard to deny that these statements, like the former ones, have sense only for some people and only within some temporal span. For example, one man may find sense in discoursing about the soul at the age of fifteen and cease to find it at fifty, while another may pass through the opposite course. Also, the grasping of sense is here a precondition for proving or securing it in any way; yet the further procedure demanded in the present case is more clearly to ascertain coherence or agreement with a selected body of other statements, but only the proper one. This may be a simple task of recollection, but it may also require physical activity, such as a trip to a shelf in a library; such activity is sometimes called "verifying," e.g., of a quotation.

Decisive is here the search for coherence: if the statement is not allocated where it fits, its sense may be seen dimly or perhaps not at all. Its grasping is already an incipient tendency to connect; a student of philosophy might not immediately see that the above wording on causality belongs to Kant, but a student of medicine would be totally helpless when faced by it. Further in this respect, it may be pointed out that there is a space for variations in how much men can do or how much they wish to do to secure a proper fit of agreement, which may be thus reached to different depths. Mathematical exactitude does not obtain everywhere. Scholarship to a great extent consists in showing that there is coherence where others failed to find it, and that there is none where they found it. The result of these

observations is that statements whose sense is established by coherence do belong to a perspective of their own, in which men
must move already to have such sense available to them. This
perspective appears to favor intellect, memory, and erudition,
but it is by no means exhausted by them. As a perspective it involves not only having seen, read, and assimilated but also
looking ahead, shaping, saying what has not been spoken of.
And it may be noted in passing that such a perspective of fitness
may be equally demanded in the non-verbal modes of speech,
in the proper sense of what is said—not intellectually at all—
by Michelangelo and Rembrandt, by Bach and Beethoven.

A third kind of statements must be introduced now, especially since these are often neglected by people for whom sense
is signification but not significance. Some examples: "An iron
curtain has descended across the continent," "To see a world in
a grain of sand!," "My love for you will never die." Dissimilar
though they are, such statements nonetheless can be viewed together. Of them all it is true in a more stringent fashion that
they can only make sense for some people and for some
time, because they are addressed only thus; for many others
they will sound like a pseudo-arrangement of words that join
no context. To speak of them is therefore difficult, expecting
only hypothetical response. Still, counting on that, it may be
said that statements like these compensate for their exclusive
address by presenting a more gripping appeal to those whom
they touch. For this uncertain audience their sense can have
more penetrating significance than any other. It is as though
they were sung rather than spoken, and human ears might be
but seldom attuned to their melody. Clearly, this kind of sense
is also shared by that human speech which has and needs no
words: art. As in all art, so in poetic speech, the sense of statements is so interwoven that it will be missed if prosaically dis-
sected into separate words. The poet does not really use words
as mere words. He is aware of what was earlier observed here:
that those discrete doses of sense—words—must not be isolated

but disposed together to gather sense. This poetic significance is thus most true to the demands of speech—except for those who never speak with a subjective appeal but always address the world at large.

But then, it may be asked, how is such significance established and secured? The answer is that it is not and need not be. Pertinent here would be that possibly apocryphal story about a thinker who attended a tragedy in a Parisian theater and asked upon leaving: "Qu'est ce que cela prouve?" A man of prose, alas, like too many philosophers. The sense which strikes with a subjective effect is not further proved. It does not require, though it will often appear in, a context of other statements to agree or cohere with. Not issuing as a word-by-word reflection of anything, it will resist any literal verification by experiment, which may even be a disastrous misunderstanding, e.g., in reference to a love declaration. In virtue of what, then, is it still sense? It was noted above that most ordinary prose statements, though verifiable, are not in fact verified: because they belong to the familiarity with which men move in the perspective of their everyday lives. In a similar fashion, a statement of subjective significance immediately belongs if it is appropriated to a medium in which the listener is ready. A lover's stammering and disjointed talk, which sounds like shreds and patches of idiocy for most, will make wonderfully proper sense for one eager and prepared to listen. Its significance is, as it were, heard by the heart, and the heart knows what it is about. The poise-controlling ego, snatching at words in surprise, may not properly hear it. But when such speech makes sense, the only proof securing it would be to repeat, reiterate, dwell with its echo, to go over and place it. Where? In a perspective prepared by sensitiveness, but not to sets of symbols: such sense will escape a computer. Sensitiveness is being ready, in one's own live way, to touch and be touched by other entities in sight. Not only men are sensitive, but the human subject is also sensitive to significance in speech.

Three short approaches have been made to the sense found in statements, and no claim of exhaustiveness is raised for them. On the contrary, these lines only suggest further possibilities for exploring spoken sense. The nets of speech are cast wide—though wider is the ocean. In those criteria of statements mentioned, the securing of sense is never limited to speech or to a moment. Possible manipulations designed to verify, acts required to see coherence, sensitive dispositions to significance—all of these stretch beyond any verbal context from which they may issue. A proof of sense is a probe appropriating it. To find sense in a statement involves for any man more than to know its language; it means to prepare, be it skill, recollection, or sensitiveness. And to probe the property of sense means to compare: to pare the intention of speech together with entities named or unnamed, as demanded. This comparing confrontation is not arbitrary; whether the mode is interpersonal or individual, it must belong to a way which is own to the human subject. There are limits of verifiability, grades of coherence, shades of significance; outside them, a man can find no sense, but inside them what he hears or says belongs to how he exists, and he will rightly claim as proper his security of grasp—until he moves further. This finite but open zone or way of living with a sight on living has been referred to as a perspective. Perspectives may or may not cross and overlap. Words from various vocabularies are simplified titles alluding to such perspectives: science, art, faith, passion, efficiency, intelligence, and many others. But two notes of convergent import should be reiterated. One, that a perspective is more than a point of view, for the human being rarely stands and looks but always moves in a perspective; at any moment of grasping sense he has already moved toward it, and with it he will move while alive. Two, that human perspectives cannot be completely described, not only because there are too many but because others are always latent. Taken together, these two observations indicate that there is a background into which any perspective advances, a background as yet unfamiliar, unappropriated, and unworded, a background beyond entities encountered.

This suggests the question about the origin of any new sense not yet proper but perhaps appropriable. New words emerge, so do new arrangements of them; any positive attempt to close such growth would suicidally starve human perspectives. Yet it must be remembered that new sense hovers on the border of nonsense. Words like "Martian," "impressionism," "brinkmanship," "flying machine," demanded by the novelty of what they may name, have their sense accepted reluctantly, often partially; but a word like "time machine" may never make proper sense. The statement, "Earth moves," a novel arrangement of old words referring to what is not new, has sense whose appropriation history is well known. And a more radically novel statement, also not meant for anything new, "Nothing nihilates"—it must at least at first sound improper. Like the Copernican statement, it offends a familiar "rational" perspective; yet, unlike the other, it attempts to reach beyond any perspective on entities. Unprovable and incomparable, it is easily rejected as nonsense. Yet the present approaches to words and their arrangements were aimed to show that their sense is secured when they are selectively compared, grouped together with what is already familiar and what has already been said; such appropriation is demanded also for new ideas and discoveries of entities. Then if speech hazards to call out the antithesis of anything familiar, owned, or secure, it passes the boundaries of known sense. But if "there is" more than men say and secure, if human perspectives remain open to advance, their background need not be dismissed as "nonsense" and may be guarded as "not yet sense." From there is drawn today what yesterday had no sense; must thought forget whence will emerge tomorrow's sense? The background— no thing, no proper word, no familiar entity—envelops the sense of human speech. Toward that ventures the wondering thought, sometimes known as philosophy, which mentions "nothing" and means "being."

Single words have sense if they belong to a gathering order; and the sense of statements is appropriated, more than verbally, within the order of perspectives. A parallel conclusion could be reached in considering the sense of larger unities of words, such as discourses, theories, descriptive reports, or works of literature. But this brief survey would be entirely inadequate if it were to leave the impression that sense is restricted to a verbal medium. Speech is a power of existing men, but they find sense not only when hearing or reading. In a situation, a groan may make more sense than the words, "I am hurt." Of course, someone might hold that speech is but a growing mixture of groans, grins, and growls with grammar. Leaving aside such quasi-linguistic phenomena, sense can be found in attitudes or actions, and not only when they are described by words. There is a variety of what might be called "living modes or patterns": simple and complex activities, thoughtful and thoughtless views, feeling and mood dispositions—all of these may sometimes have sense and sometimes none. At least some sketchy allusions to them must be made here—of necessity in words, though not words are intended. It should be kept in mind that the few examples to follow are picked at random from an inexhaustible horizon on which possible modes of living arise. Men's deeds and ideas are as open as trails over the prairie, and even harder to trace.

How do patterns of acting make sense? "Eye of newt and toe of frog, wool of bat and tongue of dog"—some such ingredients used to be mixed in a cauldron with the application of heat and pressure; today the ingredients may be iron, copper, carbon, but the pattern of activity is parallel. The former procedure used to make sense, to impress and frighten people; the latter does now. Another example: in one setting it is accepted as sensible to hang a man for his theft of a loaf of bread; in another setting the sensible handling of a triple murderer is to make him lie on a couch and relate the details of his childhood. Or something simpler: for some people there is sense in getting up long before sunrise, while for others it is necessarily proper to burn the midnight oil. None of these behavioral patterns, personal or inter-personal, has sense when taken in isolation. But any one of them can show sense when derived from a familiar ground of tradi-tions, conceptions, and experiences, and when correlated with definite results aimed at. Every human undertaking is embedded for its sense in a larger perspectival order, or what is taken as order.

What is that? It is a man's clear or dim orientation—how he is there temporally like other men, wherewith they have lived and hope to, how to act properly or what belongs to the human life. But no pattern of acting, as no pattern of words, can be expected to have sense for all men; nor can we know how long the present patterns will be accepted. This indicates that every human be-ing appropriates the privilege of inventiveness in what to do as well as in what to say with sense, and further, that for such novelty "there is" where to draw from: in the background stretches a horizon yielding what has not yet been done, handled, encountered, and hence is not spoken of. But isn't this notion of an open horizon a manner of referring to possibility? Perhaps so, except that the questionable status of possibility between what is and is not tends to confine it to a mental con-struction or a linguistic mode, while the present consideration contains the literal groping of hands and bodies; and to simplify by saying that inventive ways of drawing, manipulating, and moving are just possibilities that lie in people, is to obliterate the question where, in what inventory, a human being invents or comes across such an entity as a new but sensible action.

It would be clearly one-sided to take men's patterns of acting as mere physical bodily movements. They have been brought to attention here to stress that they have sense as actions, not as thoughts; but this need not make them blind. In the confluence of life, they are not divorced from patterns of the mind. Often they are influenced by another kind of living modes, viz., the more or less lasting views men hold with stronger or weaker rationalization. Such views deserve mention apart from word arrangements, because they need not be genuine verbal structures: men are in their grip without being ready to explicate them in words. They belong as much to character as to intellect; thus various epistemological tangles need not be entered, e.g., whether such views constitute knowledge, belief, or illusion, whether their source is experience, reason, or revelation. For a man who will not be able to settle any of this, his views nevertheless make sense and are quite secure in his thinking; and only some existential perspectives demand clarity, consistency, and self-examination in one's thought.

Pressing examples of such views into a few words may make them appear more cut and dried than they are in fact. For example, some men accept and approve decent stability in kinds of things without ever having heard of Aristotle, while others believe in evolution without knowing what Darwin meant by that word. Again, regardless of his astronomical knowledge and his ability to verbalize it, one man will view the stars as a benevolent scatter of golden lights while another will assess them as worlds to conquer. Another example: human society can be thought of as providing comfort and guidance hinging on forceful organization, and it can be thought of as a leveling frame of norms hampering divergent self-expression. It will hardly be denied that any one of such views, often incompatible with others, makes perfectly proper and familiar sense to various people and can be important for the way they live. Its sense is not isolated; its sources and consequences, illuminable for example in psychoanalytic exploration, belong together to a man's wide orientation about his being there in the world—although much of this may be submerged in forgetfulness, doubt, or naive ignorance. Like his modes of acting, any man's views have sense in a larger order; but this has not the rigid structure of logical coherence, rather the unpredictable integrity of a hand-woven mosaic design. Consequently, there is no limit to the multiplicity of views which have sense for men, nor to the continuing emergence of new ones. Their abundantly available hold on men might be so impressive as to suggest the sterile principle: "Nihil novi." But reflection could show that this pressure on any mind of all that others had thought of tends to screen and obscure the horizon to which new views may turn. The horizon, to use Jaspers' term, is "encompassing" men, thoughts, words, entities; it is as far as time.

One more kind of living mode should be mentioned, particularly to stress the unity of the human being, because it overlaps the bodily nature of his actions and the mentality of his views. It makes sense for men to feel differently in differing circumstances of life; thus a few comments are due on the sense of feeling dispositions. There is sense in feeling furious when insulted, with heightened pulse and vengeful intent; but perhaps there is also sense in subduing anger with charity. There is sense in being anxious when insecure but also in striving for—and perhaps in failing to find—security through material possessions, human fellowship, or devotion to a cause, or in challenging insecurity by making danger an occupation. There is sense in love for God, for abstract thinking, for nature's beauty, for one single person, but often so that for the subject another kind of loving, of living, would not make sense at all. There can be sense in the satisfaction with right and justice or in lighting the smiles of happiness; but these two aspirations often clash. The temporal and personal appropriation of sense is nowhere so striking as in moods, affections, and sentiments; yet the fact that they have sense warns against dismissing them as irrational.

One rather than another feeling disposition is demanded; by itself possibly silly, shallow, and stupefying, it makes sense as it belongs elsewhere beyond itself. Intertwined with and often underlying man's views and activities, these modes of feeling about how to live properly are picked, selected, chosen. They constitute for the human being the choice of respective weight and prominence of entities in the perspectives of existence. Choice by a man or for a man involves a field, a display, a horizon; if he participates in the choice to any extent, such a horizon must be open to his consciousness. But if each and every thing to be felt with sense can be displayed forthcoming from the horizon, then that is no thing and surpasses them all. Sense points to the horizon of being.

What is sense? To approach this question some lines of the preceding sketch must be recollected. Various instances of sense have been brought forward: words, statements, activities, views, feelings. In every instance it could be plausibly asserted: this has or makes sense which can be grasped. But it may not be plausibly said of any instance that sense is quite within it—in that word, in that statement, in that living pattern. Paradoxically, every instance of sense has it and lacks it, too. Sense appears like an ever borrowed evanescence. No matter how large a sensible unity is considered, its sense is always due somewhere beyond. And the availability of instances can be seen as ever owing: there is more than given words say, there can be statements or views as yet inconceivable, there is a background to yield possible novel actions or moods. And much of what used to make sense no longer does. It is hardly surprising that impatience cries out about the senselessness of it all.

The French language preserves a usage which might help to make sense of sense. "Sens," sense, is direction. Direction, of course, is not simply assignable: nothing in the world is just "down," despite the Epicureans, or just "south," without debating how a line crosses the South Pole. But any spatial entity can belong to a direction. In suggesting that sense is direction, not a tautological definition is proposed but a way of thinking. To make sense is to belong together with—whatever fits that order of belonging; but the order can be of different kinds, e.g., logical, behavioral, poetic. To the anticipated objection that this overextends the notion of order, the answer is that an order is accepted by the human subject in finding sense, though it may not be acceptable to others. But to think of sense as direction is not to take it spatially; directions of sense can rival those of space in

their multiplicity, but they are not, like the latter, indifferently
multiplied. Any structure with sense is demanded for some human
orientation in life, or else it remains but without sense; its belonging to an order is personally appropriable, which the infinite
lines in space need not be. And further, sense direction is not
reversible. "Down" is well paired with "up" and "south" with
"north." But reversing the sequence of sounds and words, or
undoing activities destroys the order of sense; only coincidence
might yield some other. This suggests that sense as direction
involves not so much space as time.

Such is indeed the trend of the preceding observations. Terms
have been used which are understandable as metaphors. Without
metaphors much thought could fail in intelligibility. Yet they
can have other intent: "orientation," not in a territory but in the
selection of a man's temporal resources; "perspective," not to
stand and look at landscape but to move through life with insight and foresight; "horizon," not as division of earth and sky
but as the bourne from which possible entities come forth, are
made to come forth to confront the human being; and "background," exceeding and receding from anything familiar and
named, anything, many would say, there is. Such words are
guide-signs for the temporal sense of sense.

Sense cannot be understood without a transcending outlook.
Whatever has sense in what is said, done, or felt must be ap-
pointed in the preceding and point to succeeding sense. Preceding roots in familiarity are languages learned, thoughts and
traditions accepted, personal tendencies developed. Succeeding
fruits depend on imagination, enterprise, susceptibility. Making
sense has always its "wherewith" and "whereto." It would seem
that to speak of sensitivity, of having sense for something—even
of the five senses—is also to point out contacts with some transcending beyond. And the understanding of sense as orienting
direction in temporal existence is therefore historical. Only the
question arises: Is sense within human history?

Men name, produce, and manipulate entities. But it must be

kept in mind that no single entity is self-sufficient in sense. When any man brings forth a new word, a new thought, a new activity, its sense is due to its belonging to an order involving other entities not made by him. A man owes his very ability to extend sense to the perspectives he has grown into. He may see novelty on the horizon as no one before him, but he does not create the horizon in being. Whenever anything makes sense to someone, it is not he who makes that sense, though he is not without a contribution in seeing, grasping, and appropriating it—as actor rather than author. Thus it is possible and proper to avoid the horns of a contemporary controversy: it is not true either that life, the world, being there as such has sense to be taken for granted, or that men must endow it with sense on their own. The making of sense is a history that intimately involves human beings in the interplay of their consciousness with entities encountered. But that history originates and moves on the background involving them all. It is not man-made, hence it is not the history of the human being: it is the history of being.

Has anything been securely proved here about being? To ask this is to misunderstand the sense of this essay. In proving, securing, and appropriating, man is involved with entities, and familiar ones; but being involves him. The sense he finds is direction in his speech and life; but being is not directed by him. The sense directions point to things in their ways; but being is no point, and no thing, ever a background for all ways to be. The easy conclusion could say that for common sense being is superfluous. Perhaps so, but is it superfluous for philosophy? Does philosophy need a conclusion? Is it still philosophy when it has said its last word? What would that word be?

William Earle

ONTOLOGICAL AUTOBIOGRAPHY

If phenomenology is increasingly winning attention in the philosophic world, perhaps it is due to the freshness with which it
enables us to approach some old philosophical problems and the
radicality of its ambitions. With its famous bracketings and reductions, it has swept aside provisionally a certain quantity of
traditional interpretation, common-sense assumption, and scientific construction to redirect our attention first of all to the fundamental living experiences themselves. After so much had been
said about them, they now reappear almost as something we
had never really looked at before except in so far as they might
illustrate what we thought we knew about them in advance and
on other grounds. And surely all this is to the good, and for
some this informal phenomenology is its only viable form. But
it most certainly is *not* sufficient to characterize either the full
method or its ambitions as they were developed by Husserl.
Phenomenology as "strict science" (*strenge Wissenschaft*) is
certainly no mere empirical or random reflection upon experience but something far more radical and transcendental. It was
at the beginning and remained to the end an effort to become *absolutely clear*. Concealed within this genuinely philosophic am-

bition, however, are problems of the most difficult order: *what is clarity, what* can we become clear *about,* and by what *procedures* can we become clear? Obviously, no philosopher has ever *sought* to become obscure or treasured it as an accomplishment; and yet what philosophers have taken to be clarity, what they have thought they could clarify, and the procedures for achieving whatever clarity could be attained have all been so variously construed as to repeat virtually the history of philosophy itself.

In what follows, then, I should like to offer a brief and I hope non-controversial account of Husserl's contentions on the question of phenomenological clarity, and then argue that there remains a residual domain which is not susceptible to any such clarity at all, and finally offer some suggestions as to what may be a more appropriate way of dealing with that domain. Since the domain in question is *human life* or what is now called "existence," what is at stake is whether there is any discipline which might appropriately be called "phenomenological existentialism" or "existential phenomenology." My contention is that there is none, and that what phenomenological existentialists aim at is more appropriately accomplished in what I shall call "ontological autobiography."

Phenomenological Clarity

Phenomenological investigations when successful are supposed to achieve an *intuitive insight.* All its procedures are controlled by this aim. The bracketings and reductions are all bracketings of what in principle cannot be reduced to intuition, bracketings of what in principle cannot *show* itself to intuition. Hence Husserl insisted on the "presuppositionless" character of phenomenology. The "natural standpoint," which was to be put "out of gear" in favor of phenomenological reflection, was so treated precisely because it lived and operated in the obscurity of its existential assumptions, that "of course" the world existed, and "of course" the variety of things we see about us and work with exist just as we see them. The deficiency of the natural standpoint is not expressed in a counter-thesis that the world did not exist, or that the things of the ordinary perceptible world did not exist, but that the very question of existence could not be raised, hence clarified, from the natural standpoint. If initially, then, "existence" and the "contingency" of existing things were bracketed, it was only in the interest of later clarifying what it *meant* to exist; existence was to be reinstated later under its clarified form.

The phenomenological position, then, aims at the immediacy of intuition; "seeing is the primordial sense of evidence," Husserl tried to demonstrate again and again. But the intuition of phenomenology must be understood equally as *insight*. The intuition in question was hardly staring at a datum, or attempting to paint its picture; it was an active insight into the constitution of the complex phenomenal object with particular reference to how its objective constitution was correlative to the subject to whom it must appear. Subjectivities were intentionally directed to objectivities; and objectivities in turn revealed upon analysis their correlation to subjectivity to and for whom they could appear as what they were. Husserl's analyses then were essentially noetic-noematic, in which the hope was to render intuitively evident the necessities which bound together subjectivity and its objective meaningful world. My present point, however, is not to rehearse these intentional analyses but to recall that the *insight* which phenomenology aspires to in principle must be insight into the *necessary*. Husserl from time to time uses the phrase "synthetic a priori"; it was the necessary and essential into which insight could be obtained. Into the contingent, the accidental, into that which could very well be otherwise, there can be no insight; at most there could be a recording of chance conjunctions, or an empirical classification and compilation; but no insight. With this even Aristotle would have agreed in his famous dictum that there is no "science of the accidental." The bracketing of the accidental Husserl formulated as the "eidetic reduction"; this was so to speak the most elementary reduction, not really distinctive of phenomenology but shared by it with other disciplines like mathematics. Phenomenology as a form of "strict science" remained always within the domain of the eidetic reduction. The essences into which phenomenological insight sought to penetrate were those essential and necessary correlations between subjectivity and any possible objective world which could have meaning for it.

Now, as virtually everyone would agree, the domain of existence is precisely the domain of the accidental and contingent. That is precisely the reason why all questions of fact were bracketed by Husserl in favor of an inquiry into essences and meanings. A fact is but a contingent illustration of an essential meaning, hence phenomenology can employ imaginative variation more profitably than factual observation. Existence is of course the one domain where something *can happen;* what can happen is precisely the accidental; and while once something has happened, it will be a determinate something or other, manifesting its own essence, which therefore can be clarified phenomenologically, *that* it has happened cannot be so clarified, is a matter of fact, and remains bracketed from phenomenology as strict science. Accordingly, no analysis whatsoever of any possible phenomenal object can disclose whether it is now a phenomenon to me; and no analysis which restricts itself to my consciousness can disclose what that consciousness is intentionally related to. And so the insight achieved in phenomenology is, for example, into the perceptible *as such,* and its correlation to the perceiving consciousness *as such;* but *what I now perceive,* of course, can be the subject of no phenomenological insight. And yet what I see is hardly of insignificance to me, although it is one of the "factual questions" inherently bracketed by phenomenology. It is of "merely autobiographical interest" and could form no paragraph in "strict science." Similarly, though it was hardly one of Husserl's favorite themes, *death* as it might appear within life might form a possible theme for phenomenological clarification, but as such it is a meaning, an essence, or an "irreality" as Husserl referred to it. On the other hand, *my* possible death, while it could certainly bear some such meaning, is mine, and I in my contingency am not, as Kierkegaard said with reference to Hegel, a paragraph in the system. I am, in fact, only of "autobiographical significance" to strict science, to any insight into essence; and so while the factual existence of any man is precisely what is bracketed by phenomenology as of merely autobiographical significance, it would be absurd for any existing man to bracket his own existence with its singularity and contingency, as of "merely" autobiographical significance to him. As an existent, it is all he has.

After having bracketed "existence," phenomenology in an effort to complete itself attempts to restore it; for, after all, in principle everything is capable of clarification. But what is reinstated, of course, is not existence which remains irreducibly contingent, but its signification, "existence," which isn't the same thing. Its essence or signification may be all that is capable of being clarified phenomenologically, but that hardly implies that they are identical. And a comparable thing happens when at the end Husserl wished to enlarge what had become a somewhat static phenomenology into an investigation of the *genesis* of significations. History with its progressive sedimentation of meaning comes into view, but again only under the aegis of *laws* and *essential* constitutions.

Human Life as a Phenomenological Residue

There is then, I believe, a domain which is irreducible to necessary meanings, which is *not* transcendentally constituted by the ego to whom it has meaning and to whom it appears; phenomenology, with its overriding interest in absolute clarity, strict science, and insight into the necessary, frankly brackets this domain and reinstates it only as a *sense* or *meaning*. But the domain of existence is not its own definition; it remains contingent, free, and unnecessary; it remains therefore a residue not soluble into phenomenological insight. There can be, I should conclude, no necessary insight or clarification of the domain that constitutes human life. And while this must seem a disappointment to those who take phenomenology as a comprehensive philosophy, in point of fact it should, I believe, be the occasion for rejoicing. For if the sense and meaning of my present life were accessible to *Husserl*, for example, what point would *I* now have in living it? My life would by that stroke be converted into a somewhat badly edited slow-motion movie whose essential plot and theme had already been grasped timelessly in a scenario, by others, and which therefore was pointless in itself, already having been grasped long ago. Could anything be more discouraging than any such view? And would not *any* such view be the one which made *every* human existence senseless precisely by having insight into its sense in advance? Traditionally, it amounts to fatalism.

And yet this is precisely the path taken by certain existentialist thinkers who wish to extend the phenomenological methods of Husserl to human existence itself. It is surely a good thing that philosophers have finally turned their attention to human life; our quarrel is hardly there. But at the same time it is of utmost importance that we consider precisely what sort of attention is exercised, what its procedures, aims, and presuppositions are. My own sentiment, for which I am trying to provide reasons, is that when the cognitive ambitions of phenomenology are directed to human life, there are reasons of principle for being alarmed at the hoped for results.

The paradox of a method which aims at being sympathetic to human existence in its own unique domain but ends by radically falsifying it can be seen in virtually every existentialist text. One of the most influential of these begins by assigning to *Dasein* the defining characteristic of *Jemeinigkeit. Dasein,* as we know, is the ontological designation for human being; *Jemeinigkeit* expresses the fact that human being is personal, or that existence is always the existence of some "me." So far, so good; and one would reasonably expect the remainder of the analysis to speak in the first person singular. It would then be frankly and openly an exploration of the sense of its author's existence. But no; that would be a delusion, would be merely ontic and not ontological. It is about *Dasein* and man *as such;* and it is not what is inherently *jemeinig* but *Jemeinigkeit,* a most deceptive category because it wishes to talk universally about what is inherently singular. And so what the analysis *indicates* as essential is at once forgotten in favor of a universal and essential doctrine of what had always been called "human nature." Gertrude Stein, who certainly could not have read Heidegger, shared similar ambitions: to write everybody's autobiography. She finally wrote it, and as might have been expected, it turned out to be her own unique life, far too singular to be *anyone* else's autobiography. If Heidegger then attempts to characterize the fashion in which human existence can recover itself from the distractions of anonymity by running forward in thought to its own personal extinction, it is instructive that Sartre finds a comparable absolute test in the realization that he cannot be God. But Jaspers, on the other hand, a good deal more aware of possibilities, finds a *variety* of *Grenzsituationen,* any of which can call my existence as a totality into question. No matter how instructive each of these analyses is, they would all be radically perverted, I believe, if they were taken as essential analyses of human existence, which however *is* exactly their explicit intention. Here we exempt Jaspers from the charge. Our present conclusion is that so long as human existence remains singular, free, and to any degree transcendental to its situation, there cannot possibly be any general, essential, phenomenological, or existential clarification of it; there is no possible conceptualization or theory which can at one and the same time express what is true of everybody and *pertinent* to anybody.

Ontological Autobiography

In a word, our lives are not pertinently touched by science or by theory, whether the science be natural science, the *strenge Wissenschaft* of phenomenology, or its illegitimate extension into existentialism. On the other hand, our singular and accidental lives are hardly unknown to us, even if they are not proper themes for eidetic analysis.

Let me then summarize the direction of my conclusions schematically:

(1) First of all, I am *not* arguing that rational validity is "reducible" to the merely personal circumstances of its thinker's life or undermining its validity by seeking to uncover the personal circumstances of its discovery. On the contrary, all essential insight is precisely that and profoundly independent of the thinker's existence. I am arguing that this very form of objectively valid, cogent insight into the necessary cannot be exercised upon human existence without radically betraying that existence. At some point we must try to express what is not independent of the thinker's life, and is it not obvious that this is the thinker's own life? A life, moreover, which is not lived in unconsciousness, but is always a living consciousness itself?

(2) While I should agree with the general existentialist theme that human existence is of overriding ontological interest, the human existence most accessible to me is my own; in general then, the basic interest of ontology must be satisfied, if anywhere, in an autobiographical consciousness. I can know what existence is like not primarily by watching others but in my own person. What I then elucidate is my life with others and *not* "human being as such."

(3) The most elementary reflection upon that existence discloses that it is always a question of something *happening;* it is what I choose, what I do, what I suffer with and among the people I know. I bear a proper name, so do they; if I ever were

to discover some inherent essential *pattern* in the whole affair, it could not retain either my proper name or theirs, and would in its necessity and generality ascend into the irrelevant. It would not express what they and what I did. If I could attain an insight into *la situation humaine*, it would not be an insight into the domain of my choice, where I still have something to decide. Nor are matters helped when human life is regarded as located in a *system* of possibilities. The system of possibilities of choice is either taken as *exhaustive*, in which case I am enclosed once more within the necessary; or it is presented informally as *mere possibilities*, in which case it loses the force of cogent insight, as well as eidetic science, and sinks to the level of interesting suggestions, to be supplemented by possibilities disclosed to every other human existence. Accordingly, I am *not* forced to raise the "question of the meaning of Being," as in Heidegger, on pain of being excluded from authentic *Dasein,* hence am not forced to orient my resoluteness by the light of death. The truth is that such questioning is a possibility only, expressive of one man's existence, Martin Heidegger, and those who are preoccupied with that question with him. Heidegger comes dangerously close to admitting this when he declares that he alone was the first to even raise the question in any explicitness. Nor, with Sartre, am I compelled to achieve freedom by realizing that I cannot become God and must therefore come to terms with the nothingness of my existence. In a word, each of these analyses is to be understood rather as an excavation in depth of the singular lives which they express, and interesting precisely in that light. Properly understood they constitute highly instructive examples of ontological autobiography.

(4) But highly delusive ones as well. The proper style of autobiography is narration, not proof or explanation. There is no insight into what happens as such; at best and finally, all that any can do is tell what happened. Sartre's repeated efforts in existential psychoanalysis to uncover the fundamental projects of Baudelaire, of Genet, and most recently of himself all presup-

pose that each singular existence *has* a fundamental project, and that it is this project which the singular existence goes about realizing. And no doubt there are lives sufficiently stylized to suggest such a fundamental project; perhaps Sartre's is one of them. But in Genet's case, the very disclosure of the project, according to Genet's own testimony, paralyzed his life for five years; he only recovered his spontaneity by taking a new turn. Now indeed perhaps the new turn is also but another expression of the same project, in which case the fundamental project is, since it remains the same, incapable of accounting for the new turn, and his life is to be understood not simply through the fundamental project but chiefly through the free spontaneity which works in his life. However, this is not "understanding it" but rather narrating it.

(5) In the cases of both Heidegger and Sartre we have, properly speaking, "ontological autobiographies," that is, an analysis of a fundamental sense of life pushed to ontology. Heidegger's is "fundamental-Ontologie," and Sartre's is "phenomenological ontology." In both, however, the analysis pushes toward a pretended universality, and the explicit autobiographical content is muted or absent. I should like to suggest that if ontology aims at what is ontologically richest, and therefore at what Being has become, it should reverse this traditional aspiration toward the universal, that which everything exemplifies or which all men exemplify, and aim at what Nietzsche aimed at when he said: Against the value of the forever unchanging, the value of the briefest, most perishable, the most seductive glints of gold on the belly of the serpent, *vita*. And even Hegel, in his reiterated demonstrations that Being as such is the emptiest of concepts, virtually nothing, whereas the richest is what these universals have become by differentiating themselves into the concrete universal, the historical and unrepeatable fulfillment of ontology.

It is then by no means certain that to be authentic is to pose a question about Being, or to confront the impossibility of being God, *or anything else formulable in advance*. It is by no means certain that there is a universally formulable sense to life, a formulable schematism of its situation or the possibilities open to its choice; but it does seem to me certain that if there *were* some such universal sense to life, then at that very instant all human life would lose *whatever* sense a free being might wish to endow it with. Hence if ontology wishes to complete itself it must direct itself to the autobiographical, without any effort to see through the autobiographical into another formulable schematism. Finally, there is no sign at all that *ontology* will yield up the answer either. Traditionally, of course, it looks like the supreme discipline; but when it is directed to human existence, what assurance have we that its favorite term, *Being*, has not been stretched out of shape and useless for its intended purpose? Even here, it appears, that human existence is under no obligation to ask ontological questions, that ontology supplies the sense only of the lives of ontologists, and that at long last, since no human existence can pretend to be exemplary for all, we are not "reduced" to pure autobiography but elevated to it and its search for its proper form of expression. And here each must accomplish the elucidation of his own life by himself without rules.

John J. Compton

NATURAL SCIENCE AND
THE EXPERIENCE OF NATURE

With a few exceptions, notably Husserl himself, phenomenologists have not generally reflected extensively on the physical or
natural sciences.[1] On the other hand, they have concerned themselves from the beginning with the foundations of the human

1. Any list of the generally relevant phenomenological contributions
would have to include, besides Husserl's writings, sections of Merleau-Ponty,
especially Chapter 3 of *The Structure of Behavior*, Boston, 1963, as well
as more recent studies: Suzanne Bachelard, *La Conscience de Rationalité:
Étude Phénoménologique sur la Physique Mathématique*, Paris, 1958; Alfred
Schütz, *Collected Papers*, I, Parts I and III, The Hague, 1962; Herbert
Marcuse, "On Science and Phenomenology" and Aron Gurwitsch, "Comment on the Paper by H. Marcuse" in R. Cohen and M. Wartofsky, eds.,
Boston Studies in the Philosophy of Science, New York, 1965; and Joseph
Kockelmans, *Phenomenology and Physical Science*, Pittsburgh, 1966. Aron
Gurwitsch's careful review of Husserl's *Krisis* is most important (*Philosophy
and Phenomenological Research*, XVI, 1956, and XVII, 1957). In addition,
there was some early work by Hedwig Conrad-Martius and Moritz Geiger
in philosophy of nature; Hermann Weyl acknowledged indebtedness to
Husserl in his *Philosophy of Mathematics and Natural Science*, Princeton,
1949; and Wolfgang Köhler departs from what he considers a phenomenological basis in his *The Place of Value in a World of Facts*, New York,
1938. (I am grateful to Alden Fisher and to Herbert Spiegelberg for many
of these references.)

sciences and have enriched the comprehension of human behavior, language, decision, moods, feelings, and perception—
the bases of interpersonal life and of culture. It may be that
phenomenology has little to add to the comprehension of physical science afforded by recent studies of its logic, language,
methods, and theoretical structure. Or it may be that the pro-
grammatic suggestions of Husserl have yet to be followed up,
that the current style of the philosophy of science is in certain
respects inadequate, and that in these areas phenomenology may
properly speak. I mean to explore the latter alternative in order
to describe the outlines of a phenomenological philosophy of
natural science.

I

Husserl, in the *Krisis,* spoke of a "crisis in the sciences," especially in physical science, by which he seems to have meant a
loss of meaning, both in the sense of philosophical content and
of relatedness to human purpose.[2] This emptying of significance
has come about in part, he held, because of the abstract and
technical, largely mathematical methodology of physics and increasingly of the other natural sciences. As a result, both as
enterprises and sources of liberating natural knowledge, they
have moved away from their roots in common life and experience. This alienation of man from science and of science from
man does not, as Husserl clearly saw, represent a failure of
science as such, but rather of our use and interpretation of it—
a failure, in fact, of philosophy.

Little needs to be added to Husserl's description in order to
bring it up to date. Today, after another world war and during
a period of rapid scientific development and enormous technical
and social change, the same diagnosis is valid. Men live in a
world created by and open to destruction through science, but

2. *Edmund Husserl, Die Krisis der Europäischen Wissenschaften,* Hus-
serliana, VI, The Hague, 1954.

they too hastily embrace or fear it, its practitioners, the power it fosters, the specialist language it employs, and the attitudes of objective analysis it sustains. We need to attach natural science to human existence, but in order to accomplish this realistically and intelligently there must be an understanding of science as a human activity; and, to this end, there must be comprehension of the total, historic phenomenon of "doing" science. Prevailing intellectualist philosophies of science, however, analyze the sciences outside this human context of development and meaning. Science is treated as a body of propositions, terms, operations, and inference rules; or as a process of experimental manipulation, of theory construction, of curve fitting, of prediction and control. Thus science comes to be considered as a species of intellectual *techne* or intellectual game, a game of devising mathematical constructs and models to fit highly specialized and selected experimental data. Now play, in its many forms, is fundamental to human existence; it is even significantly present in science itself. But science is not simply a game or a form of logical play, however useful it may be to treat it as such for special analytical purposes. And while this is an obvious truth, it is rarely deemed a philosophically important one. A phenomenological philosophy of science, on the other hand, should be expected to take seriously the incarnation of scientific work in the historic-personal-perceptual life of its practitioners and should aim at eliciting from this life the immanent purposes or intentionalities which define it.

When science is considered as a mode of man's historic being-in-the-world, a number of its essential characteristics become apparent.

(1) SCIENCE IS PERSONAL. The individual scientist sees his work against the background of his own particular vision of things, a vision affected deeply by the culture-world in which he finds himself. How he sees his problem—indeed whether he sees one or not, what concepts and alternative solutions occur or seem plausible to him, and which of these he finds most convincing—

all depend upon what he is looking for. That, in turn, is affected and modified by his skills and enthusiasms, his working conditions, his relations to his government, his religious commitments, his philosophical system, his aesthetic tastes and ideals of order, as well as guided by currents of scientific thought, the state of technology, and so on.

(2) SCIENCE IS COMMUNAL. The scientific community has evolved into a large, complex, international institution with its own communal world. The scientific community has its societies and honors, its traditions, orthodoxies, and heresies, its innovators and routine contributors, authorities, administrative boards, vast laboratory establishments, and economic and political managers. Through these many roles and facets of institutional life there has come to be expressed a distinctive orientation to the world which sets the scientific community apart from other communities.

(3) SCIENCE IS THEORETICAL. Although phases of scientific work reveal many proximate objectives, and although it is of course clear that the motivations of individual scientists are varied, yet there is a governing orientation, namely, the intent to apprehend what is the case. Science and technology are increasingly interrelated; basic and applied research are not always easily distinguishable. But these facts do not obscure the point that in the strict sense the primary product of scientists is theory; only indirectly do they produce instruments, machines, and changes in economic and social conditions.

It is quite important, moreover, that scientific method requires experimental perturbation of the ordinary states of things, and that mathematical constructs must be devised, extended, and systematically related in order to "save the phenomena" yielded by experiment. But such experimental manipulation, theoretical construction, prediction, and control are instrumentalities of a governing intent. The intent and logically relevant effect of the methodological cycle is to reduce the qualitative, perspectival, and incomplete perceptual presence of things in order to present them in fuller clarity; it is to bring the structures of events and processes in nature, their mutual relations and dependencies, to clearer, more precise, and universally communicable formulation.

(4) SCIENCE IS ONTOLOGICAL.[3] If the theoretic stance is accepted as the manner of doing science, then we must acknowledge the ontological claim that accompanies it. While science requires creative activity as much as any art, it is not literally a creative art. It is directed to the analysis of a world already at hand; it bears on an object which we customarily identify as "nature" and claims to articulate its structure.

The problem of interpreting the results of the natural sciences is this: how is one to interpret the ontological claim? What is this "nature" to which reference is made? Is it identical with "all that is," or is it dependent upon some ground? Is it to be considered "human experience," the "flux of sensations," a mental construct, or some "mode of extra-mental being"? What are the most pervasive traits which mark something as natural? Is a man natural, a culture? In short, as a way of expressing the intent of all of these questions, in what does the unity of nature consist?

It will not do simply to respond that nature is "what science studies," or that it is "what is designated by the non-logical variables or constructs of verified natural science," or even a specified sub-set of these, for it is precisely the significance of these expressions that is open to question. One wants to know what sort of thing natural science does study and what sort of reality the constructs of science do possess. One wants to know what it means to say that science bears on nature or that scientific objects are physically real. These are palpably not scientific

3. My usage of the term "ontology" in this paper is more inclusive than Husserl's. By saying that science is "ontological" I mean to assert both what Husserl would mean (that it defines a region of objects, namely nature, intended by consciousness and open to eidetic description) and also that science is "metaphysical" in his sense (that it shares with the natural attitude a tendency to impute to that region the status of a region of being in iself), which metaphysical claim must be critically interpreted.

questions, and yet upon their mode of resolution depends the entire theoretical significance ascribed to science.

One has to do justice, on the one hand, to the theoretic—one might say philosophic—function of science, and on the other, to the technical irrelevance of scientific theory to ontological questions. When Ernst Mach denied the reality of atoms and Einstein the reality of indeterminacy, it was not on the grounds of scientific fact or theory but of their particular ontological convictions. Their criteria of what would count as "real" in the physical world were different from each other as well as from those of other physicists.[4] And when, in a more recent case, J. J. C. Smart denies the reality of mental events partly because of what he calls a "scientific realism," it is not on the basis of an appeal to different scientific facts but because he treats the ontological significance of physical and physiological science differently from some other philosophers, for example, A. J. Ayer.[5] Thus, the issue can be put quite sharply in the following manner: (a) Natural science is carried on as an ontologically informative enterprise, but (b) no scientific theory as such contains an ontology directing its interpretation, therefore, (c) some ontology of nature must be invoked in order to provide such an interpretation.[6]

II

The question is what form this concept or ontology of nature should take and how it may be developed in a reasoned manner.

4. G. Buchdahl, "Science and Metaphysics," in D. F. Pears, *The Nature of Metaphysics*, London, 1957.

5. J. J. C. Smart, *Philosophy and Scientific Realism*, New York, 1963.

6. I have given a fuller development of this argument in relation to current views of the role of theory in science in my paper "Understanding Science," *Dialectica*, XVI, No. 2 (1963), 155-176. Also cf. Alphonse De Waelhens, "Science, Phénomènologie, Ontologie," in *Existence et Signification*, Louvain, 1958.

In approaching an answer to this question, we find a clue in our ordinary and pre-scientific experience which we need to consider seriously. It is simply that we inhabit nature and are in manifold, daily interactions with it. This world of our ordinary perceptions and actions is precisely the one in which natural science takes place, and it is precisely from such pre-scientific experiences of nature—from "ordinary" looking, handling, expecting, relating, reviewing, discovering, and testing—that science has come. Upon this basis, Husserl advances the following thesis:

> In physical method the *perceived thing itself* is always and in principle *precisely the thing* which the *physicist studies and scientifically determines.* . . . The thing which he observes, with which he experiments, which he sees continually, handles, places on the scales, "brings to the fusing furnace," this and no other thing is the subject of physical predicates, since it is it that has the weight, mass, temperature, electrical resistance, and so forth. So, too, it is the perceived processes and connexions themselves which are defined through concepts such as force, acceleration, energy, atom, ion, and so forth.[7]

And Merleau-Ponty suggests a similar viewpoint:

> The whole universe of science is built upon the world as directly experienced, and if we want to subject science itself to rigorous scrutiny and arrive at a precise assessment of its meaning and scope, we must begin by re-awakening the basic experience of the world of which science is the second-order expression.[8]

The position being taken here is simply that the ontological significance and unity of natural science is guaranteed by the reality and unity of the world of "ordinary" perception, because it is exactly that world of perception which is subjected to analysis from the scientific standpoint. This is sometimes called the principle of the "primacy of perception." To put it nega-

7. E. Husserl, *Ideas*, London, 1952, par. 52.
8. M. Merleau-Ponty, *The Phenomenology of Perception*, New York, 1962, p. viii. Cf. his *The Primacy of Perception*, edited by James M. Edie, Evanston, 1964.

tively, and to adapt Husserl's expression, this principle "alters the sign" of the ontological value of science. It implies that the objects of science can have no more reality than the reality of the perceived world from which they are the abstracted, idealized parts, processes, and relations—that their being is dependent upon the reality of the perceived world. Put positively, precisely by virtue of this dependence, the objects of science need to be recognized as real in their manner, for the very mark and paradigm of physical reality is primordially found in the perceptual encounter with things.

Throughout the history of science, philosophies or ontologies of nature—Aristotelian, Democritean, Platonic, Cartesian, Spinozist, Kantian, Hegelian, and the like—have operated so as to suggest methods, styles, or even specific concepts in science, and to interpret scientific results. So it is here. The specific approach to an ontological interpretation of nature which I have just described along phenomenological lines seems to me a most fruitful one to explore. It arises from concrete experience of nature and accords with the concrete practice of science. What I wish to do in the space at my disposal is to draw some of the implications which this approach may be interpreted to entail. I say "may be interpreted to entail" because I am not aware that all these points have been made fully explicit heretofore, nor am I certain that they all follow with equal strictness from the principle of the primacy of perception as Husserl and Merleau-Ponty have stated it. It is thus the scope of that principle which must be determined.

It is well, at first, and all too briefly, to rule out certain possible misconceptions of what is being said. To assert the ultimate reference of natural science to the world of perception is neither subjectivist nor phenomenalist. It would be so only if perception itself were so analyzed; but it is not. Perception as here understood is active openness to a meaningful world already and constantly at hand, a world revealed through the mutual implications of perspectives, inexhaustible in its novelty, and engaged in a lived interaction with our bodies. This is not Berkeley or Hume; nor is it Kant. The world of perception, in this view, is no synthesis of a spectatorial ego, no construct of the mind. Rather, the world as perceived is the foundation and precondition for such conceptual synthesis as may be achieved as the further dispositions of perceived things are revealed through experimental analysis.

In addition, it might be thought that an assertion of the ontological primacy of the perceived world would entail reduction of scientific concepts to perceptual data, or some reduction of scientific reality to those objects and relations with pictureable, or otherwise perceptible, models; whereas, pure empiricism in the philosophy of science has long been dead, and it is now commonplace that perceptible models, as in microphysics, must frequently be given up. But such an interpretation would be misleading. For the principle under discussion is not that scientific concepts and laws "summarize" perceptions, nor that scientific objects "resemble" them, but rather the insistence that the ultimate *reference* of scientific concepts and calculations is always to the perceived world, and that scientific objects are always to be understood as parts or relations of the things of perception considered under certain idealized or simplifying conditions. Thus microphysical processes specified by the Schrödinger equation, for example, may be considered real, although no perceptual model of the state function, that is, no ordinary wave or particle image, is possible.

On the other hand, certain interesting consequences do seem legitimately to follow from this sort of ontological interpretation of science. Let me mention four.

(1) Fundamental, I think, is the *justification provided by this view for the persistent, practical, one might say "physiological," realism of scientific work,* and thus for the continuity between certain attitudes in the laboratory and those of ordinary life.

It is at this point that all conventionalist, instrumentalist, operationalist, and idealist views of scientific theory must fail, whatever their technical interest may be. To the scientific investigator, the world of atomic reactions, ion diffusions, gene replications, and organic evolution presents itself, as does its source in the perceived world, as "already there," inexhaustible, disclosed relationally and only partially through perspectives provided by our bodily experimentation; a world never subject to our mastery, yielding only to apprenticeship, and remaining always in some measure opaque; a field or horizon suggesting ever further possibilties of analysis. It is only because this world of scientific objects is constituted in and from the perceptual world that such real independence attaches to it. And it is precisely because of this independence that we consider tested scientific theory to be not merely convenient or coherent, but to be true.

The realism of science is thus secured without creating the anomaly of a world *behind* the world, a world of mathematically and conceptually known objects behind the world of perception, a type of "naive" realism—Husserl calls it naturalism—which readily forgets its source, rejects the epistemological significance of perception, and ignores the experimental conditions that define the context of application of scientific concepts.

(2) A second implication of the primacy of perception is closely related to the first. It is natural to suppose that if the ultimate reference of scientific constructs is to the world of perception, then there is implied some sort of conformality of nature as scientifically known to nature as perceptually lived. Thus it ought to follow that *some essential characteristics of the scientific analysis of nature would correspond to and be justified by some pervasive structural features of the lived experience of nature.*

It seems obvious that this is the case in quite familiar ways. We do seek lawful relations among variables in science because we are familiar with regularities in ordinary experience; we do posit causal production in the sciences because we discern dependencies among ordinary events and processes. Is it possible to go further in this direction and suggest that it is on the same basis that we tend to distinguish scientific constructs that designate "physically real" aspects of things from those which do not? That is, given a situation in which tested theory is to be interpreted, it seems evident that not all constructs associated with the theory are or should be invested with the same ontological significance. Some specify properties or relations, such as distance, energy, or adaptive value; others specify systems, such as electrons, ions, or organisms; some are purely heuristic or calculational, such as instantaneous velocities, force vectors, intelligence scales, price indices, and the like. Upon what basis do we tend to make such distinctions? Is it a basis related to our ordinary experience of the "real" or the "natural" in lived perception?

There does seem to be significant conformality here, if one considers characteristics of the experience of nature: (a) We find *independence* essential for natural entities—that is, being already at hand, not subject to determination by thought or wish but responsive to investigative action and manipulation and thus "available," "ever surprising us," and the like. Careful measurement is a scientific device for establishing such independence. (b) *Individuality* is a second mark of reality in nature—that is, in a very inclusive sense, possessing some boundary principle, or, to put it functionally, some coordinating principle of parts or action. For this permits identification and consequently lets us return to the object, or to a similar object, and explore it. The scientific concern for invariance under stipulated transformations is a manifestation of this and may be the basis for preferring the so-called primary qualities of things in scientific explanations. (c) *Extensiveness* is a requisite of the natural as lived—that is, that it be volumetric, dimensional, that it define some region or relation in lived space-time and consequently be open to being regarded through new perspectives and revealing new facets. This may be the reason for insisting, as some physicists have, that a construct prove essential in two or more logically independent experimental-theoretical contexts before it may be considered to designate something in nature. (d) Finally, *continuity*, specifically over time, is a primary characteristic of what we experience as real in nature. This is the manner in which an "object" appears to us, as an evolving or coordinated process. Here are good old substance and causality, and perhaps, as Kant said, the roots of the scientific ascription of reality to systems with lawfully changing states.[9]

It should be obvious that these forms of the lived experience of nature are flexible and open. Whether an electron is deemed physically real, because it lacks individuality and continuity, or whether the concepts of organism, mind, and culture designate parts of nature—as seems reasonable from their general function —depends both upon the scientific development of those concepts and the rigor with which the forms or criteria of nature are applied. I would not begin to argue that phenomenological analysis will improve the clarity or applicability of such criteria in their strictly scientific use; but it is plausible that through such description their *basis*, lying as it does in the form of the perceived world, may be clarified and extended. And in this way the dependence of the scientific concept of "reality" upon perception can be shown with greater precision.

(3) A third fundamental consequence of the ontological primacy of perception is *the interpenetration of the concerns of philosophy and natural science with nature.*[10]

It is a formidable abstraction of contemporary intellectual life that all factual discussions of the world are relegated to empirical science, while philosophy is confined to second-order reflection on scientific or other forms of method, judgment, and lan-

9. For a discussion of the scientific use of criteria of physical reality, see Ernest Nagel, *The Structure of Science*, New York, 1961, Chapter 6, esp. pp. 145-152.

10. M. Merleau-Ponty, "Le Philosophe et la Sociologie" in *Cahiers Internationaux de Sociologie*, X (1951), 50-69 (now available in translation in Richard McCleary's edition of *Signs*, Evanston, 1964, pp. 98-113).

guage. But if the same natural order is indeed the reference of both scientific analysis and of pre- and non-scientific experience, then two things follow: (a) a philosophical re-evocation of the *form* of that primary experience must be suggestive for the interpretation of science, as I have just now argued. But, equally importantly, (b) the factual-conceptual *content* of natural science must be expected to amend any description of that world as perceived.

The relationship here is a most subtle one. Consider some examples. It is perhaps not strictly logically impossible to retain faith in our perception of telic behavior among living organisms while accepting a biology which treats this as a mere appearance, but such a situation seriously threatens our sense of the unity of experienced and scientifically described nature. This situation is considerably improved if further biological research, developments in cybernetics, or clearer conceptual analysis show the scientifically objective character of such behavior.

Similarly, although it is strictly possible to maintain the phenomenological reality of temporal becoming, of novelty and historicity within a Newtonian, essentially timeless universe as physically described, it is at considerable loss of conceptual (not to say existential) coherence to do so. To believe in the primacy and unity of the lived world as the foundation of physics was, in the eighteenth and nineteenth centuries, virtually impossible, or could be achieved only by reducing perceptual experience to sense-data—as Hume did—or by neglecting certain of its features and construing that experience as rigorously Newtonian, as absolute in time, space, and causal dependence—as did Kant. But with the dramatic changes in our physical world-view which have emerged in this century, the situation is completely changed. The new physical picture, from quantum and relativistic physics, is one in which time may be interpreted as irreversible and historic, in which spatial configurations evolve and depend upon the distribution of material, in which sub-atomic indeterminacy appears irreducible, and aggregates of events begin to replace well-defined particles as fundamental to physical explanation.[11]

This is a familiar story. But the interesting point is that this development reopens the pre-scientific experience of nature to more accurate deciphering. It alters the concept of nature; it aids the phenomenological "reduction" by forcing attention anew to the qualities of lived experience. It is not wholly true, as is so often maintained, that the new physics overthrows ordinary experience of nature—for that "ordinary experience" itself was overlaid by an older physics of absolute locations, times, and masses. The fact seems rather to be that these new features of the scientific face of things conform *more closely* to the con-figurational, organically interdependent, historic, imperfectly determined world of perceived nature, once these neglected features are freshly grasped. Thus the interaction of science and philosophy must be expected to modify our understanding not only of details but of the forms of lived nature as well. As Husserl once remarked, Galileo established not only a technical science but a philosophical insight, namely, that movement in lived space can be simplified geometrically. But Galileo has been superseded. It becomes the *continuing* task of philosophy to meditate the fresh findings of the sciences in order to explicate the relationship of these findings to nature as perceived.

This is to say, therefore, that the concept "nature" is an open concept—that it functions as a horizon, drawn from the outlines of the perceived, space-time world and dependent not only for its detailed determinacy but also, and for this very reason, for its very form, upon the growth of the content of science itself. We both know and do not know what nature is. We know its perceived forms, but again we do not even know what these are or mean until scientific findings more fully explicate them.

(4) A final use of our principle of the primacy of perception bears on the process of scientific discovery. The principle that

11. Cf. M. Čapek, *The Philosophical Impact of Contemporary Physics,* New York, 1961.

the perceived world is the reference of scientific theory suggests (if it does not strictly imply) that however instructive the hypo-thetico-deductive analysis of inquiry may be for *ex post facto* evaluation of hypotheses once gained, *the formation of scientific hypotheses is guided most proximately by meditation on the data of actual experiment and observation.*

The situation of the empirical investigator seeking the law of phenomenon X is interestingly similar to that of the perceiver trying to discern the pattern or meaning in the presented pro-files of an object perhaps familiar but hitherto unstudied. Such investigation proceeds along lines suggested by perceptual (or experimental) profiles, oriented by ideals of explanation, and aided by analogies and connections with other things, in an active, constructive labor of exploring hidden relationships. No new facts may be needed so much as a wrench from the old prejudices which will permit a new resemblance or relation to be seen and allow the pattern, potentially present all along, to offer itself and then to be followed up explicitly and confirmed by further observations and perspectives. This pattern of dis-covery has in fact been suggested by some logicians from an analysis of historical cases.[12] It would, in any event, be plausible on phenomenological grounds, as Husserl hints in the following passage:

> The situation as generally indicated in this, that physical thought builds itself up on the basis of natural experience, (or of the natural theses which it establishes). Following the rational mo-tives which the connexions of experience suggest, it is compelled to adopt certain forms of apprehending its material, to construct such intentional systems as the reason of the case may require, and to utilize them for the theoretical determination of things as experienced through sense.[13]

12. N. R. Hanson, *Patterns of Discovery*, Cambridge, England, 1958, and compare Michael Polanyi, "Experience and the Perception of Pattern" in Frederick Crosson and Kenneth Sayre, eds., *The Modeling of Mind*, Notre Dame, 1963.
13. Husserl, *Ideas*, par. 52.

While this must not be interpreted in any inductivist sense, such an approach emphasizes that natural science, as distinct from pure mathematics, is preoccupied with the patterns of behavior of observable things. Such a context significantly reduces the abstractness of intellectualist accounts of scientific method.

Let me sum up what I have tried to do. I have sought to outline what is, I think, the distinctive contribution of phenomenology to understanding science. This consists broadly in a style of thinking about science which seeks its total reality as a mode of man's being-in-the-world. From this approach it appears that science is personal, communal, theoretical, and makes an ontological claim. This ontological claim can then be interpreted through the primacy of perception to imply (a) that the realism of science is dependent on the realism of perception, (b) that certain criteria for determining the physical or natural reality of scientific constructs are based upon the forms of lived experience of nature, (c) that the concept of "nature" is an open concept subject to development—in form and content—through philosophic reflection on scientific findings themselves, and (d) that the process of scientific investigation reveals a special preoccupation with perceived patterns of significance in things. The importance of this phenomenological approach, however, is that it places the problem of reason directly before us, the problem of assimilating the scientific enterprise within a total understanding of man and nature. There are indeed few philosophies of science today which do this.

J. N. Findlay

ESSENTIAL PROBABILITIES

The aim of the present paper is to mull generally over the eidetic method in philosophy and to connect it with the theme of modalities in general and probability in particular. I wish to suggest that phenomenological insight into intrinsic probabilities represents an indispensable philosophical task, which the general atmosphere of phenomenological investigation, with its stress on the absolutely necessary, has tended to make people pass over. Yet the probabilistic *a priori* can claim to be an inevitable extension of the strictly necessary *a priori,* and to be in fact the most living and interesting part of the whole *a priori* field. To those to whom these notions and methods represent genuine intellectual options, not faded traditional rubrics to which no contemporary sense or use can be given, the points I am about to stress cannot seem unimportant.

The eidetic method in philosophy can be said to be an analytic method, also a synthetic method, which throughout employs the "seeing eye." Scanning ranges of things and cases roughly assembled under certain more or less interchangeable or cognate expressions, and noting the way in which such expressions are used or modified in relation to such cases, it tries to distill from the whole examination the sense of certain salient, dominant universals, some so generic as to rate as categories, others so specific as to have almost an air of chance about them, but all such as to specify themselves divergently without loss of unity, and such as to suggest and permit an interesting analysis into traits which genuinely "hang" or "belong" together and are not merely empirically associated. Further, these traits show themselves as having certain indispensable or nigh-indispensable "roles," in connection with other widely different generic and specific patterns, in building up a picture of a total viable world or of a total viable experience.

This "seeing eye" method is certainly the one described by the author of the VIIth. Platonic Epistle in a sentence (344b) which many are foolish enough to think was not Plato's, and which I shall translate as: "When all of these, names, definitions, sights and percepts are with difficulty rubbed together and are probed in questions and answers in friendly fashion and without jealousies, a wisdom and insight into each flashes forth, which reaches to the bounds of human capacity." This "seeing-eye" method is the one which is ostentatiously discouraged by certain modern philosophers of language, who see in it all the false philosophical passion for generality which prevents men from seeing the blessed loosenesses, the happy opennesses, the shifts, stretches, arrests, and hesitations that make ordinary concepts so different from, and so superior to, the stale stereotypes of philosophers, which create many more problems than they resolve. The discovery of the real character and merits of what we may call "unphilosophy" certainly represents a major philosophical breakthrough, but the superiority of unphilosophy, as regards the *special* sort of insight or conception that philosophy seeks to achieve, would not seem to have been convincingly made out. The linguistic philosophers, we may note, themselves use the "seeing-eye" method—there is no other *to* use in an unexplored field—in their own analyses of human diction. The notion of "family relations," for example, is not itself a "family-relations" notion. And Moore and others like him, who tested analyses by comparing them with concepts they had "before their minds," did much the same. Moore remained magisterial in relation to ordinary diction and used it to trap concepts rather than to delimit them. The "seeing-eye" method is, moreover, the method followed by Husserl, who, however, uses it in a comprehensive, non-piecemeal way, which in general gives his treatments, though at times a little dogmatic, a greater nearness to the appearances, to the matters on hand, than those of the analysts. Different notional regions and strata, the logico-mathematical, the natural-scientific, the psychological, the intersubjective, and so on, are each seen not only for what they separately are but also as making their characteristic contribution to the total pattern of a world as such, as constituted in or before a pure or transcendental consciousness.

The "seeing-eye" method is often called "descriptive" by those who practice it, but the term is dangerous and has in fact led to the most unfortunate consequences. It is quite properly used to enlist on behalf of what we may call real background- and framework-features of our empirical world, the interest and respect aroused in our culture by what is matter of observation, by what will come before us if we will but train our eyes firmly in the right direction. As an antidote to a view which regards necessities as not being *also* genuine matters of fact but mere reflections of the ways in which we have decided to interchange or not to interchange our expressions, such a way of speaking may be useful: necessities, when we recognize them, are certainly "part of the phenomena," are certainly written into the structure of the world. But the term "description" suggests that the investigation of the categorial or sub-categorial patterns of things and their relations is not unlike being shown round someone's farmyard, and seeing how its various sheds, runs, enclosures, and paddocks stand to one another. The term "logical geography" has the same descriptive suggestions. Many of Husserl's transcendental constitutions, immense in their subtlety, do in fact read like a mere re-description, in eidetic terms, of familiar empirical matters of fact. If I may cite an instance at random (*Ideen*, Book II, p. 56), Husserl writes: "The body is in the first place the instrument in all perception; it is the organ of perception, and is necessarily present in all perception. The eye in seeing is directed to the seen, and runs over corners, surfaces, etc. The hand glides in touch over objects. I move to bring my ear nearer to hear." These descriptions might have come, if not from Christian Wolff, then from a rather sententious textbook of physiology or psychology: there is nothing very transcendental about them. Many like such treatments, not because they bring out essential connections but because they read so much like empirical commonplaces given new excitement by eidetic language.

What is missing here is the clear realization that the sort of experience which could reveal εἴδη and their connections is not the sort of experience that with astonishment records something that it could not at all have expected, but the sort of experience which, after many attempts to *evade* the closing elenchus of a conceptual linkage, finds that it is up against the inescapable, that if it makes its bed in Sheol or takes to the wings of the morning, it will still be faced by the same connection. The experience of the necessary has not been sufficiently written up by phenomenologists or existentialists but it remains one of the most unique and astonishing we can have, an experience in which our own impotence and unsuccess mediates the understanding acceptance of something as impossible in itself. In other words, as the Platonic Epistle tells us, the experience of εἴδη and their necessary relations must be dialectical: it must arise in the active rubbing together of words, illustrations, and rough ideas, and not through any merely passive glance.

We may say, further, that the experience of the necessary is dialectical in the further sense of always involving revision: what we at first find readily formulable and entertainable, a possibility in short, has, on a deeper examination, been found incapable of a genuine carrying-out—it is an empty, an unful-fillable assignment. But we can only discover it to be unfulfill-able by first attempting to fulfil it, and by then being frustrated in that peculiar positive manner which we say mediates under-standing. Of course, once we have gone through the experience, it can leave its painless trace in linguistic usage: what we pain-fully found to be impossible comes to be avoided as a mere solecism. It goes without saying, of course, that the necessities of which I am speaking are all "synthetic"—though some often called "analytic" would be reckoned among them—a class that for me does not consist of a few, queer borderline cases requir-ing special justification, but is strewn as thick as autumnal leaves over every field of enquiry, so that it is in fact hard to isolate anything that is not overlaid with it. Facts that are quite purely "mere," like individuals that are quite definitely individuals, are things that many people claim to have encountered on their wanderings, but which are for me at best objects of devout faith rather than immediate acquaintance.

This dialectical character of modal terms means, further, that we cannot rest in any one secure use of them: what is perfectly possible on an examination which ignores certain vital relations of εἴδη to other εἴδη, may be impossible once these relations have been considered: what is mere matter of fact on one limited survey of a notional field may be wholly necessary when seen in a wider context. Philosophers of ordinary language have in fact long used this particular elenchus against those who attempt to be linguistically extraordinary. We may, in fact, require not one phenomenology like that of Husserl, achieved by a single ἐποχή or suspense of naive conviction, but a whole series of phenomenologies as numerous as the Hegelian categories or "shapes" of spirit, and separated from one another by as many suspensions and transformations. But it is not my purpose in this paper to develop any such interesting thesis. It is rather to recall that modals vary systematically in sense, or rather in use, according as one considers matters more or less abstractly. What is quite possible as a matter of mere logical form may not be so if special contents are brought in, and what seems quite possible if certain contents are abstractly considered may not be so if their necessary bearings on other contents are dwelt upon. (I am not here considering any merely *ex hypothesi* modalities which are only *relative* to situations having no necessary character.) It is never easy to be sure that any given connection or existence is really possible or contingent, even if it plainly seems so in a given language, or even seems so for our surface imagination. The language may need to be adjusted, whether Spinozawise or Russellwise, and the imagination may need to be declared out of bounds and wild. We can have haunting doubts that temper necessitarian dogmas, or that question a boundless atomism of possibilities, but where the decision will lie is a matter for insight in the given case.

It may, however, quite generally be emphasized that, whatever the encroachments of the necessary and the impossible, there must necessarily be a residual sphere, difficult no doubt to delimit, for the possible and contingent without qualification. (*Ex hypothesi* modalities are again not here in question, nor do they offer points of interest.) Even if reflection should not support—as it very well might not—the now current dogma that all existence is necessarily contingent, it could hardly verge toward the opposite dogma of holding all being to be necessary and none of the instantiations of universal types, their number and order, as well as the particular ways in which they run across one another, to be irreducibly contingent, the sort of thing that could only be known through that sheer encountering or stumbling upon them which for some counts as the sole paradigm of "experience." This need for the contingently empirical may be justified—few would feel that it needed justification —on mere grounds of contrast: if there were no merely factual element in things, there could also be no such thing as a necessity. The necessary is what you cannot get away from, no matter what you may do, and no matter what may be the case: it presupposes a variable field of alternatives, in respect of which, as Husserl says, it remains invariant. If whatever you do and whatever is the case are one thing only, then there is nothing to put necessity through its paces or to show up its form. We are really in a state where modality has become inoperative, where only simple assertion and denial are in place. The regionally or stratigraphically or otherwise necessary therefore presupposes a filling, a detailed content that is not necessary but merely factual: the merely factual or existential is, therefore, both a foil and a complement to the necessary, which latter has not the merely hypothetical status, the indifference to fact and existence with which it is often credited. (Even universal non-existence or absence of all positive character or connection, if genuinely conceivable, would itself be a mere matter of fact and existence, a limiting member to a whole series of contingent combinations.)

But I maintain that the converse entailment also holds, and that the merely factual must always specify a framework which is constraining, necessary in a more than empty sense. This is a very shocking contention which runs straight athwart much contemporary dogma, according to which there is and can be no genuine limit to the factual, such limitations as there seem to be being merely guards against certain symbolic abuses which seem to say something contentful about the world but in effect say nothing at all. I am, however, saying that, wherever there are mere facts or a merely factual element, they must necessarily fall within and give content to a definite regional mold which prescribes definite external and internal contrasts, definite external and internal dependences and independences, as well as pervasive communities and continuities characteristic of the whole region. Facts, whatever their complexity and intricacy, must ultimately concern and radiate from thematic centers or subjects, limited in type-number and simple in type-character; it is necessary that, whatever their degree of independence, it should also have the interdependence characteristic of a single theme or story. Everywhere there must be variety, not mere monotony; but such variety must stem from a smallish number of ultimate bases: mere number is everywhere welcome, even if it swells to the transfinite, but it must, except in interstitial cases, observe strict denumerability and pervasive community. These requirements hold not merely for the specifications of categories but for categories themselves and for the diversified unity they form. All these are not mere subjective requirements, geared to the limitations of understanding or language. Characters or types, we may say, would not be characters or types if they ran to unprincipled diversity or mere monotony; facts would not be facts if they illuminated infinitely numerous, unrelated topics or themes; there could be no cases of number if there were no deep gulfs and communities, and not much more of continuous connection than we postulate for sets or classes. Because there is an elastic stretch within which mere variety or diversity or discontinuity can be varied without let or hindrance, it seems abstractly evident that we could go on doing the same indefinitely, not seeing that what is possible then veers round into what is in a deep sense impossible. The Limit, τὸ πέρας, we may say, is no mere Platonic or Pythagorean superstition but a necessary property of all being, which is not to say that τὸ ἄπειρον, if duly contained and curbed, may not also have an honored place in being. Or, in other words, to be is to be a value, not of *any* variable, but of a *few*, ultimate, contrasting, interrelated variables. The *a priori* necessity of *measures* which we can nonetheless only vaguely characterize as *not being too great or too small*, also shows, at this early stage of our discussion, how thoroughly probability enters into ontology, and how we can often not so much state something to be quite necessary or quite impossible, as to have this or that relative place on a vague scale of absolute likelihood. If the foundations of things are thus indefeasibly nebulous, it is not I who have made them so.

All this will of course sound less absurd and less arrogant if I state my point in terms of intelligence and intelligibility. Experience of detailed fact and existence, one may say, is impossible in a framework which is really no framework—the familiar framework of modern radical empiricism, which is always prepared for a bad infinity of what it calls "logical possibilities," and which only feels able to guess desperately and quite foolishly regarding them. To experience things and to learn from one's experience is to do so in a demarcated region, and it is logically necessary to have an advance knowledge of the general mold of this region and the sorts of things encounterable in it. One can, in other words, only find out in detail what one already knows or conceives in principle, though of course what one finds out in detail may react upon and modify what one has conceived in principle. A strong, positive *a priori*, holding at bay the mere insolence of number and variety, is in short the logically necessary condition of there being any *a posteriori*, of there being anything that one could study or probe or learn about or learn from. And it is supremely strange that Kant, who was the first to discover the necessity of such an *a priori*, also thought that there was something puzzling and requiring explanation about it, as if radical contingency was not much more unintelligible and requiring of explanation. The need of a generic *a priori* for any detailed instantial experience may therefore be accepted, and it is what Husserl accepts when he says that whatever comes before us must embody an εἶδος, though he says little or nothing of the hard, insightful work required for distinguishing a true εἶδος from a merely factitious, interstitial type. I must, however, myself deprecate any reformulation of what I have been saying in terms of mere "intelligibility." For even if we do not follow Husserl and other idealists in conceiving the world as constituted in and for consciousness, we must nonetheless avoid that most perilous and malign of surds which makes the relation of the natural world to mind external and fortuitous; the world may, at many points, exceed our grasp by its difficulty, but it cannot exceed any positive grasp whatsoever without ceasing to be a world at all.

The aim of this essay is not, however, to remain lost among all these difficult generalities but to consider the role of probabilities in this whole *a priori* setup. As long as the contingently factual is supposed alien to the necessary, a sort of verminous growth that multiplies in its precincts, there seems no reason why the necessary should have as its offshoots various necessary or *a priori* probabilities. Whereas, if we see the contingently factual as what gives full concreteness and specific form to the necessary, we shall expect each regional *a priori* to extend far down into the detailed depth of things, and not only to set bounds to what it may contain but to "bias" it preferentially in one direction rather than another, or in certain degrees rather than others. And to exercise a "seeing eye" in the region in question is to become aware of all these biasing tendencies as well as of the inescapable principles they specify. It is a strange fact that a culture, one of whose earliest and most magnificent triumphs was the Platonic *Timaeus*, should have so far forgotten the doctrine of εἰχοτά, of rational probabilities, which throughout characterizes that work, as to have limited the probable to an unsatisfactory theory of chance encounter. The real domain of reason is in the field of the inherently plausible and the analogically coherent, not in the barren, interstitial play of dirempted possibilities.

I shall, however, beat about the bush no longer, but come down to specific examples. And here I shall choose not examples culled from the field of nature and natural science but from the field of mind, in which Husserl too plied his phenomenological arts and which almost seems, though he wholly failed to see it, the native territory of the probable. I shall first deal with a number of basic psycho-physical εἰχοτά which certainly govern us in our personal dealings, even if they may have seemed strange to ultra-empiricist philosophers, who not only believe the old view that all facts are learned from individual encounter but also the new view that all meanings are taught by acts of individual ostension. The first is the inherent likelihood of there being minds around—a likelihood recognized in the "animism" of the textbooks—and, by there being minds around, I of course do not mean there merely being reacting organisms around, but organisms whose reactions are given as problematically reaching out into a hidden dimension, a dimension *given as hidden* and also *given* as an object of permanent conjecture, but also given as capable of being appresented (to use Husserl's fine term) *through* a creature's reactions, much but not quite as a body can be seen through a cloth, all these being possibilities that we perfectly understand and can introduce to others, even though every showable instance of them exhibits the "throughness," the intrinsic indirectness which the phenomenon itself involves and requires. The world is not and cannot be the daylight world of the Wittgensteinian language-games: it is a world where the hidden and intrinsically problematic is everywhere lurking *qua* hidden and *qua* problematic, as a dimension toward which we may gesture and which is also capable of an inherently uncertain disclosure which never deprives it of its essential hiddenness. All these are not secondary growths upon primary daylight acts but the penumbra in which those daylight acts alone are possible. One cannot say, "There's a red apple" for the hearing of others without being penumbrally conscious of the intentional *sense* which this statement implies, as well as of the countless possible conscious centers in which that intentional sense could possibly be enjoyed.

But of course not merely the existence of this interior dimension is always intrinsically likely, but also, indirectly, the character of its contents. For the interior life of anything is always intrinsically, if probabilistically, geared to its outer life, much as the inner contours of a sheet of metal tend to be geared to its outer contours, concavity matching convexity and convexity concavity. For the relation of inner states of feeling, sensation, thought, attitude, and so forth to outward situations and actions is not, and cannot be, that of two disparate things empirically associated: the one represents the concentration into unity of which the other represents the dispersion into separateness, it being intrinsically likely, *ceteris paribus*, that the former will issue in the latter, and vice versa. No one who trains his "seeing eye" on his own condensed moods of feeling and thought, on the one hand, and their explication in behavior or objective situation, on the other, can doubt that we have here a connection of essence, if only an intrinsically likely connection. The one completes and fits the other. The same holds if anyone will study the language of physical analogy in which we talk of the interior life of mind, an analogy by some thought to be idle and personal and by Wittgenstein to be wholly constitutive of inner-life meanings. The truth is that it is neither: the analogies in question express the real, *a priori* affinities through which inner-life facts sometimes enter our common language.

What I have said will be even more plain if we consider the different modes of minding objects which have so exercised philosophers: the believing or disbelieving mode, the attentive or inattentive mode, the acquiescent or objecting mode, and so on. Here each mode points to a host of manifestations, interior or overt, into which it is *likely* to expand, which a too zealous interest in "necessary and sufficient conditions" too readily banishes from our "analyses." Thus belief not only has its inner core of acquiescent acceptance, and its placing of contents somewhere in an unbracketed total picture; it also has highly probable overtones of assertion, of the willingness to persuade, of the expectation that others will see things as we do, and so on. And it also involves all those probable modifications of our goal-directed behavior, removed only in the incurably abouliac or schizophrenic, in which some have seen the whole essence of believing. All these are *a priori* connections, rooted in the content of the phenomenon before us, but they are also all probabilistic connections which might not be manifest in the particular case. Husserl, with his naively simple, Brentanesque view of belief as simply a *thetic* state of mind, characterized also by an "activity" which the "seeing eye" should have told him is not always present, missed all this vivid field of probabilities, which yield up their wealth to *reine Wesensschau* as to nothing else. Obviously Brentano and Husserl would have constructed a much more brilliant, complete psychognosy or phenomenology had behavior-analysis and language-analysis been pushed as far in their time as they have been in ours. We who wish to preserve and to extend their invaluable doctrines must take account of these fundamental disciplines and their findings. But we must develop them in *a priori* fashion and not merely by borrowing pages from empirical studies. (Though what *is* the case certainly may stimulate our vision of what *must* be the case.)

I shall not make further excursions into special fields. The *a priori* probabilities of nature and of natural science are a subject of absorbing interest and almost complete non-cultivation. Husserl, in his elaborate constitution of nature, says extremely little about them. Some inductive logicians—Keynes, for example—have made timid forays into these regions, but always the noise raised by the positivists and the radical empiricists has driven them shamefacedly from the field. It is, in fact, impossible to state any genuine *metaphysische Anfangsgründe de Naturwissenschaft* in the atmosphere of our time, for they would emphasize notions like that of simplicity and analogy, "good form," and inherent probability, which now seem inherently ridiculous. I have no wish to burden this essay with further occasions for ridicule. I should like, however, to conclude by saying that I think that a treatment of intrinsic necessities and probabilities cannot end without treating the intrinsic necessities and probabilities of *being* or *existence:* it cannot be limited to the merely hypothetical study of the necessities and probabilities conditional upon the existence of this or that sort of thing. We must, in short, invade the citadel which Kant and others have sought to barricade completely and shut off finally.

Thomas Langan

FORMAL INSIGHT
INTO MATERIAL NATURES

Introduction: The Problem

The realist would like to claim that there are presented in experience objective natures belonging to the things themselves; and
that when I enjoy an insight into the sense of such a nature I
am grasping something about the way this perceived thing before me is really organized in itself, which organization in itself
is not an effect of the knowledge act through which I come to
know it. The *a priorist* points out, however, that the act of insight is an act of mind deploying its own categories, which
ought not be uncritically considered somehow the intrinsic real
constituents of things existing independently of mind. Indeed,
does not every insight yield an *a priori* truth transcending the
here and now data which may have occasioned it?

The realist of course cannot deny that the concept—result of
the insight—has a sense not limited to the concrete data of this
thing here and now in which a kind of structure was first manifested to the knower. But, he argues, this concrete thing is in
itself structured and manifests in the present perceived profile
something of the way it is structured. Thus, when I am able to

understand something of what it is to be put together in the
particular, peculiar, characteristic way this thing before me has
been formed, I then understand both the sense of that kind of
structure in general, and the fact that this thing in particular is
so structured. The realist would claim, then, that the intellect is
able to separate from the accidental and irrelevant data accom-
panying this particular thing's here and now manifestation of
its structure the peculiar sense of a possible relationship of parts,
which is that of this *kind* of structure, capable of existing in
many different individuals.

Of course the thing is structured, the *a priorist* will reply, for
the simple reason that the synthesizing activity of the transcendental ego (or the *"corps propre,"* or the "categorizing mind") has
already been deployed, forming prior to your present reflection
the perceived structured object which you are now contemplat-
ing. Moreover, the reason *a priori* truths follow insight is that
insights are grasps of categories: the understanding of a peculiar
possible way parts may belong together in a characteristic kind
of structure is nothing more than a "formal intuition," which is
to say an operation of the understanding, made possible by the
understanding itself *being* its own categories, which it then becomes aware of as the structure of the data in the *ob-jectum*
which it has synthesized.

What has the realist to answer to this contention, especially as
he himself is impressed by the irreducibility of insight and does
not want for a moment to underplay the role of *intellectus* as an
activity transcending the momentary aspects of the given?

I do not see any way the *a priorist* contention can be disproven.
Indeed, it is one of those "metaphysical contentions" the positivists are always disturbed about, precisely because such assertions can be neither proven nor disproven. The realists' patient
efforts to show there is a sense in things never really can prove
that the mind has not already put in the structure we find in the
experienced things. But I believe we can render the *a priorist*
assertion less probable.

In this study we shall be dealing with the difficult notion of "formal" insight into the way the parts of a structure "belong together." We shall see that there are different degrees of formal insight and that in some notions the dense material remainder, the dimly understood nature of the parts, is greater than in others. These notions of "form" and "matter," expressing degrees of insight, are indispensable, yet anything but clear. Unfortunately this essay does not make them much clearer. But it does show, I believe, how inadvisable it is to construe insight as deployment of clear categories to organize unclear data. With this my limited mission is accomplished: our reflections here should make it more difficult not to admit that "formal" insights into material essences are made possible by the things offering glimpses of their own organizational structure. Efforts to understand these structures lead to "formalizations," which are simply understanding grasps of some characteristic ways in which some kinds of parts can belong together. Explanation, in contrast to direct formal insight, is knowledge of the final and efficient causes accounting for the formation of the form.

I propose to begin our consideration of formal insight by examining an instance where the parts are as little "materially dense" as possible. We shall see that even in this case, the structure—a mere arbitrary figure rather than a real nature—imposes its demands on us, even beyond the express intentions of its constructor, and hence in that sense can be said to have a reality "in itself."

I. *Formal Insight and the Objectivity of Formal Structure*

Wishing to illustrate formal insight, I constructed two arbitrary figures, A and B. I intended that they should differ in only one respect: that the parallel bars be joined by different sorts of connectors which yet would be as high as the thick vertical end bars. Without knowing what the answer was, I asked myself what a third figure would have to be like if it were to continue

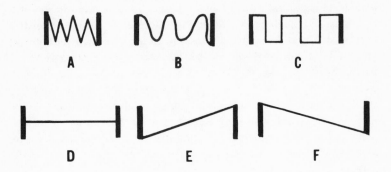

the series according to this rule intrinsic to the first two figures. I then imagined that it would have to be like C. I then presented A and B to a subject and asked him the same question. To my satisfaction, he at once produced C. I redrew A and B and presented them to an older, more reflective subject. After considerable hesitation he drew figure D. When I asked why, he pointed out that I had drawn (without intending to, I must add) A and B with B's bars somewhat farther apart than A's, so that it appeared the connector was intended to be "opening up," "so I opened it all the way." I then presented A and B, this time drawn with B's bars slightly farther apart than A's, to a subject accustomed to careful analysis. He quickly drew Figure E, then corrected himself by substituting Figure F. This last subject had intelligently grasped even more of the *given* formal features of the series A-B as redrawn: not only did the connecting bar open up all the way, it continued to respect the "given" in the first two figures, that the bar began to the left at the top and ran to the right bottom.

   In the grasp of what sort of figure belongs to the series A-B, we have a clear example of "formal insight." As the two figures were presented to each subject as a series, he saw how each was made up and what belonged to each alone, and to the two together. The last subject understood more of what was implied in the progression from one figure to the next than had the first two, and more even than the author himself had explicitly and intentionally structured into the design. Precisely there is an important point: the givens of the formal structure of the series A-B were contained in the drawn illustrations independently of the intention and limited insight of their author. First, the opening up effect was unintended, as I had not meant originally to draw B with bars farther apart than A, nor had I seen that the wavy line when compared to the zig-zag in A gave this effect. Still, it was there in fact, as I am obliged to admit once it is pointed out to me. But it is not the first subject's interpretation which puts this formal feature in the figure, for independent of any interpretation the end bars in B are in fact farther apart than those in A. Moreover, even after the second subject had pointed out the opening effect, I had not paused to see that the diagonal line proposed by the last subject fulfills still more demands established by A-B as drawn. Here the third figure can fulfill the intended end of continuing the first two only by being *formally* in certain ways. Its form depends on its end (viz., to continue figures A and B) and is *objectively* determined by it; once the initial figures are given existence (even if only in the imagination) by an efficient cause, and regardless of the cause's subjective intention, then only a limited gamut of possible figures can continue the series. Even had I absent-mindedly doodled A and B, and then *ex post facto* begun trying to see what they in fact were, they would still objectively impose their formal demands.

The *a priorist* might be tempted to point out here that such figures are necessary even when they are only imagined, and so their necessity must be necessity of mind: given A and B, C *cannot be thought* (correctly) any other way. The progression is comprehended only by a mind. In that sense its necessity is only in the mind. But its ground lies in the figures as given, not in the mind which, grasping the sense of their structures, sees what figures necessarily continue the series.

It is curious to believe, as no such figures ever existed until just a moment ago when I first drew them, that some latent, as yet unemployed but highly detailed structure of mind was just waiting around on the chance that one day an occasion would arise for its deployment. Is it not rather more reasonable to suppose that any figure whatever, once constructed (and hence *able to be* constructed), holding together as it must in some fashion just in order to be a figure, is able to be understood by a mind which itself is simply (among others) the power of comprehending the sense of all coherences? Such structures must either exist (as in the case of my perception of something confronting me) or be able to exist (as in the case of a structure I present to myself imaginatively).[1]

II. *The Distinction Between Understanding a Structure Formally and Understanding Its Causes*

We can reinforce the conviction that we understand real structures actually given in experience by turning now to an example taken from nature. At the same time we shall be able to elaborate the difficult distinction between understanding a given structure formally and a deeper "material" understanding of it in terms of its causes.

As I am being shown about a southern Indiana farm I notice a number of strange shallow craters in the rolling prairie. When I ask the farmer about them, he replies in the tone of someone enunciating a self-evident principle, "Them is sinkholes." With-

1. The imaginative presentation is carried out with the help of visual memory of real structures previously encountered. I can combine aspects of these imaginatively without understanding all that the resulting structure implies. Only through subsequent analysis of the imaginatively presented subject will I come to understand all that is implied in its *being able to hold together* the way it in fact does.

out understanding too well, I nevertheless gather that somehow the soil has sunk down into the earth. Later, a more informative friend explains that an underground current has worn out a shallow cavern in the limestone strata close to the surface, the roof of which cavern subsequently collapsed, forming the sink-hole. I now grasp the situation better, although I remain unclear as to why the roof collapsed just here rather than elsewhere, just why this occurs in limestone and not in sandstone, and just why the craters appear roughly round and fairly shallow. Still, understanding something of the cause raises my knowledge be-yond the mere formal (as opposed to causally explained) reali-zation that here is some kind of phenomenon to be explained.

But for our present concern the interesting fact is that I was able to see that a peculiar phenomenon existed and to divine very roughly in what sort of phenomena—very generally—its explanation ought to lie, before I knew anything of its causes. Thanks to past experience, I knew that craters in the prairie are rare phenomena, and I could see that neither surface water ero-sion nor wind sculpture could explain them. Here then was a Gestalt, grasped as a mere formality, to which my attention was directed by the knowledge, gained from past experience, that such forms are rare and required explanation. A child, having no experience of the ordinary, would not recognize the crater as something out of the ordinary, and so would not attend to it. But once the phenomenon has indeed become an object of at-tention, and before I am able to offer a causal explanation, I grasp something of its formal sense: shallow crater-in-a-prairie. It is my implicit grasp of the formal sense of that structure which must guide the search for a cause. For the moment, on the basis of casual observation I may be unable to advance toward an explanation, except to rule out the three common causes of minor landforms, surface water erosion, wind sculpture, and vulcanism. If I am interested, I shall keep an eye out for other such phenomena. In this way I may learn another fact about them—for example, I may notice that they always occur in the same sort of rolling, bumpy prairie. If I learn the cause of the characteristic form of those prairies, namely that they result from the weathering of limestone, I shall then want to explore the possible relationship between limestone strata and sinkholes. At that point I pass from the as yet merely formal grasp of the fact of shallow, irregular craters in rolling, bumpy landscape to a causal explanation of the fact.

III. *Formal Insight into Strictly Formal Figures and Formal Insight into Material Natures*

Our experience confronts us with a seemingly limitless variety of such formally graspable structures.[2] As in the great majority of cases we already enjoy "deeper" knowledge of most of these things, it requires keen attention to separate our formal understanding that this thing before me manifests a characteristic type of structure from our causal or teleological understanding of precisely what its importance or significance actually is. But once we have, what remains—the formal structure—is almost always more than mere form in the sense of a mere complex of mathematically locatable and calculable points and lines. Rather, the formal structure, in all but those instances of merely geometrical figures we construct, contains what, for want of a better word, is called "material content." [3] As we saw in the example of the sinkholes, much of the content—the parts—of these formally grasped material structures is perceptible in just the way I now perceive it only in virtue of past experience. My present full formal understanding—my grasp of the sense of the relationship of those parts—depends then both on the results of certain past insights and the retained images from perceptions of relevant

2. Only an intolerably tedious description of many different examples can establish this.

3. Form and matter should be understood in this context, not as Kant understood them but in Husserl's sense, where the contrast is not between synthesis and the lower stuff, but between the "founded" and the "founding" aspects of the act of knowledge.

things without which these parts would not now be present as they are. When I say that I see an unusual deformity in the terrain, or when I recognize the present prairie as a limestone soil, past experience is in some respects guiding my attention and in others perhaps "fleshing out" the actually present sensory data. The formal insight into the structure of the sinkhole which precedes the deeper understanding of it is not reducible then to the deployment of purely formal categories in the strictest sense of the term, for the nature thus known formally is grasped as a relationship of parts themselves having a material content, the sedimented results both of past acts of understanding and retained, little analyzed perceptual features. The *a priori* sense of the notion "sinkhole" which results from my bare formal insight into the phenomenon (as yet without causal explanation) is that of a "material essence." Such a structure can never be "merely formal," as a mathematical figure would be.

Contrasting our present example with the series of arbitrary figures I drew earlier, we can be clearer about the difference between formal insight into material natures and formal insight into merely formal figures.

If I grasp the sense of the series of figures as an "opening out" of the connecting line, it is not extravagant to see in that insight the deployment of an *a priori* understanding, which I enjoy because I know what it means for my own self-directing body to expand. We are familiar with Merleau-Ponty's efforts to see in all lines, points, and mere surfaces things understood, so to speak, "from the inside" by the *corps propre* in virtue of its being able itself to advance along a vector, or remain stationary in a point, or perceive itself as a resisting mass. Even if we accept the suggestion that such purely formal insight in the strict sense is the result of an *a priori* possession by the subject, an expression of an aspect of the very body which I am, still we would be obliged to see that the formal understanding I possess of a material structure such as the sinkhole could never be reduced to these terms.

When we turn to the notion of a material essence, we see at once that its notes could never be construed as developments of insights we enjoy into our very own being, nor would the *a priorists* claim they are. Rather they suggest that such notes are themselves combinations of such purely formal elements with dense masses of sensory matter to which the formal categorical elements furnish a schema of organization.

But if we subject any example of a typical material essence to careful analysis, we soon see how improbable this hypothesis really is. Let us do this for example with our notion of the sink-hole. Suppose that I now understand it to be "a minor land form consisting of shallow, irregular craters occurring in limestone prairies." If we examine the sub-notions of which this complex concept is made up, we shall find among others one relatively "formal," a much more material one, and yet a third somewhere in between.[4] The notion "minor land form" is the result of a very abstractive insight into the complete disjunction, "major-minor landform." A rather formal notion, whose basic idea, that of major surfaces within which finer articulations are to be found, is apparently *a priori*, but whose empirical element—the notion that the surface of this planet is arranged in continents, sub-continents, islands, and peninsulas, which themselves are broken by rivers, valleys, plains, canyons . . . and sinkholes, is neither *a priori* nor reducible to unstructured sense data. The notion "lime-stone prairie" is obviously less formalized, less highly abstracted, evoking a mass of little analyzed experience with terrain and soil types. If we contrast such a notion with that of a figure constructed by us out of lines and points whose full sense we live,

4. An *hypothesis* worth considering: Will it not always be the case with all our notions of "material essences" that we can distinguish a more formal part (the genus) and more material parts (the specific difference)? If we seek to understand this state of affairs *causally* we should have to look for "more universal causes" for the being of the genus. The more universal causes probably are the older and more fundamental causes standing at the beginning of a long process interior to which the finer articulations and more particular causes incurring from outside the process itself must account for the specific differences.

so to speak, from the inside, *a priori,* we shall see at once that the notions, "major-minor landforms," fall somewhere in between the more formalized notion and the densely implicit, perceptive notion, "limestone prairie," focal point of a mass of experience with different terrains, through which threads perhaps some insights into the causes of these various formations, and around which nucleus of understanding is sedimented a vast treasury of relevant perceptual experience of landscapes.

These few remarks are not intended to pass for a serious analysis of how these concepts are formed, but only to suggest how, within a single complex notion of a material essence, there are to be found sub-notions—parts of its intelligibility—which themselves are of disparate origin and varying degrees of formalization, and which yet somehow have been brought together smoothly to form a single intelligible structure. How can this be, especially as we are tempted to say that real understanding requires somehow possessing the thing understood "from the inside," the way we possess the secret of a machine we have put together ourselves to serve our own designs, or the way we understand a figure whose points, lines and extension we possess in our own body? In our knowledge of a material nature we relate one part, whose sense we are far from possessing in this "internal" way, to another, likewise little understood, either because we perceive these parts as in fact existing together, or because we can imagine them together in virtue of what little we do understand of their natures. *It is only under the guidance of the things themselves which go to make up the complex notion I have of the structure of a particular kind of nature that the parts are brought together and that I know what sort of external causes to look for in seeking a deeper understanding of them.* To the extent I enjoy that formal understanding "from the inside," which is the most intrinsic grasp of the thing, to that extent I am either master, because maker of the thing, or of the same nature, because we are both physical things, or, when another person is involved, both human.

Even in the case of the poor constructed figures, all of whose elements I may understand *a priori*, it still happened that some of the aspects contained in fact in the constructed figures themselves escaped me and were discovered subsequently only upon the application of new acts of attention to the figures themselves. Even though the relations between the parts of the figures were external, once the parts were in fact determined in these relations, certain things then followed from a correct insight into the structure and others did not. If such formal necessity results in the case of a relation of parts as external as relations ever can be, then how much denser appears the charge of potential essential intelligibility in the case of an organism, whose parts have been determined by causes as a complexus of intertwining relationships of that most intimate sort where what happens interior to one part subtly alters all the other parts; and how much more then the implications of the thing's various manifestations for each other escape our immediate grasp. For further insight into them we must reapply to the perception of them or to the dense image retained in the imagination. What could render more probable the realist's contention that our insight into the sense of represented structures is not fundamentally the result of our own construction but rather the grasp of relationships manifested by something existing in itself? Even the poorest constructed object, e.g., our arbitrary figures, *because they have to hold together some way in order even to be a figure,* manifest something about the way the world is. We cannot deduce *a priori* all the laws of possible coherence in figures; rather we must apply experientially (whether perceptually or in imagination) to presented figures and there seek to induce them. I am not talking about the psychological Gestalt laws of what is necessary for us to be able to perceive a figure, but about the formal laws governing the possible coherence in themselves of the figures.

Now, with these remarks in mind, let us return to the problem which discourages the *a priorist* from affirming that an essence is a structure belonging to the thing independently of the mind's constitutive act of forming an idea of the essence. When I say that I understand the sense of the organization of a structure, the *a priorist* points out that the sense transcends *this* thing I am presently perceiving and hence is in the knower. When the realist counters by pointing out that it is also manifest in this thing here before me, the *a priorist* insists that it is because the knower puts it there—he brings the categories which alone are the "sense" of what is concretely present here. In support of this he will point out that different people, bringing different categories to the data, will see different things in them; and some people, devoid of relevant categories, may see nothing in them at all. I believe we are now better able to deal with this problem.

I shall contend both that this thing now here before me manifests in the present profile an aspect of its organization; and that when an intelligence grasps the *sense* of that organization, the resulting notion transcends those aspects of the here and now manifestation of this thing which are limited uniquely to it. Is it proper to say that the sense of the present thing's structure is "*in* the thing"? Only by extension. Obviously the word "sense" belongs to the intentional order—sense results from understanding as typical a given relationship of parts, an understanding of how these peculiar parts belong together in this characteristic way. This grasp we have said can be the result either of understanding certain ways of being *a priori*—"from the inside"—because I myself am those ways; or it can come from recognition of the fact that somehow these real things in the world present to me now either perceptually or imaginatively do actually compose in this typical fashion. This belonging together of the parts I may come to explain through knowledge of its causes. When I perceive a real thing and I come to understand something of the way in which its parts compose, it is true to say I then grasp the "idea" of the thing and that that idea is not limited essentially to *this* thing; yet it is realized in it—it is my grasp of the actual principle of this concrete thing's organization, of how it "holds together." Hence it is not by virtue of my insight, it is not because the mind grasps the idea in a way which transcends the here-and-now accidental conditions manifested by the thing and of the thing's present manifestation to me, which in any way causes or explains the fact of *this* thing's actually being organized as it is. For that we must have recourse to final and efficient causes. Hence it is not the mind's deployment of categories which explains the organization of the thing. It explains only that part of my understanding of the thing which is most certain. Final and efficient causes found the explanation of how this thing came to be the way it is; and the way it is—the actual organization in itself—finds what we can truthfully know of it formally. Although the result of the actual intellectual insight is not limited to this time and place, it is the actual concrete structure's here-and-now manifestation in *this* perceived profile which authorizes any deployment of relevant categories in regard to *this* thing.

The problem of the relativity of interpretation needs to be dealt with here briefly, to the extent it implies, contrary to our thesis, that what is actually given is in itself structureless, taking on a sense only when interpretatively integrated into a context by a knower who perforce brings the context to the data. When pressed, those who hold some form of this position will usually concede that the given is not completely indeterminate; but they are so struck by the fact that the same thing can mean something quite different in various contexts, that they are loath to admit that it can have any "sense in itself."

Now, if by sense we mean the notion which results from an act of interpretation, in other words the *meaning* of something, this we have seen is clearly not in the thing itself, for it can only be in the intentional order. What is in the thing itself is a certain actual organization manifested through many aspects (depending on the complexity of the thing), in many perceptive profiles (depending on how the perceiver(s) happens(s) to approach it). These many aspects can and will be integrated into various interpretative schemes. But it is the actual real being of the thing itself which determines what the possible manifested aspects are and the range of possible contexts into which they may appropriately (and even conceivably) be integrated. The more organic and richer the structure of the thing, the less interpretative leeway it leaves open. A poverty-stricken arbitrary figure or a cloud, because of its lack of intertwined, mutually reinforcing fine articulations leaves room for further determination by the imagination. And a cat imposes itself more imperiously than any drawing.

But how is it that something can be structured in itself (i.e., be definitely, determinately, unequivocally *that which it is*) and yet be determinable to different meanings in the different contexts into which it may be integrated? How is it that a determinate, unequivocal something was at the same time still determinable (hence indeterminate)?

Simply because the thing was not determined and indetermined at the same time in the same respect. This can be illustrated by some simple figures. Figure I is definitely and

determinately that which it is: a vertical line and a line forming a forty-five degree angle with it, touching it at the bottom end. Now if one takes the fixed position of the figure as shown to be part of the figure (which objectively it is, in the absence of any indication to the contrary), then it cannot even be said to be a "V." We should have to move it for that, in which case we would have a different figure, figure J, which is then a V. But what happens when figure I, without ceasing to have any of the objective properties we have already noted, is integrated into a more complex figure, which means that it is then in a different context? We must acknowledge that this further determination is a real change, requiring a cause; and we no longer have figure I but figure K, a triangle. Figure I may be said to be determinable as a triangle in the sense that, given the way I is, it is compatible with its nature to be added on to in such a way as to become part of a triangle. Similarly, given the nature of the triangle, I can be extracted from it. But it is important to note this distinction: actually it is the *idea* of the kind of figure represented by I which can be part of the *idea* of K, for I and K as such—the objective beings—are mutually exclusive.

These brief considerations reinforce the conviction guiding this inquiry, namely, that if we are to avoid the paradoxes to which inevitably leads the *a priorist* temptation to deny the presented thing a determination in itself, and at the same time explain the formation of concepts in a way which respects all the facts of the intelligibility of the common world, then it is essential not to confuse the given structure manifested by the thing with the notion we may form of it. Perceptually and imaginatively, it is the structure itself which is manifest. On the other hand, it is the sense or idea of it as typical or characteristic which is understood or interpreted. The act of insight may mold itself to the structure presented, confining its results to the essence-accident distinction, distinguishing the "typical sense of this kind of thing" from the accidental aspects of its here-and-now manifestations in *this* thing through *this* profile. Or the intellectual act may be more interpretative, which involves integrating the idea of the presented thing into a more complex figure or a larger context. Such understanding will involve knowledge of its causes or *a priori* formal understanding "from the inside." In any case, the sense of the structure and the actually structured thing must be recognized as distinct and distinguishable. It is because the thing is structured in itself that we can encounter it as something *to be understood.*

William J. Richardson, S.J.

KANT AND THE LATE HEIDEGGER

The purpose of these remarks is neither to look at Kant through Heidegger's eyes, nor at Heidegger through Kant's eyes, but rather to look at Heidegger through his own eyes in so far as he sees himself at the present time in terms of his vision of Kant. I say "at the present time," for since his first and best-known interpretation of Kant, *Kant and the Problem of Metaphysics* (1929), there have been three important thematic treatments of Kant and countless lesser allusions to him. I mention here only the major statements, to which restrictions of time force us to limit our attention:

1. *Die Frage nach dem Ding* (*The Question of the Thing*), a lecture course published in 1962 but dating from the winter of 1935-1936, hence one semester after his course entitled *An Introduction to Metaphysics* (1935).

2. *Der Satz vom Grund* (*The Principle of Ground*), Chapters 9-12, a lecture course from the winter of 1955-1956.

3. *Kants These über das Sein* (*Kant's Thesis on Being*), a short essay in a testimonial volume in honor of a former colleague, the philosopher of law Erik Wolf, which dates from 1962.

None of these works has been translated yet into English, and, to the best of my knowledge, the two last to appear have not yet received very thorough analysis even by European interpreters. It seems proper, then, to come to grips at last with the inevitable question: given the famous "turning" (*Kehre*) in Heidegger's way which enables us to speak of a so-called "early" Heidegger (characterized by *Being and Time* [1927] and the first Kant book) and a later Heidegger (discernible at least since *An Introduction to Metaphysics* [1935])—does this turn in the way bring a change in the interpretation of Kant? If so, does the new vision of Kant give us any new vision of Heidegger? In the briefest terms, my thesis will be this: the Kant-interpretation of the contemporary Heidegger is not the "same" as the Kant-interpretation of 1929, yet the two interpretations, taken together, are in themselves and indicate Heidegger himself to be "one."

There is little need here to dwell upon the first Kant-interpretation of 1929, for it is familiar to all. That Heidegger saw Kant's purpose as identical with his own, namely to lay the foundation for metaphysics, is now a commonplace. How this endeavor became a *Critique of Pure Reason* is equally clear, for the metaphysics which Kant knew was the *metaphysica specialis* of the Wolff-Baumgarten tradition: cosmology, psychology, theology. All of these disciplines deal with beings, what-is (the world, man, God), and seek therefore what Heidegger calls an "ontic" knowledge about them. To ground these disciplines, Kant must explain how it is possible for man—finite as he is— to have knowledge of beings other than himself at all. In Heidegger's language, this means to explain how man has access to their structure as beings, their Being-structure, by means of what he calls "ontological" knowledge. Kant does this by defining the nature (i.e., by making a "critique") of man's reason, for reason is that power within man that makes judgments, and for the rationalist tradition all knowledge takes the form of judgments. He examines man's *pure* reason, for he must explain that knowledge which precedes ontic contact with beings, i.e., ontological knowledge of them. This for Heidegger is the sense of the "Copernican Revolution." In effect, then, the *Critique of Pure Reason* is nothing more than an attempt to establish the foundations of metaphysics by explaining how man knows the Being of beings.

How the interpretation proceeds is equally familiar. If ontic, i.e., experiential, knowledge of beings is to be explained by a synthesis of sense intuition and thought, then pre-ontic, i.e., *a priori*/ontological, knowledge is to be explained by the pure synthesis of pure intuition and pure thought (i.e., the categories of the understanding). Such a pure ontological synthesis Heidegger speaks of, following Kant's use of the word "transcendental," as the "transcendence" of human reason, to be conceived as a certain domain, or horizon, projected by reason, within which beings can be encountered as beings, i.e., in Kant's language, as objects (*Gegenstände*) of experience. Building his case exclusively on the first edition of the *Critique* (1781), Heidegger argues that such knowledge is brought about by that power (*Kraft*) within man to build (*bilden*) into synthetic unity (*ein*) both pure intuition and pure thought. This power is the *Einbildungskraft* ("imagination") and, since it institutes transcendence, the "transcendental" imagination. It performs its task through those mysterious processes that Kant calls the "schemata." It is the role of *time* in the functioning of these schemata, and therefore of the transcendental imagination, that draws the full focus of Heidegger's attention. So essential is it that the imagination is conceived not simply as the root of the sense intuition of time but as itself an original process of tim-ing (*Zeitigung*). For example, the pure synthesis of intuition and thought is achieved by the imagination through the integration of the modes of pure apprehension (which suggests the present), pure reproduction (which suggests the past), and pure recognition (which suggests the future). The imagination itself, then, by its synthesizing function, institutes the dimensions of present, past, and future, and thus originates time. Heidegger even seems to go further. Taking the transcendental imagination as the center of the entire human self, he seems to say that not only is the imagination the unifying origin of present-past-future but it derives its own unity from the unity of time itself. ". . . It is only the fact that it is rooted in time that enables the transcendental imagination as such to be the root of transcendence. Original time makes the transcendental imagination possible. . . ." [1]

That Kant saw this at least dimly in the first edition of the *Critique* Heidegger argues from the fact that time, precisely as pure self-affection, constitutes the essential structure of finite subjectivity. That is why both time, as self-affection, and transcendental apperception are both called *stehend und bleibend* ("stable and abiding").[2] On the other hand, it is even clearer that in the second edition this insight disappears, the transcendental imagination is made a function of the understanding, the self is no longer temporal. Why the change? Heidegger surmises that Kant sensed the consequences of conceiving the center of the self as the imagination rather than reason, and, indeed, as essentially temporal rather than non-temporal, and drew back from all the ominous implications.[3] Be that as it may, Heidegger readily admits that his own reading of the first edition of the *Critique* articulates not so much what Kant said as what he did not say.

What Kant does say about the self falls victim to the critique that Heidegger makes of him in *Being and Time*, namely that the *ich* of *ich denke*, even if it be conceived as a consciousness that is "not a presentation but the form of presentation," is nonetheless always the Cartesian *res cogitans*, i.e., as a *hypokeimenon*, subject—and this means for Heidegger *Vorhandenes*, a

---

1. ". . . Diese Verwurzelung in der Zeit ist es allein, kraft deren die transzendentale Einbildungskraft überhaupt die Wurzel der Transzendenz sein kann. Die ursprüngliche Zeit ermöglicht die transzentale Einbildungskraft. . . ." *Kant und das Problem der Metaphysik,*[2] Frankfurt, 1950, p. 178. Hereafter: KM.

2. KM, pp. 171-177.

3. KM, pp. 146-156.

stable, abiding entity and nothing more.[4] The point is, of course, that for Heidegger the self is more than that, it is *Dasein*, to-be-in-the-World—not at all a subject but finite transcendence, whose ultimate meaning is time. Only such a conception of the self as his own, he maintains, can ground metaphysics.

In 1935-1936 the lecture course which bore then the title *Grundfragen der Metaphysik* (*Questions Concerning the Ground of Metaphysics*) and appeared in 1962 as *The Question of the Thing* was clearly the continuation of the analysis of *Kant and the Problem of Metaphysics* (1929). But if Heidegger's principal thesis in 1929 rested on the first edition of the *Critique of Pure Reason*, the interpretation of 1935 certainly does not. True enough, his insistence will be the same, that Kant was laying the groundwork for metaphysics, and, indeed, by exploring in pure reason that field of vision (*Gesichtskreis*), that "in-between" area (*Zwischen*) between man and things, where beings-as-objects can be encountered and take their stand.[5] But whereas in the first edition of the *Critique* this domain of transcendence was instituted by the transcendental imagination, in the second edition it is instituted by the principles of the pure understanding. It is the section dealing with these principles, then, that becomes the matter for study here. We find it in the "Transcendental Analytic," Book II. The interpretation begins with Chapter 2 of the "Analytic of Principles," and after a series of generalities concerning the Kantian problematic (where apparently he supplies some of the emendations to the first Kant-book that he mentions as necessary in the preface to the second edition),[6] the author proceeds to a close and orderly analysis of:

1. The supreme principle of all analytic judgments;
2. The supreme principle of all synthetic judgments;
3. The systematic presentation of all synthetic principles of

4. See *Sein und Zeit*,[7] Tübingen, 1960, pp. 318-321. Hereafter: SZ.
5. *Die Frage nach dem Ding*, Tübingen, 1962, pp. 184, 188. Hereafter: FD.
6. FD, p. 97. Compare KM, p. 8.

the pure understanding, including: (a) the axioms of intuition, (b) the anticipations of perception, (c) the analogies of experience, and (d) the postulates of empirical thought in general. The last mentioned return again for analysis in *Kant's Thesis on Being* (1962), together with a discussion of the amphiboly of reflective concepts that follows immediately in the second edition of Kant's *Critique*. This is mentioned in passing to indicate the clear continuity between the study of 1935 and that of 1962.

There can be no question here of repeating the details of Heidegger's analysis. For our purposes it is more important to see how he comes to interpret Kant at all at this point of his career. The original title for the course was *Grundfragen der Metaphysik* (*Questions Concerning the Ground of Metaphysics*). Clearly, then, his purpose is to interrogate Being, which from the very beginning he takes to be the foundation of metaphysics. His method now is to interrogate the thing in its thingness, its Being (*Die Frage nach dem Ding*). The thing! But what thing? The sensible thing—any individual, visible, tangible thing (like a stone, a watch, a piece of wood). What makes it to *be* a thing?

Let us start, he says, with our "natural" understanding of it. But the "natural" meaning of a thing varies according to different epochs of history. The experience of nature is an essentially historical phenomenon, to be thought historically. For *us* to think upon the thingness of things means that we must do so in the context of our modern experience of nature, and this, according to Heidegger, is dominated by the scientific attitude toward the thing.[7]

Now what is it that characterizes the modern scientific attitude? Not simply a preoccupation with facts, nor even the experimental method as such, and still less mere exactitude of measurement, but a profound awareness of what Heidegger calls the *Mathematische*.[8] The *Mathematische* here means more— much more—than the individual discipline of Mathematics. For

7. FD, pp. 1-41.
8. FD, p. 52.

clarification Heidegger returns to the Greek: *manthanein*, to learn; *mathēmata*, what has been learned (or can be learned); *mathēsis*, the act of learning. Strictly speaking, we can only learn about something with which we already have come in contact. In other words, to learn means to gain further knowledge about what we already vaguely somehow know. The *mathēmata*, hence the *Mathematische*, as Heidegger takes the word, is precisely this antecedent knowledge of what is to-be-learned that makes further knowledge possible. It is only because the discipline of Mathematics deals with the type *par excellence* of this antecedent knowledge (of figures, numbers, serial relationships, and so on) that it has gradually pre-empted the name. In any case, the *Mathematische* in terms of our knowledge of things is precisely that "projective" knowledge of them by reason of which we gain antecedent access to them so that through the learning process we can come to know them better.[9] Normally the *Mathematische* would be translated as the "mathematical," but to avoid confusion and suggest its primitive Greek sense, let us translate it as the "mathematizing character" of the human mind.

It is the profound awareness of the mathematizing nature of our knowledge of things, and, indeed, as some presentative project, that makes modern science possible. To make his point, Heidegger shows how Newton's first law of motion implies that his manner of conceiving nature (for that matter, Galileo's, too) differs from that of Aristotle precisely by its character as presentative project. And it is because nature is first of all project that the method of controlled experiment becomes possible.[10]

This experience had already taken deep root in the European mind with its new spirit of anthropocentric independence well over a hundred years before the advent of Descartes, but it was he who gave it a first philosophical articulation. The *Regulae ad directionem ingenii* are especially illuminating here. Rule V, for example, proposes to disengage the simplest possible propositions

9. FD, pp. 58, 71.
10. FD, pp. 59-73.

which lie at the basis of all other scientific propositions and thus make possible a universal science, *scientia universalis*.[11] In fact, there must be one proposition (*Satz*) among the rest that underlies all others (as *hypokeimenon, subjectum*) and thereby grounds all the rest—a ground-proposition (*Grundsatz*). This underlying ground-proposition (*subjectum*) must be so absolutely radical that it suffices unto itself to serve as foundation for itself. In this sense it will be a foundation that is absolute and, because absolute, also unshakable, i.e., absolutely certain.

How Descartes proceeded and what the ground-proposition turned out to be we all know well enough. Let us content ourselves here simply to remark:

1. The *cogito-sum* of Descartes was the purest form of the mathematizing nature of human knowing, for the anticipation of the to-be-known and the coming-to-know of what had been anticipated are both identified in the single process of thought thinking itself.[12]

2. It was with the *cogito-sum* of Descartes that man first became a subject.

Previously *subjectum* had meant that which underlies the properties of the things we encounter outside us. Now it means that fundamental proposition (*Grundsatz*) which underlies universal science and therefore becomes identified with the *cogito-sum*, i.e., the existing human ego. What formerly had been called "subject," i.e., the thing, now becomes that which is thrown up against the subject and is called the "object." This condition of being thrown-up against the subject is what makes it to be a thing—its thingness (Being) consists in its object-ness.[13]

3. With the *cogito-sum* of Descartes, conceived as a fundamental proposition (*subjectum*) of all certain truths about beings, human reason itself (that power in man which does the

11. FD, p. 78.
12. FD, p. 80.
13. FD, pp. 80-82.

cogitating) becomes not only the ground of all knowing but the principle by which all beings that are known, whether as subject or object, are determined. Henceforth reason itself in itself (i.e., pure reason) will become the tribunal before which judgment upon the nature of things will be passed, and to which post-Cartesian man must address himself if he is to raise the question about the nature of the thing.[14]

When Heidegger finally comes to Kant (and this is only in the second half of his study), it is luminously clear that he conceives Kant's task as merely transposing onto the transcendental level the subject-ism of Descartes. What does this mean? It means that Kant is concerned with the mathematizing power of human reason as such (i.e., in its purity), and, indeed, on the deepest level: in terms of the *a priori* conditions of its possibility. What else does his Copernican revolution mean?

Kant's procedure is familiar enough to us. We know the objects we experience through judgments, and since reason, as a power of judgment, is for Kant the understanding, he must examine the structures of pure understanding, where "pure" in this case implies, of course (and Heidegger insists again and again on the importance of it), *a priori* synthesis with pure intuition as well.[15] These basic structures are propositions (*Sätze*) —the understanding *is* essentially the power to form these propositions [16]—but they are propositions that serve as ground (*Grundsätze*) for the possibility of beings to reveal themselves to us precisely as objects. Hence they are conditions for the objectness of objects (or rather, the thingness of things).[17] As Heidegger sees it, the analysis of the system (i.e., unity according to principles) of these *Grundsätze* of the pure understanding is the very heart of the whole *Critique*—at least in the second edition. That is why he is content to devote the rest of

14. FD, pp. 82-83.
15. FD, pp. 95, 112-115.
16. FD, p. 115.
17. FD, p. 150.

his study to an examination of them. His principal task is to show in detail what in theory is fairly obvious: how all of the synthetic *Grundsätze* of pure understanding are merely explicitating articulations of the supreme *Grundsatz* of man's mathematizing reason, namely "the conditions of the *possibility of experience* as such are at once conditions of the *possibility* of the *objects* of *experience*" (A 158, B 197). Hence, ". . . the *Grundsätze* [of pure understanding] basically do no more than again and again give expression to [this] supreme *Grundsatz,* but in such a way that in their correlation they spell out everything that belongs to both the essence of experience and the essence of the object." [18] It is for this reason that they institute the purview of transcendence where beings can be encountered as objects.

Let us conclude this survey of the *Question of the Thing* by underlining two themes which emerge out of Heidegger's entire treatment:

1. Kant here is seen in an historical perspective, i.e., as playing a special role in the entire history of modern times.

2. His entire effort to analyze the subject-ness of the subject and the object-ness of the object was in effect an articulation of his experience of the thingness (Being) of things.

The treatment of Kant in *The Principle of Ground* need not detain us. The theme of the book is: how explain the fact that the "principle of ground," or "principle of sufficient reason," as we call it, was never formulated before Leibniz? This leads him to a careful examination of Leibniz's understanding of the principle. Then, coming to Kant, Heidegger finds the principle profoundly operative in him, too, though he hardly ever mentions it—and certainly does not include it among the *Grundsätze* of pure understanding. Why? Because it is always implicit. For the

18. ". . . Die Grundsätze sagen im Grunde nur immer den obersten Grundsatz aus, aber so, dass sie in ihrer Zussamengehörigkeit all das eigens nennen, was zum vollen Gehalt des Wesens der Erfahrung und des Wesens eines Gegenstandes gehört" (FD, p. 188).

a priori conditions of possibility in human reason for knowledge of objects are also the ground of beings-as-objects, i.e., the reason-in-beings (*rationes* as *Gründe*) which enable reason-in-man (*ratio* as *Vernunft*) to achieve certain knowledge of them. Kant's search for the *a priori* conditions of human knowing, then, is a search for sufficient reason.[19]

Kant's Thesis on Being (1962) is a completely fresh approach to the same problematic, which is so manifestly coherent with the other two interpretations as to form a single perspective with them; but it deals with the problematic in terms more explicitly germane to Heidegger's own preoccupation, the problem of Being.

The pivotal text for the analysis here is the familiar one from the section on the "Ideal of Pure Reason" where Kant is offering his classic critique of the ontological argument for God's existence. "Being is manifestly not a real predicate. . . . It is the pure position [*Position*] of a thing, or of certain determinations in themselves . . ." (A 598, B 626). Let us polarize the summary around three simple questions:

1. Why is Being not a real predicate?
2. Why is Being pure position of a thing (and what role does the self-affection of pure intuition play in this position)?
3. What are these "determinations" of which Kant speaks?

First of all, "Being is not a real predicate." This is obvious enough as soon as we recall what "real" means. Deriving from the Latin *res*, "real" does not respond to whether a thing is but what it is. Hence, a "real" predicate does not attribute actuality but content (*Sachgehalt*) to a subject. In predicating Being of something (in saying it "is"), therefore, do we add any content to the idea? Of course not! That is why one hundred actual dollars are not worth a penny more than one hundred possible dollars. Being is simply not a "real" predicate.[20]

So far so good, but what does it mean to say that Being is

19. *Der Satz vom Grund*, Pfullingen, 1957, pp. 126-128.
20. *Kants These über das Sein*, Frankfurt, 1963, p. 10. Hereafter: KS.

the "pure position" of a thing or of certain determinations in themselves? "Pure" may be taken here to reassert that what is posited is bereft of any empirical content—Being accounts for the sheer positing and nothing more. But what does such a positing signify? [21]

In the pre-critical period, Kant had claimed that it was a "completely simple" notion, but nothing in Kant is quite as simple as that. He makes *Position* the equivalent of *Setzung*, and the meaning is always one of a subject setting down, positing, posing (*Stellen*)—and this in the sense of pro-posing (*Vorstellen*)—i.e., of presenting, or re-presenting, something over against itself as an object. Being as position, then, means precisely the character of posed-ness (*Gesetzheit*) of that which is posed by this pro-posing thought.[22] Its meaning will vary, of course, according to the different styles of pro-posing thought.

First of all, Kant himself speaks of a logical use of Being, i.e., the position of a P in relation to an S through the copula "is," in a simple judgment ("the stone is heavy"). He recognizes without naming, however, another use of "is," which Heidegger names for him as an "objective use," according to which he affirms the existence (*Dasein*) of something ("the stone is [existing]")! In the pre-critical period Kant refers to this as an "absolute" position, as if somehow the "is" were absolute, i.e., independent of the subject judging. To be sure, he senses some relation between an "is" of this kind and the understanding that makes the judgment, but he is at a loss to explain it.[23]

The great insight that brought Kant to full maturity in terms of his critical thought, according to Heidegger, was the discovery of the essential role that pure sense intuition plays in the function of the pure understanding. For through the affection of sense intuition something is *given* to it. To be sure, what is thus received by sense intuition is completely amorphous and must be

21. KS, pp. 11-12.
22. KS, p. 12.
23. KS, pp. 13-15.

brought into unity so that it can *stand*-as-opposed to it, i.e., become a *Gegen-stand* (object), but the object can stand *gegen*
(against), i.e., opposed to the subject, only because of the *givenness* of affection in sense intuition. The unifying function is
achieved, of course, by the categories of the understanding itself,
and the synthesis as such is a position which is a pro-position,
i.e., a judgment which proposes an object to the subject. But
now the object itself, by reason precisely of its givenness as
something opposed (the *Gegen* of *Gegen-stand*), grounds the
"is" of this judgment and differentiates it from the copula of the
merely logical order. The heart of this whole process is the synthetic, unifying power of the understanding which Kant calls
the original synthesis of apperception. Since this synthesis is a
condition of possibility for the object to be a *Gegen-stand*, it is
called "transcendental" apperception. As such it accounts for the
object-ness of objects and therefore the Being of beings-as-objects. Being here, then, is again a position—i.e., the posedness
of what is posed in the pro-posing judgments of the synthetic
unity of transcendental apperception. This is why the synthetic
unity of apperception is called the "supreme principle of all use
of the understanding" (B 136).[24]

Kant goes one step further, Heidegger claims, in the interpretation of Being as position. This is when he comes to speak of
those *Grundsätze* of the pure understanding that he calls the
"postulates of empirical thought as such." We recall that they
explain the different modalities by which an object is said to be
(e.g., whether as possible, or actual, or necessary). Now these
modalities of possibility, actuality, and necessity may be said
to be determinations of the object. In that sense they may be
called "predicates"—but not "real" predicates, for they add no
content to the object. They may be called, Heidegger suggests,
"transcendental" predicates, for what they determine is the manner in which the object is related to the understanding.[25] In any

24. KS, p. 22. Cf. pp. 16-22.
25. KS, p. 24. Cf. pp. 23-28.

case, when Kant says that "Being is the pure position of a thing, or of certain determinations in themselves," these, for Heidegger, are the "determinations" he has in mind.

By way of summary, let us permit Heidegger to speak for himself:

> . . . [Being as pure position] means the pure relation of objectivity to the subjectivity of human kowledge. Possibility, actuality and necessity are positions of different modes of this relationship. The different [kinds of] posed-ness are determined by the source of original posing. This is the pure synthesis of transcendental apperception. This is the primordial act [*Urakt*] of thought in its function as knowing.[26]

Heidegger proceeds now to examine the amphiboly of the concepts of reflection, but we can follow him no further. What we must insist on in concluding is the theme that returns again and again through the essay formally and solemnly as the author concludes each stage of the argument and moves on to another: *Sein und Denken.* In other words, what is lucidly clear is that Kant's thesis about Being states that it is a correlative of thought, where thought is conceived as the pure spontaneity of the understanding in dynamic synthesis with pure intuition (i.e., as pure subjectivity), and Being itself is considered objectivity as such.

There is the evidence. How is one to evaluate it? Does the turn in Heidegger's way occasion a new interpretation of Kant? If so, does the new vision of Kant give us a new vision of Heidegger? Recall the nature of the turning! For the early Heidegger, the focus of the Being-question is on *Dasein*, in the sense formulated in the title of *Being and Time*: "the interpreta-

---

26. ". . . Das 'bloss' meint das reine Verhältnis der Objektivität der Objekte zur Subjektivität der menschlichen Erkenntnis. Möglichkeit, Wirklichkeit, Notwendigkeit sind Positionen der verschiedenen Weisen dieses Verhältnisses. Die verschiedene Gesetztheit wird bestimmt aus dem Quell der ursprünglichen Setzung. Dies ist die reine Synthesis der transzendentalen Apperzeption. Sie ist der Urakt des erkennenden Denkens" (KS, p. 26).

tion of *Dasein* in terms of temporality, and the explication of time as the transcendental horizon of the question of Being." [27] For the later Heidegger, the focus has shifted to Being itself, as becomes unmistakably clear in *An Introduction to Metaphysics*, which dates from the summer of 1935—the semester immediately preceding the *Question of the Thing*. Here an important part of the study analyzes the text of Parmenides: *to gar auto noein estin te kai einai*, "Being and thought are identical." The same text is recalled again in *Kant's Thesis on Being* with reference to the constant refrain of the essay, *Sein und Denken*, and he adds: ". . . Being and Thinking: in this *and* is hidden the thought-worthy *[das Denkwürdige]* not only of philosophy up to the present but also of the thought of today." [28] What does the Parmenidean gnome mean?

In the briefest possible terms, it seems to mean this: *einai* ("to be") is conceived as *physis, alētheia*, the process by which beings emerge into presence as what they are, but a process which, re-vealing itself in beings as beings, conceals itself in them as itself; *noein* ("to think") is conceived not as any "rational" process in the sense of *vernehmen, Vernunft, ratio*, but simply as a gesture of acceptance, of taking under one's care (*in Acht nehmen*). In *Was heisst Denken?* (1952) it is explicitly correlated with *legein*, which Heidegger has repeatedly interpreted as "gathering together so that one lets lie forth in the Open." To-gether, *legein-noein* mean "to take under one's care what one has gathered together in the Open." *Auto* ("identical") in this context means not at all that Being (self-concealing revealment) and thinking (acceptance by *Dasein*) are the "same," in the sense of isomorphic (*das Gleiche*). Their "identity" is one of correlation (*Zusammengehörigkeit*), so that although not the

27. "Die Interpretation des Daseins auf die Zeitlichkeit und die Explika-tion der Zeit als des transzendentalen Horizontes der Frage nach dem Sein" (SZ, p. 41).

28. ". . . Sein *und* Denken: in diesem 'und' verbirgt sich das Denk-würdige sowohl der bisherigen Philosophie als auch des heutigen Denkens" (KS, p. 34).

"same" they are "one" (*das Selbe*). They are mutually correlated, because on the one hand Being has need of its There (*Da*) among beings in order that the e-vent of revealment can come-to-pass among them; yet, on the other hand, the *Da* of *Dasein* is nothing more than the *Da des Seins*—Being is its unique concern.

The theme of *auto*—the italicized "and" of "Being *and* Thinking"—recurs again and again as the years pass. By 1952, in the essay entitled *"Moira,"* it is clear that Being, conceived as process of *alētheia*, is to be thought more and more in terms of the emerging of the ontological difference, i.e., of the difference between Being and beings.[29] Sometimes this emergence will be called *Austrag* (i.e., the "issuing forth") of Being and beings, sometimes simply *Ereignis* (i.e., "e-vent") of the ontological difference. In any case, Being and beings, as they issue forth in the e-vent, remain correlatively one (*auto*), and *this* correlation is correlatively one with thought. Finally, in 1962 Heidegger gave his well-known though still unpublished lecture *Zeit und Sein* ("Time and Being"), obviously in allusion to the second half of *Being and Time* that had never appeared. The constant refrain was *es gibt Sein, es gibt Zeit:* "Being is given, Time is given." But what is the *Es* that *gibt*—what is it that does the giving? *Ereignis*—the e-vent of the ontological difference.[30]

When in the same year, then, Heidegger makes the following reflection at the close of *Kant's Thesis on Being:* ". . . What is most thought-worthy of all remains the fact that we ponder whether 'Being' or 'is' themselves can be, or whether Being never 'is,' yet nonetheless it remains true [to say]: Being is given. Yet whence does it come? to whom does it go?—this gift in 'it is given'—and what is the manner of its giving?"[31] If we may appeal here to the aforementioned lecture, we may presume that

29. "Moira," *Vorträge und Aufsätze*, Pfullingen, 1954, p. 249.
30. Cited according to unedited and unpublished manuscript, with Professor Heidegger's permission.
31. ". . . Das Denkwürdigste darin bleibt jedoch, dass wir bedenken, ob 'Sein,' ob das 'ist' selbst sein kann oder ob Sein niemals 'ist' und dass gleichwohl wahr bleibt: Es gibt Sein" (KS, p. 35).

the answer to these questions at the present time would probably be as follows: the gift comes out of the e-vent of *alētheia;* it is given to thought; it is the task of the thinker to ponder the manner of its giving.

And this is precisely what Heidegger himself has done in interpreting Kant. For Kant's thought itself was a gift out of an e-vent of Being-as-history. Recall that Being "e-mits" itself (*sich schickt*) to a correlative *Dasein* that is thereby "com-mitted" (Schicksal) in the process. The correlation of e-mitting and com-mitting constitute "mittence" (*Geschick*) which defines an epoch of time. The series of mittences constitutes "inter-mittence" (*Ge-schick-te*), i.e., history (*Geschichte*)—Being-as-history. The epoch of subject-ism that crystalized in Descartes was for Heidegger a mittence of Being-as-*alētheia,* according to which thought was experienced essentially as a pro-posing by the ego-subject, correlative with Being as the pro-posedness [*Vorgestelltheit*] of that pro-posing thought. Kant, then, for his part, was com-mitted to a mittence of Being interior to the subject-ist tradition, whereby thought was experienced as the pro-posing of transcendental subjectivity, correlative with Being as pure position. In a word, Kant's endeavor was a magnificently creative mode of forgetfulness of Being-as-*alētheia.* For all his greatness, he could not jump over his own shadow.[32] That is why Heidegger concludes the entire essay by saying: "Be all that as it may, Kant's thesis on Being as pure position remains a mountain top from which a look backward reaches to the determination of Being as *hypokeisthai,* and forward toward the speculative-dialectical interpretation of Being as Absolute Concept."[33]

If at this point we compare *Kant and the Problem of Metaphysics* (with its attempt to retrieve the *Daseins*-problematic

33. "Gleichwohl bleibt Kants These über das Sein als reine Position ein Gipfel, von dem aus der Blick rückwärts reicht bis zur Bestimmung des Seins als *hypokeisthai* und vorwärts weist in die spekulativ-dialektische Auslegung des Seins als absoluter Begriff" (KS, p. 36).

32. FD, p. 117.

in the transcendental imagination conceived as original time)
with *The Question of the Thing* (and its situation of the *Grund-sätze*-problem in the context of the whole history of modern
thought), the difference between the two does not lie simply in
the fact that the earlier work deals with the first edition of the
Critique of Pure Reason and the later work deals with the second, but rather in a change in perspective such as marks the
whole turning of Heidegger's way. Yes, the turning does affect a
change in his interpretation of Kant.

Does the new vision of Kant give us a new vision of Heidegger? In a sense I think it does, for it enables us to understand
more clearly the relationship between the two men that seems
to have been often misconstrued. For some of the most authorita-
tive interpreters seem to see a decisively formative influence of
Kant upon him, taking the Heidegger of *Being and Time* to be
the last of the great transcendental thinkers, where the turning
of the way is conceived as a breaking out of the transcendental
subjectivity of *Dasein* by the experience of Being as Non-being
(*Nichts*), followed by the meditation on Being as *alētheia*, self-
concealing revealment, that is the Source of history.[34] If it is not
too pretentious, I would like to take a position—very respect-
fully but very firmly—against any such interpretation.

The evidence already cited from the lecture "Time and Being"
indicates well enough, it seems to me, the clear direction of
Heidegger's entire effort: to probe more and more profoundly
the e-vent of *alētheia* out of which Being "is given," Time "is
given" as unfathomable gift to thought. No one will claim, I
trust, that there are any Kantian overtones here. I would like
to maintain that this position is nothing more than the term of
a long fidelity to the fundamental experience with which he

34. Among the more estimable studies, the following may be cited by
way of example: W. Schulz, "Über den philosophiegeschichtlichen Ort
Martin Heideggers," *Philosophische Rundschau*, I (1954), 65-93, 211-232;
F. Wiplinger, *Wahrheit und Geschichtlichkeit*, Freiburg, 1961; R. Guilead,
Etre et liberté, Louvain, 1965.

began the way, and, therefore, that Kant's influence was as extrinsic in the beginning as it clearly is now at its term.

As documentation, I cite the letter written in 1962 that appeared as preface to a book. Asked to explain the beginning of
his way, Heidegger refers to the doctoral dissertation of Franz
Brentano, *On the Manifold Sense of Being in Aristotle* (1862),
and writes:

> . . . On the title page of his work, Brentano quotes Aristotle's
> phrase: *to on legetai pollachōs.* I translate: "A being becomes
> manifest (i.e., with regard to its Being) in many ways." Latent
> in this phrase is the *question* that determined the way of my
> thought: what is the pervasive, simple, unified determination of
> Being that permeates all of its multiple meanings.[35]

Then he goes on to enumerate the three major forces that influenced his first steps: (1) Husserl, who suggested the method of
phenomenology; (2) Aristotle, who suggested that *alētheia*
means a process of revealment; (3) the experience itself of
ousia as presence, or presenc-ing, and therefore as a process that
is essentially conditioned by time. Hence, ". . . Time became
questionable in the same manner as Being. . . ."[36]

Asked to explain the turning itself, Heidegger writes:

> . . . This change is not a consequence of altering the standpoint,
> much less of abandoning the fundamental issue, of *Being and
> Time.* The thinking of the turning results from the fact that I
> stayed with the matter-for-thought [of] "Being and Time," i.e.,
> by inquiring into that perspective which already in *Being and
> Time* (p. 39) was designated as "Time and Being." . . .
> The reversal between Being and Time, between Time and
> Being, is determined by the way Being is given, Time is
> given. . . .[37]

Finally, Heidegger himself comes to grips explicitly, it seems,
with the alleged Kantianism of his beginning:

35. "Preface" to W. J. Richardson, S.J., *Heidegger: Through Phenomenology to Thought,* The Hague, 1963, p. x.
36. *Ibid.,* p. xii.
37. *Ibid.,* pp. xvi, xx.

One need only observe the simple fact that in *Being and Time* the problem is set up outside the sphere of subjectivism—that the entire anthropological problematic is kept at a distance, that the normative issue is emphatically and solely the experience of Dasein with a constant eye to the Being-question—for it to become strikingly clear that the "Being" into which *Being and Time* inquired can not long remain something that the human subject posits [*Setzung*]. It is rather Being, stamped as Presence by its time-character, [that] makes the approach to *Dasein*. As a result, even the initial steps of the Being-question in *Being and Time* thought is called upon to undergo a change whose movement corresponds with the turning.[38]

Is this uncritical, to let Heidegger testify on his own behalf? Perhaps. But we have only attempted to see Heidegger through his own eyes in so far as he reveals himself at the present time through his own vision of Kant. In any case, this insistence upon the singleness of Heidegger's intention from beginning to end of this way makes clear why one may maintain that the different interpretations of Kant that arise out of the early and the later Heidegger are indeed not isomorphic, the "same" (*das Gleiche*). But since they spring out of a rigorous fidelity to a single way, they are profoundly *auto* (*das Selbe*), "one."

38. *Ibid.*, p. xviii.

PART TWO

STRUCTURES OF INDIVIDUAL
AND SOCIAL CONSCIOUSNESS

Gerald E. Myers

SELF AND BODY-IMAGE

I. *Body-Image*

One's body may not appear to oneself as it really is, notably in cases of brain damage; some hemiplegics cannot recognize one-half of their bodies. Sir Henry Head introduced the psychological construct "body-schema" to explain discrepancies in body awareness, theorizing that everyone is the involuntary owner of a "body-schema" or postural model which is a necessary condition for adequately apprehending changes in one's posture and relations between one's bodily parts. A brain lesion destroys the ability to recognize one's body adequately, because it disrupts one's normal postural model. Paul Schilder elaborated and modified Head's theory, adding psychoanalytic dimensions to what he called "body-image."

> The body schema is the tri-dimensional image everybody has about himself. We may call it "body-image." The term indicates that we are not dealing with a mere sensation or imagination. There is a self-appearance of the body. It indicates also that, although it has come through the senses, it is not a mere perception. There are mental pictures and representations involved in it, but it is not mere representation.[1]

1. Paul Schilder, *The Image and Appearance of the Human Body*, New York, 1964, p. 11.

What Schilder meant by "body-image" is obscure, but I think his view was essentially this: earlier psychologists like Wundt and Titchener investigated bodily sensations but without ever noting how we experience the body itself *as a unit*. The body is experienced as a total entity having an outside and an inside filled to the surface with a "substance of heavy mass." [2] The body as a totality is not a product of sensations; it is instead the *framework* within which sensations, in their location and mutual relations, get identified. The body is a physical map, and sensations are mapped in terms of it. Since one's body may not appear to one as it really is, one's body and one's "image" of it may differ significantly. Each person's body-image, like the body itself, is a unit or larger framework within which the body and its sensations are experienced; the body-image is a necessary psychological map for identifying the bodily sensations that are mapped with reference to it. Adequate experiencing of one's body is ultimately a function of the body-image; if it is distorted, so is our awareness of our body. Finally, Schilder claimed that "in every experience the body-image is present." [3]

An impressive literature on the subject has accumulated since Schilder, although "body-percept," "body-ego," "body-schema," and "postural model" are often used instead of "body-image." Psychologists have devised interesting hypotheses involving these expressions, but their meaning is no clearer than Schilder's concept. These psychologists insist upon "image," "percept," or "schema," indicating that they are not satisfied, for example, with "body-*concept*," which can be interpreted dispositionally. That is, it is insufficient to hold that how I perceive my body is a function of how I conceive (dispositionally) of it; instead, our psychologists seem to claim that how I conceive of my body must be itself understood as a "something" experienced or introspected, as complex image or schema which can be compared—for size, shape, density, and so forth—with one's body. They sug-

2. *Ibid.*, p. 283.
3. *Ibid.*, p. 280

gest that experiencing or introspecting an "image," sensuous "map," or visual "schema" of one's body is a necessary condition for one's adequately experiencing the details of one's body.[4]

Two investigators, Seymour Fisher and Sidney Cleveland, have appreciated the question whether the dispositional notion of body-concept is substitutable for body-*image*, and they have tried to resolve the issue experimentally. Since 1951 Fisher and Cleveland have experimented with a special dimension, body-boundary or body-surface, of body-image. They have shown that our "image" of our bodily boundaries and the boundaries themselves may not coincide; our bodily perimeter and extremities may not appear to us as they are. We may chronically imagine ourselves taller or fatter than we actually are, our arms longer or shorter, our waists wider or slimmer, and so on. Brain damage or schizophrenia can cause difficulty in ascertaining whether certain stimuli originate within or without one's bodily boundary. Normal people vary in how they "feel" their body against the environment, as sharply or only dimly outlined. Some have a sharp sense of where their bodies terminate and the environment begins, others less so. Further, for some the "image" of their bodily surfaces is hard and resilient, protected against invasion, whereas for others it is soft, porous, and defenseless. Using Rorschach or Holtzman tests, Cleveland and Fisher have devised an index or barrier score with which to evaluate more exactly the body-boundary dimension of one's body-image.

Despite the extent of recent experimental study of "body-boundary," Cleveland and Fisher admit that the concept itself is obscure, but that it is not true, as one critic has argued, that

4. Merleau-Ponty understands the innovation of "body-image" as naming established associations of images, whose role is "to register for me the positional changes of the parts of my body for each movement of one of them, the position of each local stimulus in the body as a whole, an account of the movements performed at every instant during a complex gesture, in short a *continual translation into visual language* of the kinaesthetic and articular impressions of the moment." Maurice Merleau-Ponty, *Phenomenology of Perception*, trans. Colin Smith, New York, 1962, p. 99, my italics.

the concept refers only to how one responds to ink blots without any literal involvement of bodily sensations or body-*image*.[5] They devised tests to prove that one's body-image boundary is reflected in actual body experiences, that one's "barrier index" affords predictions as to whether, for example, interior or exterior sensations dominate in how we perceive our own bodies. They tested, with positive results, the hypothesis that the more *definite* one's body-image boundary the more exterior sensations (viz., skin and muscle) will dominate, and the more *blurred* one's body-image boundary the more interior (viz., stomach and heart) will prevail. This correlation between type of body-image surface and type of sensation-domination (exterior or interior) is thought by Cleveland and Fisher to be a function of two factors. The first: the definite-boundaried person is more active muscularly and thus assigns greater importance to the boundary region of his body-image than does the muscularly less active person who is oriented inwardly. The second: probably there is a greater density of sensation in the body-surface area for the definite-bounded person, whereas there is a greater density of sensation in the body's interior for the indefinite-boundaried individual, and this may reinforce these different bodily regions in the respective body-image of the two different personality types.

But Cleveland and Fisher, it appears, do not show that body-*image* is irreplaceable by the dispositional concept of body-*concept*.[6] They need only maintain that their experiments give operational significance to their construct of body-image or body-percept, and that accordingly their hypothesis does not require that their subjects readily introspect a literal, constant image of their bodies. Rather, they asked subjects to answer questions like: Were your feelings when tired, when afraid, when successful, and so on located in your skin? In your stomach? In your heart?

5. R. C. Wylie, *The Self Concept*, Lincoln, Nebr., 1961, p. 54.

6. J. J. Gibson, for example, explicitly defines body-image dispositionally: "The body percept, or 'body image' is a set of possible dispositions or poses—standing, or lying—relative to the substratum and to gravity." *The Senses Considered as Perceptual Systems*, Boston, 1966, p. 113.

In your muscles? Their findings indicated a significant correlation between the tendency to experience predominantly interior or exterior sensations and the nature of one's "image" of one's own body-boundary. But nothing in their findings seems to prohibit substituting "concept" for "image," such that the correlation may be thought to hold between the sorts of bodily sensations to which one is prone and the way in which one is *disposed* to react to ink blots, to describe one's bodily surface when queried appropriately, to imagine certain things when stimulated in certain ways, and so on.

Nevertheles, I believe an important general point, though not brought to light by the psychologists themselves, lies behind the resistance in the literature to substituting "body-concept" for "body-image." Clarifying the concept of body-image will elicit the point with its important ramifications.

II. *Clarifying the Concept*

An important difficulty in the notion of body-image is the difficulty of images themselves, specifically, of knowing whether an image is present, how much (a *whole* image, a large part of it, only a small part, and so on) of an image is present, and how to check descriptions given to it. I am of course not denying, as did John Watson, the occurrence of images, but I am convinced, from my own case and from informal interrogations, that one cannot always declare honestly whether one is conscious of an image, how much of an image is present, or how accurate is one's description of it. Those denying this seem to me to be *determined* to be certain, even if there is a risk of their being mistaken. On occasion an image is so vividly present that it seems absurd to suppose that one could ever be in doubt about an image's occurrence; yet, on occasion, if one is honest, all that one can declare about the image of one's first pet is that it "seems" to be present. Refining the definition of "image" will not help, for the difficulty is the experiential one of trying to de-

termine whether one actually does or only seems to be aware of
a genuine image; one is truly dubious about the facts and, for
that reason, about how to classify the situation. I can, after all,
seem to see something without necessarily really seeing anything,
including images.

Two examples of descriptions given to one's body-image will
illuminate the point. The first is this: my body-image is peculiar
by surrounding, enclosing, or "including" me. My body-image is
a sort of halo whose outline more or less corresponds to my own
bodily outline; I feel "inside" it once its existence is confessed.
But isn't this a trivial observation, since every image "of" me
must "include" me? I must surely be "in" every image of me?
But this objection misses the point. Suppose I have a vivid image
of myself on the beach; then of course the image of the whole
scene must include the *image of me* as well as the image of the
beach. But the image of me on the beach does not include me
but an image of me, whereas my body-image "includes" *me* and
not merely an image of me. When I entertain the image of me
on the beach, it is like looking at a compact, external scene,
whereas when I consider the occurrence of my body-image, it is
like dimly apprehending a sort of ghostly broken-fence, nearby
and surrounding, which vaguely follows in its outline the contours of my own bodily outline. It is "broken" because fragmentary, as Schilder and others insist; my body-image is rarely, if
ever, whole and well defined. It becomes known to me in bits,
though the parts are somehow connected into one unit. What our
first example of a body-image description points up, then, is one's
being enclosed by the vague, fragmentary image itself.

The second example: the body-image is experienced as a surrounding envelope, itself perhaps a few feet beyond one's actual
body surface. Between the outline of the enclosing image and
one's actual perimeter, the intervening area can be experienced
as dense or light, contracting or expanding, descending or as-
cending, vague or well defined, and so on. The space between
oneself and the surrounding outline of one's body-image is char-

acteristically experienceable as massive and oppressive or, differently, as light and airy. This intervening space becomes a locus of phenomenological variety and discovery. What this second example of body-image description points up is the experience of peculiarities in the space intervening between one's body and the surrounding image of it.

Both examples of descriptions are my own; but from informal interrogating I am satisfied that others also find these descriptions applicable to their experiences of body-image. But these descriptions are, I submit, non-literal and non-introspective. Schilder's suggestion that each of us has a constant, fragmentary body-image, which is a literal image, is fanciful; it suggests to me that I am constantly living in a sort of tattered shroud, and my introspective experience is rarely like that. But neither are my two examples of body-image descriptions verifiable introspectively; I cannot literally pick out, among my inner states, the outline of a surrounding body-image or a space intervening between it and me which is massive or light. The infinite range of body-image descriptions is phenomenologically rather than introspectively based, but this distinction needs elaboration.

Common to the different definitions of "introspection" is the idea of uncovering, identifying, or becoming aware of a *real occurrent* of some kind—a mood, emotion, sensation, image, perhaps even a physical thing. Essential to the traditional concepts of introspection is the idea of "looking inside" and either discovering something previously unnoticed or re-finding (i.e., verifying) what had been claimed to be there for notice. Introspection isolates for awareness a real occurrent and possibly its relations to other real occurrents. I want to distinguish introspection from "phenomenological reporting," which is not reporting something observed, because any "observation" is capable of verification and introspective rechecking of details within the observational experience. Phenomenological reporting is not subject to verificatory tests, not because it is indubitable but because there is no observed occurrent to be verified; there are in one's experience no literal items, like images and sensations, to be introspectively verified. As Merleau-Ponty says, "Phenomenology, as a disclosure of the world, rests on itself, or rather provides its own foundation." [7]

The earlier examples of body-image descriptions are instances of what I call "phenomenological reporting." What is reported is an experience, or a dimension of an experience, which might be reported by using the colloquial "It seems to me as if. . . ," but where, curiously, no specific images, moods, sensations, emotions, or real occurrents of any kind are either the focus of the experience or are even referred to by the report. For example, in reporting "It seems as if my body-image surrounds me," no specific occurrent is referred to or noticed; yet the report tells what my experience is like. We could say that what is phenomenologically reported is the phenomenological dimension of experience which, in the absence of specific occurrents referred to, is yet justly considered by the reporter to be described by his report. While it is true that the phenomenological dimension of experience is reportable by "It seems as if. . . ," the phenomenological use of this locution rules out any possibility of error or reality being otherwise; this use of "It seems as if . . ." excludes the possibility of "It seems as if. . . , but perhaps I'm mistaken," or "It seems as if . . . , but maybe it really is . . ." Again, the reason is not that the report is indubitable but that verificatory procedures are irrelevant; the question of warranted certainty or uncertainty about my report cannot arise. In reporting "It is as if my body-image surrounds me," introspective corroboration is impossible, since no introspectible items are essentially referred to. I may of course abandon this particular report in the future, not because I was previously mistaken but rather because the phenomenological dimension of my experience has changed.

Another feature of our samples of phenomenological reporting of body-image experiences (but not necessarily of all phenomenological descriptions) is this: the phenomenological di-

7. Merleau-Ponty, *op. cit.*, pp. xx-xxi.

mension of experience reported by :"It is as if my body-image surrounds me" is also describable as what the concept "body-image" *suggests* to me experientially; or, it is identical with my experiential "sense" of what "body-image" means. That is, the sorts of experience reported by the earlier descriptions of body-image are probably dependent upon the introduction of the concept and the consequent *looking for* an experiential dimension with which it will be associated. As we give new meaning to words, so we find new phenomenological dimensions of our experiences associated with new meanings and new words. It may be improper to equate the phenomenological dimension with the "meaning" of any expression, but it is correctly identified as what is "suggested" or associated in one's experience in the process of ascertaining what the expression might refer to. Thus, I might never have a hint of a surrounding body-image until I was exposed to the concept and began pondering its possible referents; but, given that, a new phenomenological dimension of my experience arises which is reported by "It is as if my body-image surrounds me." It is the phenomenological aspect of experience which people intend when speaking of what an expression φ "suggests" or of having "a sense of φ."

I believe that the resistance to substituting the dispositional "body-concept" for the experiential "body-image" in much psychological literature is due to an appreciation of the fact that, once the concept of body-image is introduced, phenomenological dimensions of experience occur which get neglected if talk about how we *image* our bodies is replaced by talk merely about how we *think* about our bodies, in the sense of how we are disposed to react in circumstances where our conceptions of our bodies are especially relevant. The language of body-image does indeed keep us closer than does the language of body-concept to the phenomenological aspects of our experience which arise once the concept of body-image is introduced and becomes associated with those aspects of our experience.

But the phenomenological dimensions of experience must not

be confused with the occurrence of sensations and images. For instance, "It is as if my body-image surrounds me in the center of it" does not at all require, in order to report my experience, the presence of an image of an outermost outline, imagined some few feet away from me, which more or less follows my own bodily outline. There is a universal temptation to suppose that all experience must consist of introspectible items like images, and therefore the attempt is universally made to translate descriptions of phenomenological experience into introspective language. This is especially true of the psychological literature on body-image. My point is that the concept of body-image is not an introspective but phenomenological concept; the kinds of experiences with which it becomes associated are reportable by the colloquial locution, "It seems as if. . . ," but without the presence of specific images, sensations, and so forth being referred to by the locution.

Phenomenological reporting cannot be characterized as poetry, metaphor, rhetoric, and so on. In one respect, the literal-metaphorical distinction is inapplicable to phenomenological reports (there being no verificatory procedures to define the "literal"), but such reports are literal in so far as they are direct reports of what the experiences are like. Nor should it be necessary to plead the importance of phenomenological reports for both self-understanding and inter-subjective communication. That should be as obvious to philosophers as it is to psychiatrists.

III. *Self and Body-Image*

How we imagine our bodies is intimately connected with how we feel about ourselves; a negative opinion of one's own body connects with a tendency to self-depreciation. And in learning how one's imagines one's body one learns about one's self-image; for example, as Cleveland and Fisher have shown, in discovering the nature of one's body-image boundary one realizes more fully why one is aggressive or shy, angular or lyrical in one's movements, susceptible to interior or exterior sensations, and so on. Investigations about body-image inform us about who we are, who we imagine we are, and why the two may not coincide. Body-image studies reveal much about what William James called the empirical self, the self describable as irritable or agreeable, aggressive or shy, and so forth—that is, much about personality. Phenomenological reports, of course, count importantly in these investigations of personality theory. But I want to focus here exclusively upon the relevance of the concept of body-image for what is often called the "philosophical or metaphysical" conception of the self, the view that "I" refers to a *nonphysical something*.

Ross Stagner has spoken for this conception of the self in his investigations in the psychology of personality. He distinguishes between self, self-image, and body-image, noting of course their interrelations; self-image always implies the attribution of personality traits, whereas the self is a "kind of primitive experience about which communication is virtually impossible . . . one can experience the self but this experience must be uniquely personal." [8] In the same vein: " 'I am what I am' is the succinct Biblical assertion that selfhood cannot be further defined but must be experienced." [9] Suggesting approval, Stagner refers to Koffka's remark that we can even locate the self spatially as the point dividing "in front of" from "in back of," and also "left" from "right"; it is also the point separating the future from the past.[10]

These references to the self as a kind of "dimensionless point," however literal, metaphorical, or heuristic in intent, are so

8. *Psychology of Personality*, New York, 1961, p. 185.
9. *Ibid.*
10. *Ibid.*, p. 183. Compare these observations with G. E. M. Anscombe's comment about Wittgenstein: "In Wittgenstein's version, it is clear that the 'I' of solipsism is not used to refer to anything, body or soul; for in respect of these it is plain that all men are alike. The 'I' refers to the centre of life, or the point from which everything is seen." *An Introduction to Wittgenstein's Tractatus*, London, 1959.

reminiscent of Leibniz' concept of monad, that I want henceforth to call the self of the metaphysical version the *monadic-self*.
The monadic-self is thus a spatially dimensionless, non-physical
something, referred to by the first-person pronoun. The thought
that the monadic-self is a real occurrent, an introspectible something, is as mistaken, say, as the thought that my body is what
"I" refers to. The reason is this: the distinctive use of the first-
person pronoun contrasts to the ordinary use of the impersonal
pronoun, so that whatever is the correct analysis of the personal
pronoun, it must start by marking the contrast between the uses
of the personal and the impersonal pronouns. That is, "I" is introduced into the vocabulary to refer to what *cannot* be referred
to by "it"; accordingly, if a referent is suggested for "I" which
can also be indicated by "it," then a use is proposed for "I"
which is in fact self-contradictory. The concept of the monadic-
self *as a real occurrent* involves this contradiction, for it supposes a special *something* which I can identify as the referent
of "I"; but if I could do that, I could also refer to *it* as "it,"
which would accomplish the contradiction. An appreciation,
even if largely unconscious, of the availability of the contradiction has been responsible for the occasional philosophical explanations of the logic requiring the grammatical distinction between the "I" and the "me." Thus, any theory which locates a
"something" as the referent of "I" is self-contradictory in requiring "I" to refer to that to which "it" refers.

   The monadic-self, I suggest, is a phenomenological concept,
as body-image is a phenomenological concept. Despite Ross
Stagner's claims, it appears that Hume was clearly right in denying that introspection reveals a monadic self, though Hume
failed to notice how talk about a monadic-self can report phenomenological dimensions of experience. Hume's inability to
introspect an elusive non-physical something was a consequence
of the fact that the only identifiable referent for the first-person
pronoun is the person using it, and accordingly, in the monadic-

self sense of "I," I don't exist literally; in that sense, I exist phenomenologically. My experiences are such that it seems as if
things are seen not only with my physical eyes but also by a
monadic-self; it seems as if the things I do are not only with my
physical limbs but also by a monadic-self—remembering, however, that this use of the colloquial "it seems as if" is neither the
language of metaphor nor that of illusion. I am not staring, as it
were, at perceptible or introspectible items which might deceive
me. It is rather that, once the concept of monadic-self is introduced, phenomenological dimensions of experience arise which
become associated with the concept and which are directly reported by the "as if" locution—but in the absence of specific
introspective contents which could be construed as similar to
an ordinary illusion. The force of the "as if" is to signify that the
report is not meant literally in the conventional sense of the
words used but is to be understood literally in some *other* sense
of the words. This other sense is found in the phenomenological
dimension of the experience reported; phenomenological communication always requires more sharing at the experiential level
than an understanding of words in their conventional meanings.
In the case of "monadic-self," as with "body-image," what has
to be understood (and it is partly the function of "as if" to remind us of this) is the sort of experience which "It is as if I am
nowhere but yet am the point from which all is seen" directly
reports. This is not free verse but the report of an experience.

As psychological investigations of body-image help one understand one's empirical self, so phenomenological reports with respect to body-image illustrate similar types of reports about the
monadic-self. For example, in saying, "It is as if I were surrounded by an image of my own body," the "I" referred to is not
the person named "Myers" but the monadic-self of which Myers
speaks phenomenologically with the pronoun. *I* am not seized
by an illusion of a surrounding body-image; *I* have an experience which is reported by "It is as if I were a dimensionless

point surrounded by an image of my own body." That is, the phenomenological report has a monadic-self surrounded by a phenomenological body-image. Monadic-self and body-image develop together, and what phenomenological philosophers can contribute is a fuller account of how phenomenological reports involving body-image are also reports about monadic-self experience. Doing this will afford what many people call a "deeper" understanding of our "deeper" selves.

Frank A. Tillman

ON PERCEIVING PERSONS

Sometimes when I see a facial movement, I see it not as a relic of behavior, a symptom of a mental state, but (depending on context) *as* anger, jealousy, pain, or depression. I remark this kind of perception by sometimes saying, "I saw his anger," or "I saw his depression," and so forth. Certainly we speak this way, but is it true that I see non-inferentially what another person is experiencing? Or is this way of speaking an ellipsis for "I see a person behaving in a particular way and I infer that he is probably angry"? In this essay I want to examine the idea of perception that is expressed by "I see his pain" or "I see his anger."

If I could show that we sometimes see non-inferentially what another person is experiencing, then I could display the reason why we sense that the relation between behavior and mental states is not merely probabilistic, why we appear to generalize so freely on our own case. I could also refute a generalized philosophical skepticism about the contents of other minds.

I

There are such overwhelming objections to the view that we perceive another person's mental states that one is inclined to reject it out of hand. The view seems to imply either (1) that in seeing a contraction of facial muscles I am seeing all there is to see of, say, the experience of anger, or (2) that I have the immediate awareness of another person's mental states that I do of my own.

According to (1), all experience reduces to manifestations; behavioral patterns simply occur out of all connection with the person who manifests them.

It is obvious that this view does not square with the facts, for it is always possible that what I see, in the required sense, is not what I take it to be. A man may be angry without displaying it, and he may display anger without being angry. In addition, there are, of course, mental states that do not have easily identifiable behavioral manifestations; two such are tastes and moods. As this is the case, it is always reasonable to ask whether the person is really in the state in which I perceive him.

According to (2), I am said to have as direct an acquaintance with other minds as I have with my own. But it is obvious that in normal cases I am not directly aware, in the required sense, of another person's mental states. I cannot tell when a man is shamming anger; yet in most cases that is what I should be able to tell if I were aware of his states in the same way I am aware of my own.

These facts suggest that the connection between behavior and mental states is, after all, merely a probabilistic one. Accordingly, the belief that another person is angry or in pain must be based on a type of inductive inference. One form of inference involves an analogy with my own case. I notice that my own anger or pain is correlated with certain patterns of behavior in certain circumstances. When I notice these patterns of behavior in others in similar circumstances, I can reasonably infer that they are having the same experience.

Not only is this alternative view open to the classical skeptical objections, but also it would force me to say what a mental state is, independent of behavior. It also does not explain why we generalize so freely from a single case, namely our own, and why so many philosophers have held that the relation between propositions about behavior and propositions about mental states is stronger than induction. This view seems to imply what is very likely not the case—that in order for a child to recognize the facial expression of another person, it must be so enormously precocious that prior to the recognition, say, of anger, it makes a point-by-point comparison between experience and behavior in its own case.

The gambit of introducing the concept of a criterion does not help. A criterion may be interpreted in at least three ways. (1) It may be introduced as a probabilistic indicator, in which case there is no gain over talk of behavioral symptoms. (2) It may be introduced to answer the need for a relation between propositions about behavior and propositions about mental states which is neither deductive nor inductive. A proposition specifying certain behavioral conditions is sometimes said to provide a criterion for the acceptance of another proposition specifying a mental state. But if the relation between these propositions is neither inductive nor deductive, it is difficult to know what the relation is. (3) The concept of a criterion may be introduced by the use of the expression "logically adequate criterion." If so, the concept derives its logical force from an argument reminiscent of Kant. For example, it is a fact that we have the concept of pain; i.e., we can teach the use of the term, correct someone who has gotten it wrong, and translate this concept into another language. Therefore, it is held, behavior *must* be an adequate criterion; otherwise we would not possess this concept. But notice that the concept of a logically adequate criterion does not make clear the relationship between behavior and mental states. Although this approach suggests that behavior *is* adequate, it does so without suggesting how.

I think the best thing to do is to admit these difficulties and look for a different picture of person perception. The fault of the probabilistic approach lies, I think, in the implicit assumption that behavior is an indicator or natural sign of mental states. This assumption appears to be quite natural: we take a grimace or cry to be a natural sign of anger or pain because we suppose that these are uncontrolled, spontaneous reactions. They could then serve only as evidence for mental states. Thinking of behavior as evidence is further reinforced by the picture we have of the perception of persons: it is almost a point of principle that our knowledge of others is the result of inductive inference. No doubt the philosophic skeptic forces this picture upon us; but over-attention to this way of conceiving the problem of other minds has led us to look away from the actual function of behavior.

II

I should like to propose and examine the view that behavior appropriate to pain experience, or anger, or depression, is not a symptom or natural sign but a form of action, namely a bodily gesture. Pain, anger, depression, and so on are forms of conduct. Both gestures and natural signs have meaning, but what they mean is very different. I shall argue that the picture of perceiving persons should be conceived more on the analogy of reading language than reading a barometer.

The best evidence I have for this view consists of facts that are fatal to some of the views I have rejected.

1. That I can simulate pain behavior when I am not in pain, and that I can forbear acting in pain when I am, suggests that pain "behavior" is something I accede to and can control and perform. To say that I exhibited pain or anger is not merely to say that my facial muscles moved in fairly well-defined ways.

The movement was under my control in the sense that in most cases I could have inhibited it had I so decided. Of course there are physiological changes which I cannot control or which interfere with my control of postural and facial gestures—increased heartbeat, distribution of blood, suspension of digestion, and simple reflexes. But the fact is that I do manage to inhibit and modify reflexes that involve skeletal muscles. My pain and anger deceptions are very often successful.

This means that there is no simple correlation between my "behavior" and my mental states. Biological changes are usually too generalized to be correlated with any one specific mental state. My facial gesture of anger is not a passive indicator, like a swollen jaw or an infected tooth. Human ability and skill intervene and make the movements associated with anger, pain, depression, and so on complex in the way a barometer or other natural sign is not.

But examples of pain and anger deception are the exception. And I should not want to rest my case that a significant portion of our seemingly spontaneous behavior is gestural on such a narrow base. So I shall try to show that we exert more control over ordinary movements associated with mental states than we commonly suppose.

2. Our body is at one and the same time the medium of our emotion and our articulation of it. Even though some of our gestures are causally related to internal and visceral changes, and our gestures themselves are partly conditioned by our musculature, our ability and skill intervene. Our gestural movements conform to certain social conventions. We learn very early how deep physiological reflexes must be controlled and what socially acceptable forms they should take. The transformation of the physiological smile of an infant at three weeks into the social smile at two months is a good example.[1] Most of our gestures

1. R. A. Spitz and K. M. Wolf, "The Smiling Response: A Contribution to the Ontogenesis of Social Relations," *Genetic Psychology,* XXXIV (1957), 57.

are based on natural and instinctive movements which we have muted or intensified, elaborated and refined, and made to serve specific purposes in conformity with social sanctions and rules.

It is obvious that a great number of our acts are symbolic or emblematic, e.g., saluting the flag to show allegiance, kneeling to show reverence, thumbing the nose to show contempt. These specific gestures have little or no direct connection with universal biological responses. We are not surprised to find that these gestures have no meaning for people in other cultures; they would be as opaque to some people as the exposure of the tongue in certain pieces of Mayan religious sculpture is to us.

It is not at all obvious that behavior we commonly think of as spontaneous and unmediated is also bound by convention. There is evidence that such seeming biological constants as pain, anger, and sorrow, are expressed in radically different ways by various groups. The following examples are intended to quicken our sense of strangeness about what we ordinarily take for granted.

> If we saw someone cut his finger, we would not find it strange if we saw him quickly put his finger to his mouth, purse his lips, and grimace. Yet as George Murdock once reported, an Indian from the Western plains of the United States would find this highly amusing and even silly. It is not his way of showing pain or distress.[2]

Anthropological literature is rich in alternatives;[3] for example:

> The Chinese show anger by opening their eyes widely and staring fixedly at the person who is the object of anger, whereas to us this act would mean surprise or fright, depending on circumstances and other supplementary gestures. It is common for the Chinese to express surprise by sticking out their tongues.[4]

2. From an unpublished lecture given at Yale in 1957.
3. W. Labarre, "The Cultural Basis of Emotions and Gestures," *Journal of Personality*, XVI (1947), 49-68.
4. O. Klineberg, "Emotional Expressions in Chinese Literature," *Journal of Abnormal Social Psychology*, XXXIII (1938), 517-520.

These movements represent a covert culture—codes of the face and body that vary from group to group. Our bodily gestures are as colloquial as our language.[5]

There is no sharp line between physiology and culture. Most human behavior falls between the extremes of simple reflex and obvious symbolic behavior. Most behavior consists of physiologically conditioned responses that have been modified by custom. Pain is no exception; it is impossible to separate the sensory from the motor parts of pain responses. And behavior resulting from motor impulses is shaped by the customs of when, where, and how pain is expressed. It is difficult to find a human movement which is not tainted by custom and yet sufficiently rich to be associated with a mental state.

The fact that a great deal of our behavior conforms to rules has consequences for an account of our perceptions of other persons.

3. We sense that the relation between the behavior of others and their mental states is not merely probabilistic; we seem to generalize too easily from our own case. This is because our gestures and bodily stances are intimately connected with a set of social conventions. Our bodily behavior acquires a socially shared meaning.

It is a fact that a very young child recognizes the meaning of a facial gesture, but he could hardly do so on the basis of observed correlations or the analogy with his own feelings. Nor

---

5. We have hardly done justice to the wide range of face-to-face skills that punctuate a social encounter: re-enactments of logical pauses, subtle changes of rate and volume of movement, to say nothing of gestures that are introduced along with speech acts. In a certain context a gesture may have a propositional as well as an expressive character. If someone has repeatedly slammed a door in my presence and I say, "That is the seventh time you slammed that door," the next time he slams the door my look, suitable to that circumstance, is often enough to say what I just said, and with perhaps greater force. Gesures have what Austin called an "illocutionary force" as well as "perlocutionary" effects. I have developed this point in a paper on "Expression and Speech Acts."

does he identify his own mental states before he identifies the
behavior of another. This is about as worthless as the genetic
hypothesis that in order for there to be a language there must be
a first person who learned it. A child cries indiscriminately in
pain or anger, but he soon learns the difference. Being angry
involves knowing how to be angry, and the same is true of pain
and other states. Knowing how at least involves a knowledge of
when and where to be angry or in pain; it involves a knowledge
of the customs and sanctions of our group. Even when we
are not in pain or angry, we know what we do when we are.
This is the basis of our successful deceptions. If this account is
correct, then I am not forced to say what pain is, independently
of my bodily behavior. Nor need I maintain that we find out
what pain is before we recognize it in another. Since behavior
is construed as gesture, it is as important to consider the recipient as the performer. My ability to recognize my pain and your
gesture of pain must occur at the same point in the logical order
of my understanding. My gestures and my linguistic acts have
that much in common.

But conformity to rules is not alone sufficient for a bodily
movement to be said to have a meaning analogous to linguistic
acts.

4. There is an obvious gap between the fact that gestures and
bodily stances conform to custom and my contention that our
bodily movements acquire a socially shared meaning. For example, we learn when and where to expectorate. There are even
legal injunctions restricting such activity on public conveyances.
But the fact that there are such rules and that people normally
conform to them does not turn the act of spitting into a gesture.
But this act, in suitable circumstances, *can* be a gesture. The act
of spitting is a way of showing defiance, denigrating or insulting
a person, or desecrating an object.

When an action functions as a gesture, in addition to there
being rules in force which both gesturer and recipient acknowledge, there is also an intent—in the case of spitting, the intent

to insult or defile. The act succeeds only if the intent is made clear and it is in virtue of the commonly acknowledged rules regulating spitting that this intent is displayed, in this case by breaking them.

I think that the factor of intent is also present in some cases of pain and anger behavior. When a person is in pain, it is generally his intent to show his pain in socially acceptable ways. The presence of an audience is sometimes essential. A child who has hurt himself cries very little or not at all if no one is present. In adults, involuntary cries of pain in soliloquy occur only in the extreme. When we are in pain we usually use the well-defined acts recognized by our culture for expressing ourselves. An adult male does not cry in pain, but he is likely to grimace. We expect others to respond to our pain or anger, and we sometimes take elaborate steps to control their responses and to prevent, sometimes, their recognizing our obvious intent.

This is the point at which we link our pain and anger behavior with certain moral practices; by acting the way we do we get other people to notice our needs or states of mind, to comfort or console us, or to assuage or relieve our pain and take warning from our anger.

Unless we acknowledge that there are rules involved in such behavior, and that we generally intend to communicate, it would be as difficult to explain the meaning of a bodily movement as it would be to explain why the American flag is lowered at nightfall on the basis of observed correlations between the flag's going down and the setting of the sun. Making use of a facial grimace or a frown in order to display pain is rather like diverting and modifying a small amount of smoke in order to signal the presence of a special kind of fire. Although there is an obvious correlation between smoke and fire, the significance of the signal could not be understood apart from conventions, in this case a code for understanding smoke signals.

III

If this account of behavior as gesture is correct, then we can understand why we sense that the relationship between propositions about behavior and propositions about mental states is stronger than induction; and why we sometimes see a bodily configuration as pain, anger, or some other state. This account would also force us to take a different philosophical attitude toward human bodily behavior and suggests a different model for the perception of persons.

1. If we give full significance to some bodily behavior, it would always make sense to ask about another person, "What is he doing?" or, "What does he mean?" unless there were obvious reasons for thinking that his behavior was a matter of reflex, e.g., the movement of a person's leg after a physician taps it.

It is a well-documented fact that the attitude or purposes one assumes tend to structure the visual field.[6] For example, if I am searching for a lost pencil of a certain length and color, the visual field suddenly restructures itself so that objects with just those qualities stand out. During such tasks we see no more than we need to in order to complete the task.

To see the human body as a physical object is not at all difficult, but to see it as possessing just physical qualities is a perverse practice in most social circumstances. An exception would be the case in which I become separated from my friend in a large crowd. In trying to find her, I would see people who possess only the attributes—perhaps hair color or height—that she possesses. A physiologist or logical behaviorist who looks at just the muscle contractions of my face, but not at my anger or my depression, is seeing in an analogous way. This kind of seeing naturally invites the question, "What is the cause?" rather than "What is the facial movement for?" And seeing a facial move-

6. H. L. Teuber, "Perception," in *Handbook of Physiology*, Chapter 65, III, American Physiological Society, 1960.

ment as a symptom of a mental state is just an instance of this kind of selective seeing.

I do not mean to suggest that the logical behaviorist actually sees this way. But his philosophic account of the perception of mental states does commit him to holding that this account of seeing is adequate for the perception of persons. I have tried to show why such an attitude toward perception is not appropriate to perceiving human bodily behavior. But if he persists in holding such an attitude, then it is perhaps only because he believes that eventually behavior, as he interprets it, will be the ultimate basis for any satisfactory account of human mental states. If he is correct, then his eventual account would effect a considerable simplification in the philosophy of mind.

I would like to show that the present account of behavior as gesture may also effect a considerable simplification of its own.

2. I propose that our perception of others is a matter of seeing a certain gesture as anger, or pain, and so on. And the problem of our knowledge of other minds is the problem of reducing the ambiguity of a particular structure with meaning.

If behavior is not merely symptomatic of a mental state but gestural in that it conforms to conventions and is used with the intention of conveying something, then we recognize the meaning of a gesture in much the same way as we recognize the meaning of a speech act.

There is a suggestive parallel between the structural ambiguity of a configuration of movements and the ambiguity of a sentence token. For example, if someone uttered the words, "John jumped higher than Mary," then, exclusive of context, those words could mean ambiguously either "John jumped higher than Mary jumped" or "John jumped higher than Mary is tall." The addition of "Then Mary stopped jumping in competition with John," or some extra-linguistic feature of the context, would reduce the ambiguity.

Ambiguity also infects other kinds of structures than sentences. Certain drawings created by psychologists are also ambiguous.

Leeper's composite drawing of two women, sometimes called the bride and the mother-in-law, is one example. We perceive alternately the face of two women, the young woman or the older one. The ambiguity of this composite structure can be reduced by placing alongside the drawing a single line, the main curve of which is the outline of one or the other of the two faces. Once the line is perceived, only that face will emerge that the line resembles; and great effort and the use of memory is required to make the other face emerge.[7]

In an analogous way the ambiguity of a gesture can also be reduced. Our attitude toward another is one in which we expect his actions to mean something to us, unless we have reason to think otherwise. By hypothesis we know the learned conventions we associate with certain mental states. When a particular bodily structure is ambiguous, the problem of the perception of others is the problem of reducing the ambiguity by adding more of the context. It is then sometimes impossible to see another person's gestures as anything but pain or anger or some other mental state.

7. The analogy between reducing the ambiguity of a gesture and reducing the ambiguity of a sentence occurred to me while reading J. A. Fodor and R. F. Freed, "Some Types of Ambiguous Tokens," *Analysis,* XXIV (1963). I owe to them and to N. Chomsky the idea that questions about ambiguity are questions about syntactic and semantic structure. See Noam Chomsky's "Perception and Language," *Boston Studies in the Philosophy of Science,* Dortrecht, Holland, 1963.

Fernando R. Molina

HUME AND THE PHENOMENOLOGY
OF BELIEF

For the purposes of ordinary, everyday communication there are, it seems to me, no pressing questions regarding the nature of beliefs. There are, of course, occasional problems that relate to the lack of clarity or downright ambiguity of our beliefs, just as there may be, for example, important questions concerning the implications of our beliefs. In the case of our beliefs about morality, the last sort of question assumes particular importance. But ordinarily and for the most part, the *fact of believing* itself seems reasonably clear as regards its general nature, no matter what specific theoretic or practical problems may, as already noted, be occasioned by it.

Threatening the apparent clarity which attaches itself in our uncritical moments to any concern that we might have with the nature of belief is a tension which in my judgment is generated by two mutually discordant facts about beliefs as these beliefs occur at so many points in our lives. The first of these two facts is that beliefs are taken to be *states* or *possessions* of individual human beings. For a belief to be shared is for a number of individuals to *have* that belief. We become impatient

and often angry at individuals because of the beliefs to which
they cling, beliefs which they will *not give up.* Frightful tortures
are devised to make individuals suffer for or part with *their*
beliefs.

Common sense and ordinary modes of discourse are not alone
in this relegation of belief to an essentially subjective status,
that is, to an existence which is not much more than a psychological state of a subject. William James, for example, in his
classical *Principles of Psychology,* writes that in its inner nature
belief ". . . is a sort of feeling more allied to the emotions than
to anything else." [1] Charles Sanders Peirce also referred to the
"feeling of believing" [2] and to the "state of belief" which is ". . .
a calm and satisfactory state which we do not wish to avoid.
. . ." [3] Even Gilbert Ryle finds it meaningful to speak of "believe"
as being in the family of motive words. To believe, according to
Ryle, is to have ". . . a propensity not only to make certain
theoretical moves but also to make certain executive and imaginative moves, *as well as to have certain feelings."* [4]

The second fact which I wish to note regarding the nature of
beliefs, a fact which I shall term the "reality moment" of beliefs,
is likewise attested to by both ordinary and philosophical thought
and modes of speech. Syntactically this feature of beliefs is represented by the use of the word "that" as it introduces the noun
clause.[5] Augustine's belief *that* there is a God, for example,

1. William James, *The Principles of Psychology,* New York, 1950, II,
283. Italics dropped.
2. C. S. Peirce, *The Philosophical Writings of Peirce,* ed. Buchler, New
York, 1955, p. 10.
3. *Ibid.,* p. 10.
4. Gilbert Ryle, *The Concept of Mind,* London, 1953, p. 135. Note that
Ryle at least does not identify the believing with the feeling. But it does
seem reasonable to distinguish a person's propensity to make certain
"moves" and to have certain feelings from *what he believes* such that he
"has" such a propensity. (Italics mine.)
5. The aspects of that propensity which for Ryle is believing are said
to "hang together on a common propositional hook" (*The Concept of Mind,*
p. 135). I submit that it is not, for example, the occurrence of the phrase
"thin ice" but rather the sense *that* the ice is thin that characterizes our
beliefs. As regards the *language* of belief, Ryle's point seems well taken.

would be nothing but an interesting biographical sidelight were it not for this feature of beliefs. What is essential, to continue with this example, is the *believed-in-fact* that there is a God with such-and-such a nature, not that Augustine is in a so-called "state" of belief. Military heroes do not die *because of* the psychological state in which they find themselves; they die because of the objective status of certain principles which they regard in a certain way, namely, in a believing way. Believing, I am urging in a preliminary way which I shall attempt to clarify further as the discussion develops, is in its nature far more like *perceiving* than like *feeling*, if by the latter we mean some kind of subjective psychological state. (I find it both interesting and relevant that we say of a person who has "shed" certain beliefs that he "saw through" them.)

There are, in ordinary usage, at least two examples which in my judgment reflect the fact that what I have called the reality moment is indeed a feature of beliefs. When asked to assent to something which we cannot believe could be a fact, we reply, "I don't believe it; *that* can't be!" rather than "I do not believe the proposition which you have just uttered to be true." Also, when similarly approached with regard to some fact which we find difficult to believe because of the fact's (not the belief's!) improbability, we reply, "How could *that* be?" Our immediate concern with the alleged fact *whose reality* we verbally deny or question belies any theory of belief that omits the reality moment in its account, in that this concern tends to show that the alleged state of our self referred to is in fact a *regard* of the fact as existent in belief, or non-existent in disbelief, or as unlikely in doubt.

On the side of the professional philosophers, it seems a reasonable speculation that some awareness of the reality moment of belief may have been the occasion for Peirce's statement that belief is ". . . certainly something more than a mere feeling . . ." [6] James, on the same topic, is more explicit, and, in his definition of belief already cited, he puts in apposition with the word "be-

6. Peirce, *op. cit.*, p. 177.

lief" the phrase "the sense of reality." [7] Here James the phenomenologist exhibits more trenchant insight than James the psychologist. In his latter capacity, his commitment is to study the *phenomena* of the mental life (as well as their conditions), examples of such phenomena being ". . . feelings, desires, cognitions, reasonings, decisions, and the like . . ." [8] But as phenomenologist—and admittedly this is a distinction which I superimpose on his thoughts, although, I maintain, justifiably so—it is clear that James studied phenomena *accessible to* the mind without prejudice as to whether such phenomena should themselves be properties, acts, or aspects *of* the mind. Thus, for example, James can write as he does in the *Psychology* that not ideas but *things* are associated in the mind. [9]

Philosophers acquainted with and sympathetic to Husserlian phenomenology will recognize in James's phrase "the sense of reality" an old friend, namely the concept of intentionality, the fact that awareness is *of* an object. I should mention that I have introduced this point at the conclusion of these preliminary observations instead of at the beginning because, although I am in my own reflections forced to the conclusion that the believing consciousness is *of* the "believed-in" object, I feel that this proposition should be a conclusion to an examination of the believing consciousness and the way we speak of it (to the extent that speech may express fact), rather than a deductive conclusion from the now axiomatic and seldom questioned concept of the intentionality of consciousness.

It is, by the way, an interesting fact that Hume, whose *Inquiry* provides the main text for this study, had to overcome a far greater limitation than James in providing us with a phenomenology of belief. Among other things, James had an acknowledged acquaintance with Brentano's reflections on belief; Hume had only a starkly conceived associationism from which to make his

7. James *Psychology*, II, 283.
8. James, *Psychology*, I, 1.
9. James, *Psychology*, I, 559.

systematic moves and *in spite of which* to achieve and express his insights into the essential features of belief. After first quoting from the *Inquiry* at some length, I shall single out and criticize Hume's systematic moves concerning the nature of belief, that is, those moves which at least in spirit follow from his associationism. Next I shall argue that Hume's unsystematic observations quite accurately represent the true nature of belief and, further, do so in a way that is simpler and more consistent with Hume's own metaphysics of experience than his systematic pronouncements on the nature of belief would seem to indicate. In a concluding section to this study I shall attempt a phenomenology of the believing consciousness, with help from William James.

Consider first the following excerpts from Hume's *Inquiry:*

. . . the difference between fiction and belief lies in some sentiment or feeling which is annexed to the latter, not to the former, and which depends not on the will, nor can be demanded at pleasure. It must be excited by nature like all other sentiments and must rise from the particular situation in which the mind is placed at any particular juncture. Whenever any object is presented to the memory or senses, it immediately, by the force of custom, carries the imagination to conceive that object which is usually conjoined to it; and this conception is attended with a feeling or sentiment different from the loose reveries of the fancy. . . . belief is nothing but a more vivid, lively, forcible, firm, steady conception of an object than what the imagination alone is ever able to attain.

(Note carefully what happens next and *how little relation it has to what has gone before.*)

This variety of terms, which may seem so unphilosophical, is intended only to express that act of the mind which renders realities, or what is taken for such, more present to us than fictions, causes them to weigh more in the thought, and gives them a superior influence on the passions and the imagination. . . . But as it is impossible that this faculty of imagination can ever, of itself, reach belief, it is evident that belief consists not in the

peculiar nature or order of ideas, but in the *manner* of their conception and in their *feeling* to the mind.[10]

Regarding this passage, it is first to be noted that the distinction between fiction—or mere imagination—and belief is said to
consist in the presence, in the case of belief, of "some sentiment
or feeling" which does not depend on the will and which is connected to the ideas which, as it were, constitute the "body" of
the belief. I would like to propose as scarcely needing argument
that there is no *essential* difference of feeling or sentiment between the deliverances of the imagination and of the believing
faculty. Hume, I suggest, is here simply saying that almost all of
us *have* feelings in conjunction with our beliefs, whereas only
artists and the like have feelings that amount to much more with
regard to the products of their imagination. Many of our beliefs
are, simply stated, cold-blooded; take, for example, my belief
that the copies of the *Saturday Review,* to which we subscribe,
will arrive once a week. Hume has apparently made the virtually
universal error of confusing the concerns and feelings that often
accompany our beliefs with the believing itself. The proposition
"I believe that X exists" is not synonymous with, nor does it entail, the proposition "My believing regard of X's existence is
necessarily accompanied or conditioned by the presence of concern or other sentiment." On logical grounds, if not on phenomenological ones, Hume can be excused, for his form of associationism provides him only different sorts of impressions and
their correlated ideas with which to work.

It follows, then, that our concern with Hume lies with those
thoughts presented by him which, while they may not be dis-
coverable by the application of his principles, are at least trib-
utes to his vision as a phenomenologist, no matter what "axiom"
he begins with. My main candidate for evidence that Hume's
vision outstrips his axioms occurs in the lengthy passage cited,

10. David Hume, *An Inquiry Concerning Human Understanding,* New
York, 1952, pp. 16-22.

specifically where Hume attributes to the "vivid, lively, forcible, firm, steady conception . . ." of which belief is said to be the expression ". . . that act of mind [an already illegitimate importation] which renders realities, or what is taken for such, more present to us than fictions. . . ."

Hume may very well have a penetrating insight here, but if his views are to be theoretically consistent, he has no right to it. Simplemindedly put, an idea is an idea, and an idea present to the mind is an idea present to the mind, and such an idea is no more or less present as far as Hume's theory of ideas is concerned. But that's not what he is saying at this point. He is asserting that this particular conception—that is, an idea plus feeling—expresses that "act of the mind" that renders *realities*— *not* ideas but *realities*—"more present to us" than fictions. Strictly speaking, Hume can only say in this context that belief renders *ideas* more present than fictions. But an idea is either present or it is not! What I am suggesting is that on Humean grounds Hume has not made his point. On a more broadly construed phenomenological basis, however, what Hume says is interesting.

Note, first of all, that Hume is speaking of "realities" or of "what is taken for such," rather than of ideas or of configurations of ideas. I propose that Hume is correct in speaking of realities, or at least in *not* speaking of ideas. The fact is that when I examine the act of believing I am not examining ideas at all but rather *what I take to be the case*. To be sure, the object of my examination involves the first person singular in that it is what *I* take to be the case. That *I take it* may be a necessary condition for believing, but it is not a sufficient condition. With Hume, I too want to say that realities or what are taken as such are "more present." They are not present as in perception; they are, if you wish, present in a "believed-in" way. The complete characterization of the believing awareness must include at least these two moments: the moment of judgment, in the sense of receipt or

acceptance, and the moment of presence or of existence or reality—choose whichever word best captures the spirit of Hume's
phrase, "realities or what is taken for such."

Actually, I am not completely sure that the "I take it . . ." is
the best possible way to represent the subjective, the *noetic,*
moment of the believing awareness. My point is that in believing
I don't seem to be doing anything, certainly not judging in the
neo-Kantian sense in which to judge is to constitute, to set up
that reality which "then" appears to me. On the contrary, what
impresses me is the passivity of belief noted by Hume when he
stated that belief, unlike fiction, does not depend on the will.
My phrasing "what impresses me" here is not entirely unhappy
because it does represent the fact that I *find myself* passively
believing; that is, I accept as fact or reality, Kierkegaard not-
withstanding, that belief is essentially a passive state vis-à-vis
the believer, my implicit taking to be the case what in fact
seems to be the case (hence my earlier choice to compare believing positively to perceiving and not to feeling).

Actually, I am asserting at least two things: first, the distinction without separation of the believing subject and the believed-
in, and second, the epistemological independence of the believing awareness; that is, the act of becoming clear as to what the
believing awareness is in no way presupposes that it be "in
truth." There need be no real inconsistency here, of course, for,
since this is a phenomenological analysis which proceeds without
reference to the real world but with reference only to my experience of what I take to be the real world, it is possible to refer
to what I take to be the object or event believed-in without
existential commitment. As to the distinction without separation
of the believing consciousness and the believed-in, that is a
straightforward distinction from phenomenology—namely the
distinction between *noesis* and *noema,* the manner of entertain-
ment and the object entertained.

Let me restate my main theses briefly before concluding with further remarks on how Hume has a better solution available to this problem than what he himself proposed.

(1) Negatively put, believing is in its essence not a matter of ideas *as ideas* or of feelings *as feelings*.

(2) Believing is, however, a matter of accepting or acknowledging what is *taken to be* the case or of what *appears to be* the case.

(3) Since we are doing phenomenology, it does not matter whether the world *is* as "characterized" by the belief. (Of course, this is not the case on the part of the believer *qua* believer.)

(4) The object of belief is given to awareness in a "believed-in" way—but is not, for that reason, taken to be less real. It follows that believing is *phenomenologically* a relation *to the world* or, if you wish, the world-phenomenon, not to one's ideas.

Now consider how Hume could have dealt with this problem in a better way. The furniture of the universe, what we hear, see, or desire, for example, consists of impressions. Impressions are generally, if not without occasional error, distinguished from ideas in that the latter have less force and vivacity: ideas are faint and dull copies of impressions. In the *Treatise,* simple ideas are said to differ in degree and not in nature from the simple impressions from which they are derived. The crucial point here is that the proposition that our perceptions are of real things is a proposition, the justification of which would at least in part lie in an introspective consideration of the force and liveliness of our perceptions, these (perceptions) being presumably "states" of mind.

Now if an idea, because of its connection by association with some present impression (which usually is followed by that impression of which the idea in question is a copy), is thereby entertained by the mind "in a believing way," we can then say that this idea is conceived in a vivid, lively, forcible, firm, and steady way. But liveliness and forcibleness are distinguishing characteristics of impressions, and impressions are what constitute what

we take to be the real world. Thus an idea believingly entertained by the mind is being entertained or is appearing in that
way that makes it *approach*—to borrow from the mathematicians
—an impression. That is, the believingly entertained idea meets
those conditions that qualify it to be taken to be part of the
furniture of the universe.[11]

In the example of causality and of the other side of objects,
the unseen side, this Humean-based scheme seems to work
particularly well. This "filling-in" activity by which the mind
falsifies any "pure" sense data theory of perception may very
well be what in Kant would be the action of the productive
imagination. To be specific, at least as regards Hume, it is this
activity which accounts for the fact that the phenomenological
problem about causality is a problem about our idea or, better
yet, our *sense* of the necessary connection of the effect with its
cause rather than with the universal expectation of the effect as
a merely temporally sequential spatio-temporally contiguous
companion to an event termed its cause. The effect of a cause,
in brief, is not a feeling of expectation in my mind; it is a real
event that hasn't yet occurred—*but wait!*

Hume was very much aware of this "externalizing" function
("projection" in the language of Whitehead) that mediates between the past experiences that condition the occurrence of belief
and the nature of the believing consciousness itself. In Book I of
A Treatise of Human Nature he refers to the

> . . . common observation . . . that the mind has a great pro-
> pensity to spread itself on external objects, and to conjoin with
> them any internal impressions, which they occasion, and which
> always make their appearance at the same time that these objects
> discover themselves to the senses.[12]

Hume's point here is consistent both with the interpretation of
his ideas which I am urging and with the proposed phenomen-

11. Strictly speaking, from attending to the phenomenology of believing
we *come to* understand the meaning of Hume's criteria of liveliness and
forcibleness!

12. David Hume, *A Treatise of Human Nature*, Oxford, 1955, p. 167.

ology of belief; namely that the believed-in object or event is regarded as *out there* in the world and that this is so no matter what views one holds regarding the subjective base or origin of the fact of believing!

If it be said of this scheme that it too quickly and too often leads to the introduction of *belief* where ordinarily *knowledge* would serve, I can only reply that belief is a phenomenon of far greater significance than is usually granted. I suspect this failure to see how widespread the phenomenon of belief is rests on the social fact dictated by intellectual modesty, namely that the notion of belief be used in cases where we are not able to present evidence in principle, no matter *how right we know we are!*

This mention of evidence suggests another problem to which this phenomenology of belief must offer a solution if it is to be an adequate treatment of the question. This problem centers on what James termed "the reality of the unseen." In one sense, of course, this is the paradigmatic example to which an adequate concept of belief must relate; yet at the same time it is the type to which the Humean schema seems least applicable. I say this because Hume's empiricism strictly construed would clearly entail the meaninglessness of an idea correlated with what to him would surely be a non-existent impression.

I propose to solve this problem by expanding the Humean schema with a suggestion, and then to illustrate the solution with an observation, both suggestion and observation coming from the thought of James. If this attempt at solution is in any way successful, it should serve to specify further the phenomenology of belief being proposed here. You may recall James's already cited equation of *belief* with the *sense of reality;* this latter phrase clearly expresses the already discussed distinction without separation of the believing consciousness and the believed-in object. With James, who here follows Kant, I agree that the reality that is the object of belief is not identifiable with the "intellectually or sensibly" intuitable properties that an object may *have.*[13] Unlike James, however, I submit that this reality (*reality-phenomenon*, in the language of phenomenology) which is definitive of belief does not inwardly leave the object as it finds it (cf. James, *Psychology*, II, 296), but rather it does precisely the opposite; reality as sensed by the believing awareness is an *objective reality*, and the fact that it is sensed is to the believing consciousness an accidental fact which is in no way essential to the reality of the object believed-in. Finally, if objective reality so defined is actually a phenomenon which can be present to or sensed by a mind, then, granting its distinguishability from the "ideas" or qualities which, using James's term, it enriches, there is in principle no difficulty in expanding the Humean schema to include objective reality as a new type of idea which is entertained in a believed-in way and which "approaches" an impression and hence appears to populate the universe. It is surely a phenomenon of this sort which James described in *The Varieties of Religious Experience:*

> It is as if there were in the human consciousness a *sense of reality,* a *feeling of objective presence,* a *perception* of what we may call *"something there,"* more deep and more general than any of the special and particular "senses" by which the current psychology supposes existent realities to be originally revealed.[14]

The absolutely important point at this stage is to avoid the difficulty encountered in slightly different ways by both Hume and James, for each occasionally confused the *sense of* reality with a *sentiment about* reality. The latter is a psychological state in the full-blown sense; the former is not. The phrase "sense of reality" connotes an intentional (in Husserl's meaning) polarity in which *the reality sensed,* as it were, preempts the psychologistically presumed dominance of the sensing. By that I mean, as already suggested, that an accurate phenomenological descrip-

13. James, *Psychology*, II, 296.
14. William James, *The Varieties of Religious Experience*, New York, 1958, p. 61.

tion of the believing consciousness would include reference essentially to *the reality that is felt* rather than to *the feeling of reality*. Neither Hume nor James was able to consistently transcend his psychologistic bias in order to report this phenomenon accurately, although it does seem that each philosopher was aware of it.

Frederick J. Crosson

THE CONCEPT OF MIND AND
THE CONCEPT OF CONSCIOUSNESS

This essay is not meant to be another skirmish in the cold war across the English Channel, despite the provoking discourtesies that have been exchanged. It is rather an attempt to state, with as much precision as I can, a fundamental difference between language analysis and phenomenology, or at least between some analysts and phenomenologists.

While I am aware of differences between philosophers in the analytic movement, and will focus primarily on Gilbert Ryle, I shall refer to other analytic philosophers to instantiate premises or attitudes which I believe are common.

To set up the difference which seems to me fundamental, let me quote first of all from G. E. M. Anscombe. In an essay on memory, she notes that one who learns to use "was red" after a red light has gone out has learned a "new use of 'red' whose outstanding feature is that 'red' can be said when there is no red." [1] Now what explains, what grounds, what justifies this new and appropriate use of "red"? She rejects the appeal to memory as

1. G. E. M. Anscombe, "The Reality of the Past," in M. Black, ed., *Philosophical Analysis*, Ithaca, 1950, p. 40.

an explanation and ends up by claiming that the search for a justification is a mistake.

. . . only the account of meaning given by Wittgenstein enables one without begging the question to introduce mention of actual past events into one's account of knowing the past that one *has* witnessed. This is made possible precisely by that feature of his method which is most difficult to accept: namely that he attacks the effort at justification, the desire to say: "But one says 'was red' because one knows that the light *was* red." One says "was red" in these circumstances (not: *recognizing* these circumstances) and that *is* what in this case is called knowing the past fact.[2]

For Husserl, on the other hand, of whom Fink says, "Seeing is—for him—the original evidence," [3] remembering is a phenomenon of consciousness, not of language.

Recollection (*Wiedererinnerung*) can make its appearance in different forms of accomplishment. We accomplish it either by simply laying hold of what is recollected, as when, for example, a recollection "emerges" and we look at what is remembered with a glancing ray (*Blickstrah*) wherein what is remembered is indeterminate, perhaps a favored momentary phase intuitively brought, but not a recapitulative memory. Or we accomplish it in a real, re-productive recapitulative memory in which the temporal object is again completely built up in a continuum of presentification, so that we seem to perceive it again, but only seemingly, as if.[4]

So it would appear that we have two different approaches here to the exploration of the concept of remembering: one directs its attention to the use of "remember" and of past tense verbs, the other reflects on the *experiences* of remembering. The approaches

2. *Ibid.*, p. 59.
3. E. Fink, "Das Problem der Phänomenologie E. Husserls," in *Revue Internationale de Philosophie* II (1939), 253. Cf. Husserl's "Principle of Principles," *Ideen* I ss. 24.
4. *The Phenomenology of Internal Time-Consciousness*, trans. J. Churchill, Bloomington, 1964, ss. 15, p. 59. I pass over the difference between retention and recollection and also the problem of the constitution of memories.

might, of course, be complementary were it not for the fact that
the very possibility of the second approach is rejected by analysts.
It is the ground of the rejection that I wish to explore.

I

As a young Oxford don, Gilbert Ryle passed through a period
when phenomenology exercised a good deal of influence on him.
He studied in Germany, and a perusal of journals in the twenties
will uncover his reviews of Ingarden, Heidegger, and others.
This information should come as no surprise to anyone acquainted
with phenomenology who has read *The Concept of Mind*. No
intention of detracting from the originality, acuteness, and importance of this work is behind the suggestion that ideas like
"bearing in mind," sensory "expectation-propensities," or "perception recipes" have Husserlian roots.[5]

But in spite of the remarkable range of agreement between
phenomenology and conceptual analysis, there is one point which
seems to divide them sharply: the question of consciousness. In
The Concept of Mind, Ryle affirms that consciousness, as there
described, "is a myth." Exactly what he is rejecting and why
he is rejecting it must be seen in some detail.

The general aim of his argument is to show that "the mind is
not the topic of sets of untestable categorical propositions, but
the topic of sets of testable hypothetical and semi-hypothetical
propositions." [6] Statements—whether first-person or third-person
—about the way one acts, thinks, feels, and so on are statements
about one's overt acts and utterances, not about ghostly occurrences in a private theater of the psyche. He combats then what

5. It is suggestive, I think, that when Ryle wants to analyze what is
involved in perception, he has to leave ordinary language and introduce a
"technical" or at least non-ordinary language to do so. The question suggested by this departure is the following: granted that an impressive set of
philosophical questions can be dealt with by ordinary language, is the
concern of philosophical reflection coextensive with that set?
6. G. Ryle, *The Concept of Mind*, New York, 1949, p. 46. Hereafter: CM.

Sartre has called "the illusion of immanence," and he has recognized his agreement with Sartre with respect to this negative goal.

But he has to admit that there are apparent exceptions to this general evacuation of the private world—for example, pains. "Only the wearer knows where the shoe pinches." Ryle responds to this observation by contending that this is no argument for an inner perception: it is true that the cobbler does not witness my tweaks, but it is also true that I do not witness them. "I feel or have the tweaks, but I do not discover or peer at them." Moreover, to say, "I had a twinge" "does not assert a relation, as 'I had a hat' does . . . the phrase 'my twinge' does not stand for any sort of a *thing* or term." [7] We do not observe twinges as we observe robins.

What is important here is less his positive account, which is sketchy indeed (I shall return to this), than what he is rejecting. It is clear that he is being guided, as Wittgenstein would say, by a picture: a picture of consciousness as the observer of data, the subject facing its objects and knowing these inner objects by perceiving them. This is of course the classical picture of modern post-Cartesian philosophy: as Hume says, "To hate, to love, to think, to feel, to see; all this is nothing but to perceive." [8]

That this is in fact Ryle's picture of consciousness becomes clear when he takes up the concept of consciousness explicitly. It is, he says, supposed that

in being conscious of my present mental states and acts I know what I am experiencing and doing in a non-dispositional sense of "know" . . . I am actively cognizant of it. Though a double act of attention does not occur, yet when I discover that my watch has stopped, I am synchronously discovering that I am discovering that my watch has stopped.[9]

The key word here is "discovering": it translates once again

7. CM, pp. 205, 209.
8. D. Hume, *A Treatise of Human Nature*, Oxford, 1888, p. 67. Cf. Descartes, *Response to Third Set of Objections* (re the Second Meditation).
9. CM, p. 160.

Ryle's assumption that consciousness is the passive registrant of events, whether "inner" or "outer."

Against this view he brings a battery of arguments: (1) no one has recourse to such a ground to vindicate statements about himself: no one says, "I know I am afraid *because* I am conscious of fear [I observe my fear]"; (2) episodes or events are the wrong sort of accusatives to follow the verb "to know" [this of course depends for its force on the assimilation of "being conscious to 'knowing'"]; (3) people make mistakes about their frame of mind; (4) consciousness of consciousness leads to an infinite regress.[10]

With this philosophical use of the term consciousness thus disposed of, introspection can be and is given short shrift. Its unreliability, the disagreements among psychologists who claimed to be using introspective method, the impossibility of detachedly observing passionate agitations, and the infinite regress dilemma serve to dispatch it. Ryle admits the existence of "retrospection" but denies that it yields any privileged access to ghostly episodes.

In sum, Ryle accepts as the essential component of any theory of consciousness the subject-object structure of classical British empiricism. Since he finds insuperable objections to this manner of conceiving of one's awareness of oneself, he rejects the philosophical idea of consciousness *in toto* and takes on the task of showing that the supposed deliverance of one's self-knowledge can be accounted for on other grounds.

No doubt the "revolution" in British philosophy and the development of his own view are not unrelated. In his writings in the twenties and early thirties on phenomenology, he invariably focuses on the *Gegenstandstheorie* of Meinong, which he identifies with Husserl's theory of essences and categorical intuition. Mixing oil and water, he describes Husserl as holding that we can have "a knowledge by acquaintance" of these "objects of a higher order." Phenomenology is then

10. *Ibid.*, pp. 161-162.

a sort of observational science (like geography); only the objects which it inspects are . . . semi-Platonic objects.[11]

(It is needless to remark here that although Husserl's language might give rise to these misconceptions, he explicitly denies them.[12]

Now this view had been undercut by Russell's theory of definite descriptions, which, as John Wisdom remarked, opened up a whole new era in metaphysics. For it showed how philosophical problems might be dissolved by a proper analysis of the language in which they were formulated. So, Ryle argues, the meaning of a word like "for" is not something which we know by intuition— "which I take to be a synonym for knowledge by acquaintance or perception" [13]—rather the meaning of not only syncategoremmatic but also categoremmatic terms is the use or set of uses to which they can be put.

(Husserl does of course claim that "essential intuition is . . . analogous to sensory perception," [14] but this is in virtue of its being an *originär gebender Akte*, an unmediated presence, and not in virtue of its being observed or peeped at that the analogy holds. But our aim here is not to tax Ryle (and others) with having misread Husserl, it is rather to compare their own proper views.)

Ryle's conclusion then is that the subject-inspecting-object conception of consciousness cannot account for, and is not required for, the understanding of language in general and psychological or mental statements in particular. There are, we might say, no objects, whether meanings, essences, or ghostly events, for the subject to inspect—and if a subject doesn't inspect objects, what is there left for him to do?

11. G. Ryle, "Phenomenology," Part I, in *Aristotelian Society Supplement*, XI (1932), pp. 72, 73.
12. E. Husserl, *Logische Untersuchungen* II, 1, First Investigation, ss. 34.
13. "Phenomenology," p. 73. Cf. Ryle's "Theory of Meaning," in M. Black, ed., *The Importance of Language*, Englewood Cliffs, 1963.
14. *Ideas*, trans. Gibson, London, 1958, ss. 23, p. 92.

II

In contrasting the phenomenological description of consciousness to Ryle's picture of it, the first point to be made concerns unreflective awareness.

> Every Ego [writes Husserl] lives in its own experiences, and in these is included much that is real (*reell*) and intentional. The phrase "It lives them" does not mean that it holds them and whatever is in them "in its glance," that it apprehends them after the manner of immanent experience (*Erfahrung*), or any other immanent intuition or presentation.[15]

Unlike Ryle's account of consciousness, according to which "a mind cannot help being constantly aware" of its states and operations—and this means "actively cognizant" of them [16]—Husserl begins with a level of implicit awareness in which the ego lives its experiences (*Erlebnisse*) which are directly had or felt, but not articulated, discriminated, reflected on. As Sartre succinctly phrases it, "toute conscience n'est pas connaissance." There is a consciousness which "is not *positional*, which is to say that consciousness is not for itself its own object." [17] Its object is, for example, some pleasant landscape, and my pleasure in it is not the object of my awareness, as if the awareness were different from the pleasure. Pleasure is not an event or process apprehended by consciousness (cf. Ryle's "mind aware of its states"), as if I could say, "Hullo, I'm getting some pleasure out of this." Rather, my pleasure *is* my consciousness of the pleasant landscape.

But all this explication of my lived experience is of course reflective and discriminated. And it is here that the critical issue arises. For I can say that I am pleased only by transforming the

15. *Ibid.*, ss. 77, p. 215.
16. CM, pp. 154, 160.
17. J-P. Sartre, *Transcendence of the Ego*, trans. F. Williams and R. Kirkpatrick, New York, 1957, p. 41.

implicit level of awareness to the explicit level of articulation, and this transformation is not as automatic as Hume's "perception" seemed to be.

Let me note in passing that Ryle's account of consciousness and reflection (or introspection, for he equates these) curiously does not note the most obvious criticism of the latter, namely its utter redundancy. For if consciousness is already actively cognizant of itself, then surely the postulation of a second act of attention which "deliberately scrutinizes" its states and operations is a work of pure supererogation.

Here again Ryle's rejection of reflection is due to his identification of it with introspection à la Locke.[18] That is, it is again his "picture" of consciousness as subject-regarding-object which guides him. Reflection is for him the observation of (psychic or mental) *facts*, entities, and not, as it is for Husserl, the explicitation of a lived *act*. Moreover, it is characterized as inspection in terms of the passivity of the observer (the reflecting consciousness) vis-à-vis what is already *there*, and not, as it is for Husserl, as a transforming act. Husserl does indeed describe reflection as an immanent perception, but he has already sharply distinguished between "immanent perception" and "interior perception," the latter of which is modeled on the natural attitude conception of psychic facts.[19]

Husserl says:

. . . *every variety of "reflexion" has the character of a modification of consciousness*, and indeed of such a modification as every consciousness can, in principle, experience.

We speak of modifications here just in so far as every reflection has its essential origin in changes of standpoint, whereby a given

18. CM, p. 159. Incidentally, he explicitly attributes this view to Husserl: "By immanent perception he [Husserl] refers to the direct recognition or inspection that I can have of my own mental states and acts, when these are concurrent with the inspection of them. I take it that he is referring to what we call introspection." "Phenomenology," *loc. cit.*, p. 81.

19. *Ideas*, ss. 78, p, 219, ss. 38, p. 124. Cf. E. Husserl, *The Idea of Phenomenology*, trans. W. Alston and G. Nakhnikian, The Hague, 1964, Lecture II, and P. Ricoeur, *Philosophie de la Volonté*, Paris, 1949, p. 12.

experience or unreflective experience-datum (*Erlebnisdatum*) undergoes a certain transformation (*Umwandlung*)—into the mode, that is, of reflective consciousness (consciousness of which we are aware).[20]

The transformation here spoken of is, if I understand him, what Eugene Gendlin means by explication, and implies neither a distortion of the original experience nor, clearly, a mere redoubling of it. It is thanks to the retentional structure of the temporality of consciousness that:

> The experience as really lived at the moment, as it first enters the focus of reflexion, presents itself *as* really lived, as being "now"; but not only that, it presents itself as just *having been*, and so far as it was unnoticed as precisely such, as not having been reflected on.[21]

The paramount point to seize here, of course, is that Husserl is speaking of the reflection on *acts*, not the *Dasein* of some psychic entities, and an act can be grasped only in its realization. It is given *in* reflection, not *to* reflection, and the reflection accompanies it; it does not hypostasize it. Ryle is right to disown the bastard notion of psychic facts; the question is whether he does not throw the bath out with the baby. I am not aware of remembering because I recognize my "images" to be such by their familiarity, faintness, and so forth.

Ricoeur concisely summarizes Husserl's thesis concerning reflection:

> In discovering unreflective consciousness as it was before reflection, reflection discovers itself as a modification on the unreflected *erlebnis:* thus reflection comes to situate itself in relation to the unreflected which it reveals just as it was.[22]

Reflection, that is, does not objectify in the empiricist's sense but rather exists as a modification of the unreflected *erlebnis.*

20. *Ideas*, ss. 78, p. 219.
21. *Ibid.*, ss. 77, p. 216. Ryle seems to waver on this retentional character (CM, p. 160), but the notion is clearly present in his book.
22. *Idées*, trans. Ricoeur, Paris, 1920, p. 250, n.1.

III

My concern here has been a methodological rather than a substantive one, addressing itself more to the question of how we can analyze the concept of mind than to what we find there. It would be foolish to deny that conceptual analysis is also guided by the lived experience of the analyst. But map-making is as important as exploring the terrain if we want to understand what we are doing, and directions on how to get there may be a long way from a chart of the region.

My claim then is that, lacking a conception of consciousness which avoids the subject-inspecting-object picture, the analyst's explanation of how the analysis of the concept of mind is possible is hauled up short at the simple affirmation of "a fact of natural history."

Let me document this. One instance is the explanation by Anscombe, quoted earlier, of how we come to use the past tense. Another is Sydney Shoemaker, who after a superb critique of empiricist attempts to account for self-knowledge concludes: if we still are inclined to ask how first-person psychological statements (about memory and self-identity) are possible, "the only answer is that it is just a fact of human nature that human beings can be so trained that they are able to make such statements." [23]

Finally, Wittgenstein accounts for the use of the word "pain" by denying that it *refers* to any sensation and suggesting that it *replaces* the "primitive, the natural expressions of the sensation and [is] used in their place." [24] Its use is, one might say, simply a fact of our natural history. I mention this particular example because Ryle, some ten years after the *Concept of Mind,* has

23. S. Shoemaker, *Self-Knowledge and Self-Identity,* Ithaca, 1963, p. 243. This kind of explanation is clearly on the level of what Husserl called the "natural attitude."

24. L. Wittgenstein, *Philosophical Investigations,* Oxford, 1958, p. 89.

doubts about following Wittgenstein on this score. In a paper prepared for the Royaumont Colloquium, he notes that while swearing is not a report of anger, nor yawns of fatigue, the attempt which he had made to assimilate avowals of pain to this category "will not do." For an avowal of pain can be a response to a question, from a doctor for example. It can give him information, it can be a report. But here, for the second time so to speak, he pulls up short. What could it be a report *of*, if there is no interior man?

He ends up remarking of such first-person declarations, "Their conceptual place is not yet fixed." [25] Given my understanding of his concept of mind, I cannot but sympathize with his puzzlement.

---

25. G. Ryle, "La Phénomènologie contre *The Concept of Mind*," mimeograph, last page.

John R. Silber

BEING AND DOING:
A STUDY OF STATUS RESPONSIBILITY
AND VOLUNTARY RESPONSIBILITY

The doctrine of Original Sin, according to which man exists in
a fallen state, in a diseased condition, having begun his earthly
career under a burden of guilt derived from Adam, is repugnant
to most contemporary minds. Its repugnance derives not from
its mythological elements which might be cut away by a Bult-
mannian re-section, but from its foundation in and dependence
on a notion of *status* [1] *responsibility*: it finds man morally wrong
and morally blameworthy for his diseased *condition* or *state of
being* rather than for any specific *conduct* of a morally blameworthy character. The doctrine of Original Sin is radically at
odds, therefore, with the legal definition of criminal conduct and
the contemporary philosophical view of moral obligation, both
of which are based on a notion of *voluntary responsibility*. According to the latter notion, man is morally wrong and blameworthy, not for what he *is* but for what he *does*. The concep-

---

1. "Status" here means the (legal) condition or state of being of a person,
not of course his social status or prestige.

tions of status and voluntary responsibility are both ancient, both enshrined in mythological lore. Yet it is a curious and important historical fact that the conception of voluntary responsibility has become dominant in both ethics and in criminal law, while the conception of status responsibility has scarcely survived. The latter conception is generally rejected by ethicists as being itself an immoral notion; and while it is not totally rejected by criminal courts, lawyers, and legal theorists, it is accepted into criminal law only under severe limitations, with grave doubts, over vigorous opposition, and for extra-moral considerations.

I

A brief review and illustration of the legal position, though hazardous for a philosopher, may prove useful. In common law countries it is taken for granted that no man should be treated as a criminal or convicted of a crime unless he has done something wrong and knew what he was doing. Generally speaking, the behavior of a man is to be treated as criminal conduct only if there is a concurrence of *mens rea,* the awareness of the wrongfulness or unlawfulness of the conduct, and *actus reus,* the physical manifestation of *mens rea.*[2] An act or occurrence cannot be criminal unless the basic functions of intelligence and volition are present. The consensus of legal thinking on this point is well summarized by Professor Herbert Packer:

> To punish conduct without reference to the actor's state of mind is both inefficacious and unjust. It is inefficacious because conduct unaccompanied by an awareness of the factors making it criminal does not mark the actor as one who needs to be subjected to punishment in order to deter him or others from behaving similarly in the future, nor does it single him out as a socially dangerous individual who needs to be incapacitated or reformed.

2. Jerome Hall, *General Principles of Criminal Law,* 2nd ed., 1960, pp. 253, 177, 70, 230.

It is unjust because the actor is subjected to the stigma of criminal conviction without being morally blameworthy.[3]

Criminal sanctions are generally applied only in those situations in which moral blame would be appropriate. If criminal punishment is understood, in the words of Professor H. M. Hart, as "a formal and solemn pronouncement of the moral condemnation of the community,"[4] then we can more easily understand and accept the moral indignation and high-pitched rhetoric of the district attorney as an expression of the lawyer's professional sense of the dependence of criminal law on morality. And unless morality provides for status offenses and status responsibility, we should find in criminal law a tendency to deny legal force to status crimes or status responsibility.

Morality, as interpreted by most contemporary philosophers, makes no such provisions. H. L. A. Hart, in complete agreement with Kant, lists among the distinctive features of morality the *"voluntary character of moral offenses."*[5] In developing this point, Hart writes:

> If a person whose action, judged *ab extra*, has offended against moral rules or principles, succeeds in establishing that he did this unintentionally and in spite of every precaution that it was possible for him to take, he is excused from moral responsibility, and to blame him in these circumstances would itself be considered morally objectionable. Moral blame is therefore excluded because he has done all that he can do. . . . [I]n morals "I could not help it" is always an excuse, and moral obligation would be altogether different from what it is if the moral "ought" did not in this sense imply "can."[6]

In due course I shall examine Hart's statement in detail. For

3. Herbert L. Packer, "*Mens Rea* and the Supreme Court," *The Supreme Court Review,* 1962, p. 109. Cf. American Law Institute, Model Penal Code, Tentative Draft No. 4, Comments, §2.05 (1956).

4. H. M. Hart, "The Aims of Criminal Law," *Law and Contemporary Problems,* XXIII (1958), 401.

5. H. L. A. Hart, *The Concept of Law,* p. 173.

6. *Ibid.,* pp. 173-174.

the moment I enter it in the record as a clear statement of the generally accepted view of the essentially voluntary character of moral responsibility—a character which makes lawyers properly reluctant to apply criminal sanctions in a situation unless there is (a) action and (b) the action is voluntary and intentional. Lawyers would be prone, moreover, to excuse any action that is unintentional, undertaken with due care and precaution, or unavoidable.

This is illustrated by the decision of the Supreme Court in *Robinson vs. California.*[7] Robinson was convicted under a California statute which made narcotics addiction a criminal offense. Under the terms of the statute,[8] "No person shall use, or be under the influence of, or be addicted to the use of narcotics, excepting when administered by or under the direction of a person licensed by the State to prescribe and administer narcotics. It shall be the burden of the defense to show that it comes within the exception." During Robinson's trial, the judge instructed the jury that this statute made it an offense for a person "either to use, or to be addicted to the use of narcotics." The judge said further: "That portion of the statute referring to the 'use' of narcotics is based upon the 'act' of using. That portion of the statute referring to 'addicted to the use' of narcotics is based on a condition or status. They are not identical. . . ." In explaining the State's burden of proof, the trial judge said, "All that the people must show is *either* that the defendant did use a narcotic in Los Angeles County *or* that while in the City of Los Angeles he was addicted to the use of narcotics." [9]

The trial judge instructed the jury that Robinson could be convicted under the statute if they found simply that his status (or chronic condition) was that of being addicted to the use of narcotics. It was therefore unclear to the Supreme Court whether the jury, in finding Robinson guilty, found him guilty of the *act*

7. 82 S. Ct. 1417 (1962), or 370 U.S. 660 (1962).
8. Section 11721 of the California Health and Safety Code.
9. My italics.

or merely the *status* condemned by the statute. In delivering the opinion of the court, Justice Stewart complained that the statute is not one "which punishes a person for the use of narcotics, for their purchase, sale or possession, or for antisocial or disorderly behavior resulting from their administration." Rather, he said, "We deal with a statute which makes the 'status' of narcotic addiction a criminal offense. . . . California has said that a person can be continuously guilty of this offense whether or not he has ever used or possessed any narcotics within the State, and whether or not he has been guilty of any antisocial behavior there."

In order to categorize this statute properly, Justice Stewart considered whether it would be possible to "make it a criminal offense for a person to be mentally ill, or a leper, or to be afflicted with a venereal disease. In light of contemporary human knowledge," he concluded, "a law which made a criminal offense of such a disease would doubtless be universally thought to be an infliction of cruel and unusual punishment." He concluded that the statute under which Robinson was convicted fell into this same category because drug addiction is an illness, and that a law which "imprisons a person thus afflicted as a criminal, even though he has never touched any narcotic drug within the State or been guilty of any irregular behavior there, inflicts a cruel and unusual punishment." The length of imprisonment was held to be irrelevant. Justice Stewart declared: "Even one day in prison would be a cruel and unusual punishment for the 'crime' of having a common cold."

Justice Douglas, concurring, compared narcotics addiction to insanity. He noted that while insane people "may be confined either for treatment or for the protection of society, they are not branded as criminals." And he concluded:

> I do not see how under our system *being an addict* can be punished as a crime. If addicts can be punished for their addiction, then the insane can also be punished for their insanity. Each has a disease and each must be treated as a sick person.

. . . He [the addict] may, of course, be confined for treatment for the protection of society. Cruel and unusual punishment results not from the confinement, but from convicting an addict of a crime. . . . A prosecution for addiction, with its resulting stigma and irreparable damage to the good name of the accused, cannot be justified as a means of protecting Society, where a civil commitment would do as well.

Both Stewart and Douglas agree (a) that drug addiction is a disease, (b) that the California statute under which Robinson was convicted made it an offense simply to be a narcotics addict, whether or not one performed any antisocial actions or even used the drugs himself within the jurisdiction of the statute, and (c) that it is wrong to make being sick a crime. The first two points involve questions of fact and interpretation of statute, but (c) expresses Stewart's and Douglas' reluctance to recognize crimes of status or to hold a person criminally liable for his condition, for *what he is* in the absence of any record of *what he does or has done.*[10]

The opinion of the Supreme Court in *Robinson vs. California* thus illustrates the abhorrence lawyers generally feel for status responsibility in criminal law and their refusal to use this concept in defining crime. The opinion illustrates their confidence in and approval of the dominant concept of moral obligation which allows only for voluntary responsibility, according to which only action or conduct (*actus reus*) that is voluntary and intentional (involving *mens rea*) can be morally blameworthy. Conditions of moral blameworthiness as defined by the voluntary conception of responsibility are accepted in *Robinson vs. California* as

10. Justice Harlan, concurring, did not agree that narcotics addiction is an illness nor, consequently, that to subject narcotics addicts to criminal sanctions would amount to cruel and unusual punishment. But, like Stewart and Douglas, he denied the right of the state to convict a person for his addiction to narcotics rather than for their use. Since, according to Justice Harlan, addiction is not more than "a compelling propensity to use narcotics," he reasoned that the California court had in effect authorized "criminal punishment for a bare desire to commit a criminal act." And he refused to permit the substitution of a wish following from status for an action, an *actus reus,* in the definition of a crime.

limiting conditions for the application of criminal sanctions. The
moral inappropriateness, indeed, the immorality of status responsibility, of blaming one for what he *is* rather than for what
he *does*, is seen to be the driving force behind the court's
decision.[11]

It might seem, however, that a serious and extensive reliance
on the concept of status responsibility in criminal law is found in
those cases in which a person may be convicted of a crime and
suffer criminal sanctions on the basis of strict liability. Many laws
concerned with public welfare—e.g., laws pertaining to food
adulteration or mislabeling of drugs, and so forth—permit criminal conviction in cases where there is complete absence of *mens
rea* and even absence of *actus reus* by the accused.[12] But even

11. But the reluctance of our courts to use the concept of status responsibility in criminal cases has not been universal. Many states using the
common law have applied criminal sanctions to the offense of vagrancy.
Prior to *Robinson vs. California* a vagrant could be anyone, from a healthy
beggar,[a] to a prostitute,[b] to a narcotics addict,[c] and it is clear that such
laws punish a state of being or a condition and abandon the requirement
of conduct, *actus reus,* in the definition of the criminal offense. Confinement
for vagrancy is a punishment, in the words of Justice Holmes, "for being
a certain kind of person, not [for] doing a certain overt act. It follows . . .
that the conduct *proved is not* the offense, but only grounds for inference
that he is that kind of person."[d] But not only does the decision in *Robinson
vs. California* stand in opposition to crimes of status, this opposition is likewise found in the Model Penal Code and the Uniform Narcotic Drug Act.
(a. Ala. Code Title 14 §437 (1958); b. Tex. Pen. Code Ann. art. 607
(1952); c. N.J. Rev. Stat. Ann. §2A:170 (1953); see 37 N.Y.U. L. Rev.
109-113 (1962); d. Commonwealth vs. O'Brien, 179 Mass. 533, 61 N.E.
213, 214 (1901).

12. In *United States vs. Dotterweich,* 320 U.S. 277 (1943), the Supreme
Court recognized the validity of a law which, in the words of the court,
"dispenses with the conventional requirement for criminal conduct—awareness of some wrongdoing" (320 U.S. 280). Here the court upheld the
criminal conviction of Dotterweich, the president of a company which had
made two interstate shipments of drugs that were either mislabeled or adul-
terated, although it had not been shown that Dotterweich was either personally aware of the mistaken shipments or negligent in his administration
of the company.

And in *United States vs. Balint,* 258 U.S. 250 (1922), and in *United
States vs. Behrman,* 258 U.S. (1922), the Supreme Court so construed the

this is not a serious exception to my general point about the criminal law's avoidance of status responsibility, for the criminal law is nowhere under more vigorous or sustained attack, both from within, in actual litigation, and from without, in legal scholarship, than in its reliance on strict liability.[13]

Even so, it must be acknowledged that there is an increasing reliance on strict liability in tort law, particularly in cases involving the determination of responsibility for defective products, and this development has not brought shrill objection from legal scholars. But here again I find no more than a highly qualified exception to my descriptive point about the rejection of status responsibility in criminal law. In the first place, tort law is a branch of civil, not criminal, law: the defendant in a tort action is neither *indicted* by a grand jury of fellow citizens nor *accused* of a *crime* and *prosecuted* by a public official. And most important, he is not subject to a *criminal* sanction of fine or imprisonment; a judgment against him does not *ipso facto* imply an assumption of his moral blameworthiness or the stigma of criminal conviction.[14] In the second place, the courts have justified their reliance on strict liability in tort actions either on the principle of overriding public welfare or on grounds that reveal varying degrees of personal responsibility by tort-feasors, even though,

---

Harrison Narcotics Act that knowledge that one was selling narcotics was not made an element in the offense of selling them. And the court raised no objection to the provision of five years' imprisonment as the maximum penalty under the statute for an offense which could be proved against a person who did not knowingly engage in the activity proscribed by the statute.

13. See H. L. A. Hart, *The Concept of Law,* p. 162, *passim;* Henry Hart, "The Aims of Criminal Law," *Law and Contemporary Problems,* XXIII, 422-425; Hall, *op. cit.,* pp. 342-351, 375; Packer, *op. cit.,* pp. 109, 110, 147, 148; American Law Institute, *Model Penal Code,* Tent. Draft No. 4, §2.05, and Comments, p. 140; F. B. Sayre, "Public Welfare Offenses," *Columbia Law Review,* XXXIII (1933); R. A. Wasserstrom, "Strict Liability in Criminal Law," *Stanford Law Review,* XII (June 1960); G. Williams, *Criminal Law* (1953), pp. 70-76, 285-286.

14. This is not to deny that some acts which give rise to tort litigation do involve the moral blameworthiness of the agent.

admittedly, the degrees would be insufficient to sustain the ascription of personal responsibility on the basis of the voluntary conception of responsibility.

To illustrate, in *Suvada vs. White Motor Company* we find the court saying:

> Recognizing that public policy is the primary factor for imposing strict liability on the seller and manufacturer of food in favor of the injured consumer, we come to the crucial question in this case, namely, is there any reason for imposing strict liability in food cases and liability based on negligence in cases involving products other than food. . . . Without extended discussion, it seems obvious *a*) that public interest in human life and health, *b*) the invitations and solicitations to purchase the product, and *c*) the justice of imposing the loss on the one creating the risk and reaping the profit are present and as compelling in cases involving motor vehicles and other products, where their defective condition makes them unreasonably dangerous to the user, as they are in food cases.[15]

In this opinion there is no suggestion that moral blameworthiness attaches to the defendant. The court speaks of "imposing the loss" not of "imposing the blame" or "imposing the penalty." In *a*) the court stresses merely the important public concern that products which are advertised and sold be safe for public use. In *b*) and *c*) the court points out that the party who creates the risk (whether by manufacture, advertising, sale, or promotion) and reaps the profit is *in justice* the one to bear whatever loss may be incurred if such products are defective. Here the court recognizes responsibility for a loss even though the loss is not the consequence of a voluntary, intentional act. The manufacturer or seller of a defective product is responsible for the loss, not because voluntarily or through negligence he occasioned the loss, but because he is the one who shaped the situation in

15. *Suvada vs. White Motor Company et al.*, Zion 2d 182 (Sp. Ct. Ill. 1965). I inserted *a*), *b*) and *c*). I wish here to thank Professor Wayne Thode of the University of Texas School of Law for informing me of the extensive use of strict liability in tort law, and for his general criticisms of this paper.

which the loss might occur. The *status* of the manufacturer or seller, rather than his specific *act*, provides the basis of his responsibility; and yet the manufacturer or seller creates his status through prior acts, even though those acts have nothing directly to do with the loss. This is, then, a mode of responsibility which does not fit the models of either voluntary or status responsibility but rather suggests a conception of responsibility containing elements of both. This mode should commend itself to the attention of philosophers and criminal lawyers for having at least some of the subtlety and complexity characteristic of human life.

It will be seen, I believe, that this conception of responsibility in tort law is appropriate for the concept of human action that I wish to support. But it cannot be regarded as a qualification of my basic point that in both criminal law and contemporary ethics there has been, generally, a rejection of status responsibility and an assumption of the validity and adequacy of the voluntary conception.

II

Thus far we have merely observed the rejection of the concept of status responsibility in criminal law, as represented by the Supreme Court, and in morality, as articulated by H. L. A. Hart. But whether this concept has theoretical or practical advantages of its own has not been considered; nor has the conceptual or practical adequacy in law and morality of the prevailing concept of voluntary responsibility been critically assessed. So far we have accepted passively the view of the many that the concept of status responsibility—because it conflicts with the voluntary conception—is immoral and should be rejected. But Plato has warned us about the views of the many.

If we probe beneath the surface we shall discover, I think, (1) that moral and criminal offenses cannot be understood either as voluntary actions devoid of status or as states of being devoid of intentional activity; (2) that neither status nor voluntary responsibility is adequate in law or in ethics, that both are high abstractions defying sensible application in either field; (3) that human action, which cannot possibly be understood either as pure status (being) or pure voluntary intentionality (doing), is the complex, active being of living persons who function at various points on a continuum of action—a continuum that approaches vanishing points at the opposite extremes of pure being and pure doing; (4) that the continuum of human action is divisible into, or can be ordered in terms of, actions of distinctive types whose properties are functions of the proportion of static and voluntary elements; (5) that a sound concept of responsibility must be so fitted to the continuum of action over which it applies that it can designate the modes of response available to or obligatory for persons functioning at any particular point on that continuum.

Nothing less than an entire theory of human action and responsibility could establish all these points. In the rest of this paper I shall confine myself (a) to showing some of the perplexities that arise when one tries to understand certain moral experiences in terms either of the doctrine of the Supreme Court in *Robinson vs. California,* or that of Hart; (b) to the partial analysis of Hart's paradigmatic statement of the character of moral offenses and moral obligation; and (c) to suggesting the value and power both for law and ethics of a concept of responsibility containing both status and voluntary elements.

If we take a more careful and critical look at the work of the Supreme Court in *Robinson vs. California,* we find apparent in the court's decision the practical absurdity of trying to separate the being and the doing of human agents—an effort required by the distinction between status and voluntary responsibility. The court agreed that the California statute under which Robinson was convicted would have been valid had it required proof of the actual use of narcotics within the state's jurisdiction. Yet if the court was correct in defining narcotics addiction as a disease, and if one characteristic of this disease is the compulsive use of narcotics, it is difficult to understand how a statute inflicts a cruel and unusual punishment by holding one responsible for having the disease, whereas the punishment would not be cruel or unusual if it were applied only to those acts which are the inevitable consequences of the disease. To use the example of the court, if "even one day in prison would be a cruel and unusual punishment for the 'crime' of having a common cold," why would the punishment be any less cruel or unusual if it were for the "crime" of having sneezed, coughed, or blown one's nose?

The court was obviously on absurd ground philosophically when it tried to separate acts of addiction from the status of addiction. If the court was right in holding that addiction implies use and that use is criminal, how could it deny that addiction is criminal? But if addiction is not criminal, then it would seem to follow logically either that addiction does not imply use or that use is not criminal.[16]

The court could have avoided this absurdity by boldly asserting that because the status or condition of addiction and the use of narcotics are inseparable, the condition-and-use together are the disease, and that therefore neither the state of addiction nor the use of narcotics can be punished as a crime.[17]

16. Justice Harlan, as we noted, *supra* note 10, avoided this pitfall in his concurring opinion.

17. This appears to be the direction taken by the court in *Driver vs. Hinnant,* 356 F.2d 761 (4th Cir. 1966). The court held that the constitutional provision against cruel and unusual punishment precluded North Carolina's punishing a chronic alcoholic for public drunkenness. In language reminiscent of *Robinson vs. California,* the court said, "The upshot of our decision is that the State cannot stamp an unpretending chronic alcoholic as a criminal if his drunken, public display is involuntary as the result of disease" (356 F.2d 764). . . . "The alcoholic's presence is not his act, for he did not will it. It may be likened to the movements of an imbecile or a person in a delirium or a fever" (356 F.2d 765). See also *Easter vs. District of Columbia,* 361 F.2d 50 (D.C. Cir. 1966), in which the Circuit Court recognized chronic alcoholism as a defense to the charge of public intoxication.

The court was reluctant to take this step for many reasons. Paramount among them is the fact that the court would have had to blur the distinction between the condition or state of being of the accused and the actions of the accused. This blurring would, in turn, destroy the traditionally accepted "factual" basis for the distinction between voluntary and status responsibility.

The refusal of the court to take this step is not entirely regrettable. There may be important uses for the fiction of pure *actus reus* and voluntary responsibility, despite their philosophical limitations. Indeed, it is one of the beauties of the law—sufficient perhaps to revive the lost faith in a Divine Order—that the Supreme Court can serve the interests of philosophers while making serious philosophical mistakes. However impossible it may be to separate the use of narcotics from the status of addiction, it is quite clear that we do not want the police arresting citizens in the absence of any anti-social behavior. Political liberty was served by the decision in Robinson, despite the fact that the decision reveals the artificiality and absurdity of sharply distinguishing action from being, or voluntary from status responsibility.

If we turn to an examination of the philosophical doctrine of voluntary responsibility as presented in Hart's paradigmatic statement, there are many points to be considered. One remarkable feature of Hart's characterization of moral offenses and moral responsibility is that he restricts himself to a pejorative context, to a context of moral failure. Hart's characterization of

---

Future developments may be presaged in the dissent of Justice Fortas to the Supreme Court's denial of certiorari in *Budd vs. California* (*Budd vs. California*, cert. denied, U.S. Supt. Ct. Bull., B-79 October 17, 1966). "Our morality does not permit us to punish for illness. We do not impose punishment for involuntary conduct, whether the lack of volition results from insanity, addiction to narcotics, or from other illnesses. The use of the cruder and formidable weapon of criminal punishment on the alcoholic is neither seemly nor sensible, neither purposeful nor civilized."

the distinctive features of morality in terms of moral offenses
might be explained by the fact that the description is given in
the context of a discussion of the similarities and differences of
law and morality. There is very little in the rules of law or ethics
concerning obligations to praise others or the right to claim
praise for ourselves. The rules of law and morality derive their
importance from the fact that they are so often transgressed;
hence most of the thought and ingenuity expended in these
fields has of necessity been directed to the recognition, evaluation, and just handling of transgressions. We no more need to
praise the morally virtuous than to pin medals on those who have
kept out of jail. The norms of ethics and law define a high level
of expectation. In law they are occasionally exceeded, but only
in those moral systems providing for supererogation is there even
a logical possibility of exceeding ethical norms.

But these considerations do not, in my opinion, account adequately for the negative character of Hart's exposition. Hart's
selection of the pejorative context derives, I believe, both from
his view of morality and from his idiosyncratic, if not dogmatic,
linguistic restriction of the term "responsibility" to situations of
failure.

Hart's view of morality is essentially rule-oriented. Hart dis-
cusses moral offense only as action that offends against moral
rules or principles. If the possibility of moral offense or moral
achievement is restricted to the compliance with or transgression
of moral rules or principles without regard to the fulfillment or
loss of moral values, moral achievement will at best be the neutral absence of moral offense. In this particular context we cannot expect Hart to say everything about ethics, and perhaps he
would wish to supplement his account of morality with a discussion of values. But recent English and American ethical thought
has been so dominated by the discussion of rules and their many
kinds that I doubt it. This is rather a bias in contemporary English and American ethical discussion that needs correction by
channel crossing and an extended vacation on the Continent.

Hart's restriction of "responsibility" to contexts of failure would preclude, for example, our substitution of a context of moral achievement and compliance for his context of moral failure and offense, although there is nothing about the English language (or any other language) that prevents it. Suppose we use most of Hart's own words to describe an action which has not offended but has accorded perfectly with moral rules or principles. Consider the following: [18]

> If a person whose action, judged *ab extra*, has been *in complete accord with* [has offended against] moral rules and principles succeeds in establishing that he did this unintentionally and in spite of every precaution that it was possible for him to take, he is *denied* [excused from] moral responsibility and to *praise* [blame] him in these circumstances would itself be considered morally objectionable. Moral *praise* [blame] is therefore excluded because he has *had too little or nothing to do with it* [done all that he could do].

We may continue:

> . . . in morals *"I didn't really do anything"* [I could not help it] is always *a reasonable disclaimer* [an excuse], and moral obligation would be different from what it is if the moral *achievement* ["ought"] did not in this sense imply *performance* ["can"].

Hart would surely object to the substitutions; he would never countenance my speaking of responsibility for a morally or legally exemplary act. Yet there is nothing odd about this usage. A morally good person would immediately object to being credited with responsibility for an apparently exemplary act which he performed either inadvertently or not at all; he might likewise feel some disappointment if another person were credited with responsibility for an exemplary act which he had in fact performed and for which he was in fact responsible. This is perfectly intelligible talk and not unheard of. We also find the honorific use of "responsibility" in such statements as the follow-

18. Hart's original phrases are in brackets following my italicized alterations.

ing: "He is a thoroughly responsible person," or "He was responsible for saving the child's life," or "He deserves no credit since he was not responsible for it." There is nothing odd about these statements, but let us suppose there were. What has one proved if he establishes that a given usage is odd besides its oddness? Surely "odd" does not imply "wrong" or "mistaken." Nor could the fact of linguistic oddness, if it were a fact, offset the most important non-verbal fact about responsibility, namely that personal involvement provides the basis for responsibility whether in contexts of success or failure. Hence we have the right to use the word "responsibility" when there is personal involvement, whether it be praiseworthy or blameworthy.[19]

With these preliminary observations out of the way, let us now consider Hart's discussion of the voluntary character of moral offenses point by point, beginning with the first sentence:

> If a person whose action, judged *ab extra*, has offended against moral rules or principles, succeeds in establishing that he did this unintentionally and in spite of every precaution that it was possible for him to take, he is excused from moral responsibility . . .

I find two ambiguities in this sentence which are not apparent or troublesome if one accepts dominant contemporary views about intention and action. For example, does "did this" refer to an action performed unintentionally by a person, or does Hart hold that all action involves intention? If he holds that in every action the agent must have an intention, it follows that "did this" cannot refer to an *action* but only to an event which, judged *ab extra*, might have appeared to be an action. I assume that Hart accepts the dominant view that intention is an essential ingredient in action, hence that there could be no action which was not

---

19. The relevance of this discussion should be apparent in due course. If responsibility is limited to pejorative contexts, it will be difficult if not impossible to present in ordinary English a continuum theory of responsibility in which voluntary and status elements are combined. The increased difficulty would be, moreover, the gratuitous consequence of linguistic dogmatism.

intended.[20] But whether Hart takes the broad or the narrow view
of action—i.e., whether "did this" refers to an action or merely
to an event—is of no great importance in this context, because
Hart clearly insists that moral offenses are voluntary and that actions or events (whichever word is appropriate) neither intended
nor the result of negligence are not voluntary and therefore are
excusable. Consequently the undetermined scope of the term
"action" results only in an unimportant vagueness so far as this
passage is concerned.

There is a vagueness or ambiguity in the word "intention,"
however, which is of critical importance. Does Hart restrict the
meaning of intention to that which is consciously intended, or
would he accept the view that there are subconscious, unconscious, and organic modes of intention in addition to the conscious modes in their varying degrees of focus and intensity?
Examining this passage alone does not reveal which alternative
Hart accepts. It can be seen, nevertheless, that these alternatives
confront Hart as a dilemma: the consequences of either option
are inimical to his position and support the view of action
and responsibility that I wish to urge. If Hart accepts the narrow conception of intention, he must sacrifice factual support for
his position; if he accepts the broader conception of intention, he
must blur the distinction between voluntary and involuntary to
the point that moral offenses cannot be accurately designated by
their distinctive voluntary character.

If we take the latter alternative and recognize varying degrees
and kinds of intentionality, we recognize our personal involvement to varying degrees in complex series of events. This recognition involves our acceptance of the sequence as *our action,*
even though we may not have fully or even consciously intended
it. On this view, we preserve the essentially intentional [21] char-

20. As will soon be evident, I accept this view provided it is interpreted
in the context of an expanded notion of intention which is not generally
accepted in philosophical circles.

21. Here, of course, "intentional" has a common sense and not a phenomenological, technical meaning.

acter of all action while recognizing the degrees of action corresponding to the degrees and kinds of intentionality and personal involvement. This position, which I take, is more adequately supported by the few relevant facts available than the former alternative, which restricts intention to consciousness. But Hart cannot approve this latter alternative and its factual support without destroying his thesis that moral offenses are essentially voluntary. For if we admit that personal involvement in action need not be accompanied by conscious intent in order for the action to be morally imputed to the person as agent, we destroy the basis for any sharp distinction between that which is and is not voluntary, thereby destroying the foundation for any sharp distinction between voluntary and status responsibility, and we alter radically the conditions or criteria of moral excusability. It is, then, clearly impossible to speak accurately or precisely of the essentially voluntary character of moral offenses.[22]

I presume, therefore, that Hart accepts the former alternative and restricts intention to that which is consciously intended. He holds, I believe, that a person succeeds in establishing that he did X unintentionally, if he can show that he did not consciously intend to do X. But what justification can Hart offer for restricting the meaning of intention to conscious intention—for assuming, that is, that there is no such thing as subconscious or unconscious intention? Perhaps he would rely on Stuart Hampshire's argument that "The sleeping and unconscious man is not an agent. . . . It is a necessary truth that he has no intention under these conditions." [23] It would seem that Freud's demon-

22. I shall consider later the question of whether the acceptance of this view alters the relation of implication between "ought" and "can" in such a way that, as Hart alleges, moral obligation would be transformed into something altogether different from what it is.

23. Stuart Hampshire, *Thought and Action,* p. 94. Consider also Hampshire's statement: "A more decisive difference between consciousness and unconsciousness lies between the necessity of intended action in one case and the mere natural movement without intention in the other" (*idem*). When done by linguistic fiat, as in this instance, philosophy becomes as easy as it is irrelevant.

stration of censorship in dreams and, indeed, the manifest content of dreams apart from any Freudian interpretation, force us to recognize the intentions of the dreamer; his personal involvement seems to color everything. Yet, like many American and English philosophers who ignore Kant's adage that concepts without percepts are empty, Hart perhaps assumes that the logic of language will supply our want of information. By restricting the meaning of intention to conscious intention and the meaning of voluntary action to that which is done intentionally, Hart can preserve the sharp distinction between voluntary and involuntary and, thereby, the basis for his insistence on the voluntary character of moral offenses. His theory gains clarity, precision, and some coherence by this move to linguistic rationalism, but it loses its factual support and plausibility.

I do not reject Hart's and Hampshire's restriction of the meaning of intention to conscious intention on the basis of my intuition of the "logic" of the term "intention," or on the basis of my "right" to replace their definition with one of my own. I urge, rather, that there are relevant facts about human action which are denied when one insists that a person has to be conscious of what he intends in order to have an intention. Just as the anatomy and organic functions of the whale force us to admit that a whale is not a fish, regardless of the logic of the term "fish" or the definitions of venerable dictionaries, the anatomy and dynamics of human behavior and action force us to recognize unconscious and subconscious, no less than conscious, intentions.

Factual support for the broader conception of intention, and for the theoretical implications regarding responsibility that follow from it, is found in abundance in the daily affairs of ourselves, other individuals, and nations. How am I to regard those movements of mine which are judged by others, *ab extra*, to be my actions and which may reveal to others one or more of my overriding, long-range intentions, but which I can truthfully report were not a part of my conscious intention at the time my movements took place? Consider the way, for example, men and nations pick fights and exacerbate quarrels to their enormous advantage while truthfully and conscientiously denying all conscious intent or desire to fight. Consider Oedipus' attack on Creon; did he really believe that Creon was guilty or was this just the sort of conduct to which Oedipus was habituated? Consider Odysseus' trifling yet possibly sincere excuses for failing to support Hecuba in Euripides' play; what did he really intend? Consider the actions and intentions of Hitler and Chamberlain prior to the outbreak of World War II. In these cases we have factual proof of action possessing an intentional structure, or a goal-direction, radically at odds with its conscious intention.

And such actions must be judged morally. We are prepared, I believe, to say that both Hitler and Chamberlain were morally blameworthy men, the one for his almost diabolical craving for universal destruction (however much he may have spoken of peace and German fulfillment),[24] and the other for his cowardice and preoccupation with immediate selfish advantage (however much he may have spoken of reasonable compromise in the interest of peace).[25] Are we not prepared to recognize, moreover, the corporate moral guilt of the Englishmen who cheered Chamberlain on his return from Munich and of the Americans who relied on Washington's Farewell Address to justify avoidance of entanglements on behalf of freedom in Europe? But did these Englishmen and Americans consciously intend to behave as cowards or to evade their moral obligations on the Continent?

More prosaically and perhaps more convincingly still, consider the Christmas dinner at which the spinster aunt, in the shrill voice of Carry Nation, delivers a temperance lecture while the father is opening a bottle of wine saved for the occasion. Are we to

24. Mircea Eliade lays great stress on the National Socialists' selection of the Nordic myths as an expression of national purpose: the goal is *ragnarök*—total destruction of gods, heroes, and men! See *Myths, Dreams and Mysteries*, pp. 26-27.

25. When Chamberlain said that he brought back from Munich "Peace *in our time*," he let the cat out of the bag. It is not hard to find the intent behind that phrase or behind the equally famous "Après moi, le déluge!"

deny that the aunt's dislike of the father for having destroyed
her only immediate family by marrying her sister, and the aunt's
envy of her sister for being the mother in another family, are
expressed in her action? Are we to believe that she does not desire and intend to hurt this family, to dampen the pleasures of its
Christmas feast? Yet who would call the aunt a liar when later,
in tears, she apologizes for having spoiled the celebration while
she continues to insist that her only concern was for the welfare
of the father and mother and children who are going to destroy
their health by drinking? The aunt can claim, with complete
justification, that her love for the family has been fully demon-
strated by her generous and loving support in times of extreme
hardship at great personal sacrifice to herself. But it is equally
true that she is resentful of the family and full of hate. And
because her actions are *hers*, it is not surprising that they should
reveal much more of herself than she consciously intends to express: what she *does* is a function of *all* that she *is*, all her loves,
hates, and wants, and not merely the expression of what she
consciously intends when she acts. In this case all of her action,
including its disruptive consequences and its good and bad will,
was intended and was done intentionally, despite the fact that
her conscious intention was merely to save the family she loved
from alcoholism. The most accurate account of this situation is
one which simply accepts *as fact* the presence of unconscious
and often ambivalent intentions.

Four years ago in Austin, Texas, a man charged with the murder of his wife claimed in his defense that he had killed her
while he was sleeping or immediately on awakening. Psychologists and psychiatrists testified to the possibility of this occurrence. And if the man had lived happily with his wife for twenty
years, one might be inclined to excuse his act on the grounds
that it was unintentional. According to the evidence, however,
the man and his wife fought frequently, and he had planned on
two occasions to divorce his wife in order to marry another
woman. By his own admission he dreamed that he was killing an

intruder who was chasing his nieces; then he awakened to find that he had killed his wife. I would accept as factual that the man killed his wife while in an unconscious or subconscious state. But I see no reason for concluding, as Hart or Hampshire would, that the man did what he did unintentionally and, consequently, that he is to be excused from moral blame for killing his wife.

Hart insists that a person is to be excused from moral blame if he can establish "that he did this unintentionally and in spite of every precaution it was possible for him to take." Now if we admit that the man killed his wife while in a non-conscious state and that consciousness is required for intention, it follows that in this case the man did what he did unintentionally. And unless we consider him reckless or negligent for having continued to sleep in the same bed with his wife after having quarreled with her,[26] we have no basis for claiming that he failed to take every precaution it was possible for him to take. We cannot fault him for having failed to consult a psychiatrist or marriage counselor; recourse to such professional help presupposes a level of education and sophistication which the accused had not attained.[27] On Hart's view, we must conclude, therefore, that the man was neither negligent nor intentional in his behavior, hence that he did not offend voluntarily, hence that he is excused from moral responsibility and blame.[28] This, in my opinion, constitutes a *reductio ad absurdum* of the view that limits ascription of moral blame and responsibility to voluntary, consciously intended acts, the view that moral offenses must be voluntary and that in order to be voluntary they must be consciously intended.

There are at least two ways of avoiding this absurdity and

26. Survival of the institution of marriage would require the negligence of most of the adult population if such a consideration were made a rule of law.

27. We will discuss later the problem of accounting for negligent conduct on a theory which recognizes only a conscious level of intention and awareness.

28. Hart would not necessarily excuse him from legal responsibility. Hart would not accept without serious qualifications Jerome Hall's position that "Penal law implies moral culpability" (Hall, *op. cit.*, p. 347).

acknowledging the moral responsibility of the agent in this case. First, we may hold that, since the man had no conscious intention to kill his wife, his bodily movements in killing her do not constitute an action, and hence that killing her was not voluntary. In this way we preserve the usages of Hart and Hampshire. But then we are forced to abandon Hart's thesis that moral offenses are voluntary: we are forced to predicate the man's responsibility on his being, or status, rather than on his voluntary action. We now avoid the absurdity of excusing him by morally blaming him for *being* a man who killed his wife even though he did not kill her voluntarily or intentionally.

Or, second, we may describe what the man did in terms of action, intention, and volition developed on a continuum view of responsibility. We may hold that there was a degree of voluntariness in his action proportionate to the degree and kind of intentionality and, consequently, a corresponding degree of moral blame. We would have to assess the degree and quality of his intention by reference to what he had thought, said, dreamed, and done about his wife in the preceding months and years. And to the degree that the man's intentions, as so assessed, were apparent in his bodily movements of killing her, we would describe those movements as, to that degree, his voluntary action. This second way, by far the soundest in my judgment, provides a better fit of facts to theory than the first way. It imposes, moreover, very little strain on traditional linguistic usage and offers qualified support for the traditional view, represented by Hart,[29] of the voluntary character of moral offenses.

On the second view we recognize that there must be some element of intention and some degree of voluntariness in a series of bodily movements if those movements are to be called an action and if the action is to be subject to moral judgment. At the

29. I have indicated at several points in this paper that Hart's statement represents, or is representative of, the generally accepted view of the voluntary character of moral offenses. I selected Hart's statement for examination because it epitomizes the view that has been dominant among ethical writers from Aristotle to Kant, as well as because of its clarity and brevity.

same time, moreover, we recognize the essential co-presence of elements of status responsibility. The mixture of kinds of responsibility reflects with accuracy the mixture of being and doing in personal action. It reflects the fact that what a man *does* is a function of what he, in the context of his situation, *is,* and that what he *is* within this context is revealed by what he *does.* The partial truth of the voluntary conception of responsibility is acknowledged through the recognition that what a man *does* is the *ratio cognoscendi* of what he *is,* and the partial truth of the status conception of responsibility is acknowledged through the recognition that what a man in context *is* is the *ratio essendi* of what he *does.* This view can also accommodate the existential point that what a man is and does determines or creates what he shall be and do; that his existence can give rise to a new essence.

We are compelled, then, largely by factual considerations, to reject the view that intentions are necessarily or always consciously intended, that a person must be conscious of his intention in order to act intentionally. We are forced, that is, to reject the view that a person can establish that he acted unintentionally if he can show that he did not consciously intend to do what he did. And when the concept of intention is extended, the character of moral offenses and the criteria of moral excusability are altered. We recognize, for example, the possibility of being morally blameworthy for what we do on the basis of unconscious or subconscious intentions in the absence of any conscious intention to violate moral rules or principles or to neglect any values that should be enhanced.

And we have taken only the first step toward confronting factually and acknowledging theoretically the larger range, scope, and depth of mental concepts. The enlargement of the concept of intention must be accompanied by a comparable enlargement of the concept of awareness. The importance of this step can be seen most clearly in the present context if we ask whether a person can be morally blameworthy for negligent conduct. Hart recognizes, of course, the difference between intentional or purposive action and action which is done with knowledge or conscious awareness but without intent. He insists, therefore, that the person whose action violates some moral rule or principle must, in order to excuse his conduct, establish not merely that he acted unintentionally but also that he did not know he was running any avoidable risk of violating them. He must establish that, in Hart's words, "he did this . . . in spite of every precaution that it was possible for him to take." Thus, in order to be excused morally the person is required to prove that his conduct was not reckless. But it is important to note that he is not required to prove that his conduct was not negligent. As exemplarily explained in the *Comments* to the Model Penal Code,

> recklessness involves conscious risk creation. It resembles acting knowingly in that a state of awareness is involved but the awareness is of risk, that is of probability rather than certainty.[30]

Hart's view clearly requires that a person who would excuse his action must succeed in establishing that his conduct was neither intentional nor reckless: he must show both that it was not his purpose or intent to violate the rules and that he was not aware that he ran any avoidable risks of doing so. But on Hart's view a person is not required to show that his action was non-negligent, for negligence, unlike recklessness, does not involve any state of awareness:

> It is the case where the actor creates inadvertently a risk of which he ought to be aware, considering its nature and degree, the nature and purpose of his conduct and the care that would be exercised by a reasonable person in his situation.[31]

If Hart takes a narrow view of mind, intention, and awareness, and if he holds that moral offenses must be voluntary—by which he means that they must be avoidable by means available to the agent at the time he acts—how can the agent be blameworthy for failing to take a precaution of which he was not aware and

30. A.L.I., Model Penal Code, *Comments* on §2.02, p. 125.
31. *Ibid.*, p. 126.

which was therefore not available to him at the time he acted?
If the agent is aware of reasonable precautions which he is neglecting to take, he is acting recklessly. But if he is not aware of
any reasonable precautions that he is neglecting to take, in what
sense can it be possible for him to take them? In what sense can
he be *voluntarily* negligent and therefore morally blameworthy
for his negligence?

It makes no sense to include among possible precautions those
of which one is not consciously aware, unless it is recognized
that there are various modes of awareness, including peripheral,
subconscious, and unconscious modes, and that there are purposive acts of forgetting, repressing, neglecting, and so on. If
we accept the fact that persons express through their actions
intentions of which they are not fully or even partially conscious,
and if we give credence to the psychoanalytic and psychological
evidence of repression and other forms of subconscious or unconscious awareness and activity, then—but only then—have we
a sound factual basis for extending the concept of moral blameworthiness to truly negligent behavior. For it is only after we
accept this evidence as factual that we have a basis for identifying the presence and effects of the person in such conduct. It
is another shortcoming of the traditional view that moral offenses
must be voluntary in the sense that they must be avoidable by
means of which the agent is aware, that it limits moral blame to
actions which are either intentional or consciously reckless, and
hence that it cannot impute moral blame for truly negligent
conduct.[32]

On the basis of the extended view of awareness and inten-

---

32. In my consideration of the case in which the man killed his wife
(*Texas vs. Blomquist*, 1962), I dealt superficially with the question of his
possible "recklessness or negligence" because I had not yet introduced the
technical distinction between negligence and recklessness. In retrospect it
should be clear that the theory as represented by Hart is reduced to an
absurdity when applied to this case, because in terms of the theory the
man's conduct was morally excusable. It was, in terms of the theory, neither
intentional, negligent, nor reckless.

tionality, by contrast, it is possible to hold a person morally blameworthy and legally culpable for genuinely negligent conduct. And by extending the meanings of these mental concepts— in response to factual evidence, be it noted, and not to the "logic" or usage of these terms—we need not abandon but only qualify the traditional requirements that morally blameworthy acts be voluntary and that legally culpable conduct involve *mens rea*.[33] In holding a person morally blameworthy or legally culpable for truly negligent behavior, we recognize the presence of the person existing and functioning mentally on some level in the process of acting. We recognize degrees of moral blameworthiness or legal culpability appropriate to the degree and kind of personal presence in the action. The greater the degree of consciousness in awareness and intention, the greater the degree of voluntariness and *mens rea*—hence the greater the degree of moral and legal responsibility.[34] Once again we confront increasing or decreasing continua of awareness, intention, *mens rea*, and so forth, on which our judgments—on continua scales— of the presence and degree of personality, voluntariness, action, responsibility, blameworthiness, and culpability are based.

Because there is still much doubt (a good deal of which may be fully merited) about the soundness and relevance of data provided by depth psychology and psychoanalysis, I do not want

33. Professor Herbert Packer, *op. cit. supra* note 3, has urged the consideration of negligence as a conceptual halfway house between strict liability and *mens rea*. If we accept as factual a side of mental life of which we are not directly conscious but which, according to many psychologists and psychoanalysts, accounts for slips of the tongue, deliberate forgetting, and other failures which can be grouped under the general heading of negligent behavior, a substantial element of the *mens rea* requirement could be reintroduced into criminal and tort law under rules concerning negligence at points where at present rules of strict liability are used, or where negligence is treated as if it were devoid entirely of *mens rea*, and hence where rules of negligence are applied exactly as rules of strict liability.

34. A continuum theory of human conduct and responsibility may have been behind and is certainly required by the A.L.I. proposal, in §2 of the Model Penal Code, of four modes of culpability, which in descending order are: purpose, knowledge, recklessness, and negligence.

to rest my case against the traditional, simplistic concept of voluntary responsibility exclusively or even primarily on such data. By restricting ourselves to familiar experiences in daily life—without appeal to psychoanalytic interpretation—we can expose the inadequacy of the view that a person can excuse himself for morally offensive conduct by showing that he did what he did unintentionally and after taking every possible precaution. According to Hart's statement, if a person meets these criteria, "Moral blame is therefore excluded because he has done all that he can do . . . [and] in morals 'I could not help it' is always an excuse." But we can show, I think, that "I could not help it" is not always an excuse, because moral responsibility can have no meaning in human affairs unless there are times and situations in which one is morally responsible (deserving of moral praise or blame) for what he is, whether he could have helped being what he is or not. That is to say, I wish to show by reference to uncontested facts of human experience that the concept of moral responsibility (and, by limitation, moral offense) involves some minimal element of status responsibility and cannot be based solely on voluntary responsibility. To show this at least sketchily will be the burden of the final part of this paper.

III

It is often mistakenly assumed in philosophical discussions of action, intention, person, and responsibility that everyone is clear about the precise, and even logical, difference between an event and an action, between an action and its consequences, between a voluntary and an involuntary action or movement, between a person and a thing. But in fact there is great uncertainty and fuzziness on all these matters: wherever we look we seem to find one item or concept fading by imperceptible degrees into another from which it is alleged to be factually or even logically distinct.

We find, for example, not merely the gradations of personality, agency, and responsibility in the sequential observation of comatose, vegetative, senile, idiotic, infantile, stupid, sleeping, insane, neurotic, normal, wakeful, rational, articulate, intelligent, or imaginative persons; we also find a spectrum of action, personality, and responsibility in the daily life of any ordinary human being. Consider the following experiences of X:

1. While walking aimlessly in his garden, he steps on a thorn and feels a terribly sharp pain.

2. While playing badminton in his garden, he steps on a thorn and feels some pain.

3. While in a desperate struggle with an intruder in his garden, he steps on a thorn and feels no pain at all.

4. While asleep he dreams of a stranger who is killed and whose estate is inherited by his brother.

5. Working in his garden while hungry, he thinks suddenly of eating bacon and eggs.

6. Working in his garden, he thinks of his brother who is on military duty in the war zone, and he offers a silent prayer for his safety. In the midst of the prayer the thought crosses his mind that if his brother is killed he will inherit his brother's estate.

7. Hungry but still at work in his garden, he decides to cook those eggs and bacon.

8. As he is going inside, he thinks, "I don't want my brother dead; what a scoundrel I must be for having a thought like that."

9. He prepares lunch.

10. His brother comes in unexpectedly on a military leave granted so that he can recuperate from a wound and lead poisoning; X invites his brother to eat with him.

11. X decides to slip a fatal dose of powdered lead into the eggs before serving his brother.

12. X puts the poison in the eggs.

13. He serves the eggs to his brother.

Here we have a continuum of situations from events to moral
action in which a gradual increase of personal involvement and
responsibility is shown. At what point shall we speak of action
rather than mere event? At what point does the personality of X
express itself in what happens or in what is done? At what point
do we speak properly of moral responsibility or moral blameworthiness? Of legal responsibility or culpability? [35]

X's personality and personal involvement are apparent from
the outset. Even the way in which X feels pain in #1 has elements of action about it. The intensity of his pain is a function,
presumably, of his degree of abstraction while walking and of
his normal pain threshold. If he has a low threshold and a vivid
memory of such experiences, the pain may be excruciating, and
he may relive the shock for hours or days. If his threshold is
high, a single "Dammit!" and the removal of the thorn may be
all there is to it. Now are we to suppose, in the interest of precision or clarity, that X's reaction to stepping on a thorn is
just a *reaction,* a psycho-physical event in which there is no
personal involvement and no element of action? Can we doubt
that X's response will be not merely indicative but largely
determinative of his action in a situation of moral crisis in which
the threat of pain is involved? If X were to serve later in the
army and be taken prisoner, how would he respond to the
mere threat of physical torture? Can we assess his moral responsibility by asking, "Could he help whatever he does?" If
his pain threshold is low and his memory of past pains and his
imagination of pains to come are vivid, can he help divulging
secrets on the mere threat of torture, whereas he would not
divulge them even after torture were his pain threshold high
and his imagination and memory less vivid? Does it make any

35. My discussion of these thirteen situations will of necessity be very
brief and sketchy; it should serve, nevertheless, to carry the reader on his
own through many of the considerations which I find relevant.

more sense to say, "He could not help doing what he did," than to say, "He could have avoided being who he was"? Or does it make any more sense to say, "He could have avoided doing what he did," than to say, "He could have avoided being who he was"? If what a man does is not a function of what he is, in what sense can his action be his? But if what a man does is a function of what he is, such questions make no sense. The proper question for the assessment of moral responsibility should rather be: "What kind of person is he—that is, under what conditions, both external and internal, does he do or would he do what he did?" I see no way of determining whether or not X can be different from what he is or could be different from what he was at any particular time. Likewise, I see no way to determine whether he can do differently from what he does or could do differently from what he did at any particular time. But there are ways to determine to some extent the conditions under which X does what he does and is likely to do what he will do—that is, we can come to know something about his character, including his moral character, and a statement of his character is a description of his being-doing.

Now if X screams and cries when he steps on the thorn in #1, we may be able to talk to him about his behavior and train him so that he will exercise greater control the next time. When he shows greater control the next time—stiff upper lip, and so on —are we to say that praise is inappropriate, for it is only another event and not an action for which X can be praised? Hardly. The fact is that we train children to exercise control— and hence to *act* to a minimal degree—even in the way that they experience pain. I can hear a critic saying, "But you train the child to control his response to the pain, not to alter his experience of it." It is probable that control would be impossible in cases of intense pain if there were no way of altering the experience itself. The unity of mind-body in human experience has been seriously underestimated by philosophers since

Descartes. They have also underestimated or ignored the personal controls that we know are operative, but which we are not aware of as operating in such basic processes as perception.

But if one questions the presence of minimal personal presence and therefore a minimal element of action in #1, what will one say about #2 or #3? If we argue that the adjustments in the awareness of pain in 2 and 3 are merely bodily adjustments having nothing to do with the person involved, we shall be left with a high abstraction instead of a richly concrete person. The extent of the reduction in the awareness of pain in 2 is not merely a function of the attention areas in the brain; it is likewise a function of X's involvement in the game. If he doesn't like the game, the pain is likely to be far more intense than if he were extremely fond of it. The greater his competitive involvement, the less intense the pain. If he is playing with a young woman in whom he has a strong romantic interest, his pain may be either lessened or intensified according to his courting technique, quite apart from the question of whether he will feign greater or lesser pain for courtship purposes. His personality will express itself instantaneously in the midst of play prior to his conscious assertion of secondary control. I see no reason to deny that the initial response is his personal response, not merely an organic reaction, though I should not want to deny the greater element of personal involvement expressed through his secondary control.

I acknowledge that pain must not be too intense if the element of personal action is to be found in the very perception of it. Pain so intense as to produce almost instantaneous loss of consciousness is clearly of a different sort. But this consideration should not blind us to the minimal expression of the person in the experience of less severe pains.

In a situation like 3, we should condemn a soldier or an athlete who did not suppress virtually all awareness of pain. (I introduce athletes into a situation like 3 out of consideration

of American pro football, which is much more like 3 than 2.) If
he continued to feel pain from a thorn to the point that it inter-
fered with his fighting, we should probably deny that "he did all
that he could to control the pain." (Note that we speak of controlling pain when we can mean nothing other than controlling
the way we experience it, rather than the response we make
to it.) We should be inclined, I think, to say that a football
player who felt enough pain from a thorn in the foot to be
seriously distracted by it while engaged in hand to hand "com-
bat" cared too little about winning the game and "had not done
all he could do" to win it. Whether or not we regard his failure
as morally blameworthy depends on how seriously we take the
game and whether we view it as a moral struggle, but not on
the character of his action. His personal involvement, minimal
though it be, is sufficient to justify imputation of some very
small degree of moral blame.

By the time we come to situation 4, I should suppose the
presence of personal involvement and responsibility would be
generally acknowledged. It was Plato, not Freud, who first
stressed the moral significance of dreams and who insisted that
it was important to consider a person's dreams when assessing
his moral character. It is universally acknowledged that dreams
reveal the desires of the dreamer: starving men dream of sumptu-
ous meals; sexually deprived persons dream of sexually pleasing
objects; bed-wetting children dream of toilets while they wet
their beds. Now if we add to these commonplace observations
Freud's theory of dream censorship, we find an important similarity between 4 and 6. Freud would credit X morally for his
dream work, for his censorship of his dream. He would assert
that X's love or respect for his brother, or at least his acknowledgment of his brother's right to live, was expressed in his sup-
pression of the true content of his dream and in his provision
of the manifest content. Freud would say that X was a better
man for dreaming what he dreamed in 4 than if he had dreamed

directly of his brother's death, for his dream in 4 shows that he disapproved of his own desire.[36] Without trading on the metaphysics of psychoanalysis, I should argue that X's incompatible wants were revealed in 4: his affection for his brother is in conflict with his desire for his brother's estate. And I should argue that we can never make sense of personal or moral responsibility unless we recognize the expression of the person and hence a mode of personal action, if not in one's dreams at least in one's wants and desires.

By moving from 4 to 5 we confront essentially the same issues, but in a context in which the rejection of Freud's or Plato's interpretation of dreams poses no threat to my position. But I do not wish to deny what seems to me the clear moral relevance of dream behavior. I contend that no one would hire a baby sitter who frequently dreamed of killing kittens or chickens, much less one who dreamed frequently of killing children. We all know perfectly well that our dreams reveal ourselves, our persons. When I was a child of eight—and long before I had heard of Freud—I dreamed on two occasions of the deaths of my parents. In these dreams I basked in the emotional glory of being the "poor little orphan." When I awoke I was ashamed of myself for indulging in those gratifying thoughts of having everyone sorry for me at the cost of losing my parents. I considered then, and now consider, that a moral fault (admittedly of trivial importance) was revealed in those dreams. But I would not know what it means to be me, or what my moral quality as a person were, unless I based my judgment on all indices of myself. I might add that in dreams in which I have "done the right thing" in a situation of great temptation I have awakened mildly pleased with myself. Only a fool would ignore what he can learn of himself through his personal activity in dreams.

For the sake of those who reject Joseph along with Plato and Freud, however, there are always 5 and 6. If in a fully conscious

36. Sigmund Freud, "Moral Responsibility for the Control of Dreams," *Collected Papers*, V, 154-157.

state I think of the attractive consequences of my brother's death
in a situation in which I am concerned for his well-being (I
need not be praying about it), I must obviously recognize my
ambivalence toward him. And if I have no basis for wishing
him ill, must I not recognize my personal involvement and
agency in the morally blameworthy thought of the attractive
consequences of his death? Let me emphasize once more that
we are speaking here of microscopic blame. X could not be
called a basically morally bad person because he had the dream
in 4 or the thought in 6, unless they were interpreted later in
light of 11, 12, or 13. But the continuum of personal activity
and responsibility is what I wish to stress. And I think we find
in 6 a significant though minuscule instance of personal agency,
responsibility, and, indeed, moral blameworthiness. The degree
is far greater, moreover, than in situations 1 through 5.

Situations 4 through 6 show that a person's wants are a
part of him and an expression of his personal agency. A man
who will not assume responsibility for his desires and wants
may just as well deny responsibility for his mind-body. I believe
that what I say accords with the findings of clinical psychology
in so far as the person who does not recognize himself in his
desires and wants, and in the subtle ways in which their intensity bespeaks his control of them, antecedent to consciously
deliberate control, is suffering some degree of mental illness.
(Ego is no longer master; repression is terribly extended, and
so on.)

In situations 1 through 6 we have the gradual emergence of
clearly recognizable action from events in which faint but
significant traces of personal activity are found. In situations 6
through 13 we have actions in which there is a gradual development of conscious deliberation and moral responsibility. Numbers 11 through 13 can be described as one action or as three,
but the quality of the decision in 11 is not fully revealed until
the occurrence of 13. X's decision in 11 may not have been
fully determinate even in the mind of X at the time it was

made. His decisiveness *becomes* complete as his action develops. But even at 13 there may be irresolution: 13 may be followed by a 14 in which X snatches the plate away before his brother can eat. The person of X may change and develop in the tension of the situations. But his being will never be separated from his doing; he is and does together and at once. It makes no sense at any point to say that he could have *done* differently unless he could have *been* different.

Of course, there were alternatives open to X at every point from 1 through 13, and, as we noted, alternates remain open after 13. But were there alternatives which X could have taken while being what he was at each instance? This is the question we cannot answer with any empirical guarantees. Only the metaphysicians of free will or determinism can fight this issue through. But we can recognize the important differences in the quality or kind of alternatives available to X. We note that his awareness and conscious deliberations are on an increase from 1 through 13. His alternative at 1 may be little more than the possibility of accepting or rejecting himself as the person he is and deciding on a course of training to raise his pain threshold. Indeed, in all situations from 1 through 5 his action or activity is not so much planned as happening. And his act of praying in 6 is a sudden impulse (though a morally significant and revealing one). But in 7 there is planning. He decides on a course of action—which is itself an action or part of one—before he goes inside or gathers the food and the utensils and begins to cook. Time passes between the action of 7 and the cooking of the eggs. And in every moment of time there are occasions in which his person can express itself in different ways if his person is such that the expression comes forth. But time, the *sine qua non* for alteration of plans, for the expression of ambivalence or contrary desires or intentions, for deliberation and thoughtful consideration, is provided. And the person whose action has been undertaken and sustained through prolonged moments of time, in which deliberation and consideration of alternative desires, wants, intentions, and plans may express themselves through the alteration of the course of that action, is more fully identified and identifiable with that action than a person whose action is of less duration down to the point of being almost instantaneous. Enduring action in which the full capacities of the person are engaged is what is properly meant by voluntary action: it is expressive of the volition of the person; it reveals what the personal agent wants to come to pass in the world and what he wants to be.

Concerning voluntary action we can say that there was time and opportunity for the agent to do differently from what he did had he been a different person from what he was. Hence we are prepared to blame him more for such action, because his personal identification with and in such action is greater. In blaming him severely only for voluntary actions, however, we are not denying that we are blaming him for what he *is* as well as for what he *does*. We blame him more severely because his fully conscious mind and deliberative choice are expressed in temporally extended voluntary action. We blame him less severely for impulsive or responsive actions or for dream actions, precisely because far less of himself is expressed in or identified with them.

We have just examined an event-action continuum in which we observed the gradual increment of personal expression as we moved from cases of predominantly event-like reaction, through those involving sudden responses, dream work, impulsive thoughts, or desires, to cases of maximally conscious, voluntary, and deliberative action. The continuum was one of increasing personal involvement and expression, increasing voluntariness, and increasing responsibility. Throughout we found, moreover, the co-presence of personal being and personal doing, and we observed the artificiality that results from the separation of the person's being from his doing.

We observed and considered only a small aspect of the ontological foundation of action and responsibility. Action and responsibility depend on far more than the being and doing of the agent himself; they depend also on the being and doing of other agents and finally upon the general matrix of action, including all of the ontological conditions on which action depends. The ontological matrix of action no less than the intentions of the agent sets the determinate limits of action and the degree and quality of responsibility.

Let us resume our consideration of X by supposing that each of the following situations is an alternative successor to 13:

14. **X snatches away the eggs just before his brother eats them.**

15. **X's brother begins to eat, feels sick almost at once, and stops eating before consuming a fatal amount; X throws away the eggs (a) in happy relief that the plan has failed, or (b) in anger that his plan has failed.**

16. **X's brother eats the fatal meal and dies.**

17. **After serving the poisoned eggs, X leaves the house for a few minutes; while he is gone his mother enters, partakes of the poisoned meal, and (a) both she and the brother die, or (b) the brother feels sick, does not eat, and only the mother dies.**

In 14 X is still in control, as much as any voluntary agent is in control of his action; that is, his action has not yet set in motion or been caught up by forces that may result in a disrelation between his action and his plan or intention. In 14 we see that the determination, expressed with increasing clarity and force from 11 through 13, is still far from steadfast or overpowering. In 14 we find that determination is shaken by competing aspects of X's personality and interests; his action now expresses perhaps either his prudential concern for his own safety and well-being, his continuing but ambivalent love for his brother, or his respect for law. X's movement in 13 may have been impulsive: an expression on his brother's face may have reminded X of a happy incident from their childhood. Alternatively, his movement may have been deliberate: he may have known even as he was serving the plate and carrying it to the table that he would have to snatch it away at the last; perhaps he only toyed with the idea of murder and even savored the moral test he was putting himself through. The range of possibilities is almost infinite.

But 14, whether impulsive or deliberate, forces us to reassess X's blame. Our judgment made on the basis of 11 through 13 is no longer adequate. If X's action from 11 through 13 was deliberate while his action in 14 was impulsive, can we allow our judgment based on 11 through 13 to stand? Shall we argue that 11 through 13 prove that he intended to murder his brother and that it is immaterial that he was stopped by an expression on his brother's face rather than, as in 15, by the fact that his brother does not eat the poisoned food? Shall we argue that he was stopped in either case by an accident in so far as he was concerned? We must argue, I think, that he is to be credited morally for his response to his brother's expression in a way that he is not to be credited for his brother's refusal to eat the food—though both accidents, if that is what they are, partially determine his moral worth. Much of X is centrally involved in his response to his brother's facial expression: it is not just the expression but the expression as seen by X that accounts for X's throwing away the eggs. The expression as seen by X shatters his resolution and alters his intention, whereas there is no break in X's intention in 15(b). We must give X moral credit for his response to his brother's expression, or for his deliberate consideration in which his love for his brother was reasserted, or for his thought of his brother's right to live and the wrongness of murder, no matter how intensely he may have hated his brother. We must give X moral credit, though to a lesser extent, even if his action in 14 expresses nothing more than his prudent concern for his own safety; there is an important element of moral goodness in the man who is law-abiding even for the wrong reasons—he does not destroy some of the values that the laws protect. Or are we so carried away by the moral dare-deviltry of formalistic, voluntaristic ethics that we find no moral worth in law-abiding conduct which is prompted by selfish motives?

The situation in 15 seems radically different from 14, but it is only gradationally different. In 15 the action has clearly moved beyond X's voluntary control. But did X have voluntary control over his brother's expression in 14, or over the present strength of his love for his brother, or over the education that developed whatever sense of duty and respect for the lives of others that may have moved him in 14? We know what X was in 14, but we must not slip back into the mistake of supposing that X could have *done* differently in 14 any more than in 15 without having *been* a different man in these situations.

Since the situation in 15 is nonetheless beyond X's voluntary control, what should we conclude concerning his responsibility? His maximally voluntary responsibility must be assessed by reference to his reaction to the failure of his plan—to the truncation of his action. In 15(b) we find that his resolution was complete: X did his best to kill his brother and never wavered in his intention. We can say, as I suggested in another paper,[37] that X murdered unsuccessfully. But that is a misleading way of putting it, for it is a brute fact that in 15, X did not murder his brother. The continued existence of his brother provides an ontological refutation of any charge of murder. X has been saved from the crime of murder by his brother's sensitive digestive system. Although X did all he could to bring it about, although his voluntary involvement was complete, his action was terminated short of its completion. His action was defined by his intention to kill his brother, but his action was terminated (a) after he had done all he could to realize his intention but (b) before his action had been completed by his brother's

37. See my "Human Action and the Language of Volitions," *Proceedings of the Aristotelian Society* (1963-64), LXIV, 199-220.

death. In 15(b) we have a situation in which the ontological matrix of the action does not support the volitional matrix, and the discrepancy is effectively articulated, in my opinion, by the traditional language of volition. X *willed* to kill his brother and is morally blameworthy for his acts of volition, even though he did not succeed.

But is X as morally blameworthy for having willed, but failed, to kill his brother as he would have been if his action had fit his intention—if, that is, his volitional act had been completed by his brother's death? [38] Unless we banish from ethics all concern for the realization of values, our answer must be that X is not so blameworthy. In spite of his volition, X is not guilty in 15 of having destroyed a human life with all its values! If in 16, X can be held responsible morally for his brother's action in eating the eggs and for the action of the poison within his brother's system, why should he not be relieved of some responsibility and blame if these intended and probable consequences of his efforts in preparing and serving the eggs do not take place?

The traditional answer has been that X intended the consequences and did everything in his power to bring them about; hence they are a part of his action, and he is morally accountable for them whether they happened or not. Persuasive as this answer is, it overstates the case. It ignores the absence of certain elements of being or status requisite to full moral responsibility. The man who has attempted murder, as X has in 15(b), is as guilty *volitionally* as he can possibly be. But he lacks the *being*

---

38. We raise this question while recognizing that to *will* something, unlike merely to wish it, involves a determined effort on the part of the agent; within the limits of his capacities, the agent does everything he thinks is required for the fulfillment of his intention. If one *wills* something to happen, its failure to come to pass cannot be imputed to the volition of the agent, for if he wills it he does what he can to bring it about and does nothing to prevent it. As the article just cited, *supra* note 37, will show, I do not accept any para-mechanical theory of the relation of mind to body or any of the other horrible things that Ryle alleges are accepted by those who use the language of volitions.

or *status* of a murderer. It would be a *reductio ad absurdum* of the theory of voluntary responsibility to assume that he would not be far more blameworthy had he acted in an ontological matrix that supported his intent and brought about its full realization. On the other hand, it would be a *reductio ad absurdum* of the theory of status responsibility to assume that the man who has attempted but failed to commit murder has no moral guilt as a murderer, just because his victim is still alive and unharmed. His volitional offense still stands.

Much more needs to be said about the ontological matrix of action. But it is already clear that it can alter the agent's action despite his intention or volition and, hence, that it can alter his moral and legal responsibility. If we limit our considerations merely to X's awareness of himself and ignore what the law or his family might think of him, we must recognize the difference in what he as a person is in 15 and what he is in 16. According to 15, X is not a murderer, although he has a murderous will in 15(b) and may have no better than an ambivalently murderous will in 15(a). In both 15(a) and 15(b), however, there are redemptive possibilities open to X that are closed by 16. Reconciliation with his brother is only the most obvious. By considering the difference between X in 15 and X in 16, we see plainly his finitude both physically and morally: he is dependent with regard to both his moral guilt and virtue on many ontological factors that are not under his control, not even in the weakened sense of being expressions of his volitional being. This fact that his moral virtue or guilt depends on ontological factors beyond his control is not acknowledged by the traditional view of moral responsibility, according to which one deserves credit or blame only for what he has done voluntarily. The traditional view necessarily ignores this fact because it has ignored the ontological foundations of voluntary action.

In 15(a) we have a situation that is similar in many respects to one of the situations we considered in interpreting 14. X's resolution is still divided and incomplete. He is still ambivalent;

in many ways he is still the man he was in 6 and 8. *Fortunately* [39] he is not a murderer with regrets and remorse but only a man who has come very close to being one. He is protected from or relieved of some moral blame by the collapse of the ontological matrix required for the completion of his murderous intent. X's moral blameworthiness under 15(a) must, nevertheless, be substantially greater than it is under 14, no matter how we construe X's motives in 14. There is an incremental rise in X's blameworthiness as we move from the interpretation of 14 as motivated by X's respect for law to 14 as motivated by prudence. In 14 *his* being and doing are largely decisive; but in 15 his intended action is truncated by the collapse of the larger ontological matrix for which X has far less responsibility. Since X has far less to do with the truncation of his action in 15 than with his own termination of his action in 14, there is no basis for reducing his moral blameworthiness in 15(b) at all, or in 15(a) more than slightly in so far as it is based upon elements of voluntary responsibility. But X's blameworthiness based on elements of status responsibility is not substantially greater in 15 than in 14, though it rises sharply in 16.

In 16, X's act is fulfilled, completely realized. His intention and volition are fully and accurately expressed in and supported by the ontological matrix which includes his brother's act of eating and digesting and the poison's causal efficacy. X would not and could not be a murderer without the support of this or some other matrix over which he has no control. In 16 there is no increment of intention, determination, or voluntariness in X's action over what was present in 15(b); the increase in his moral blameworthiness in 16 over 15(b) must come therefore from an increase in his status or ontological responsibility. The fit of intention and volition to the ontological matrix is perfect: the full action is expressed in this absence of disrelation between

39. I use the word "fortunately" in order to assert again the shocking fact that luck, accident, or fortune play important and partially determining roles in the shaping, no less than in the assessing, of moral responsibility.

intention and occurrence, between volition and being. The full action is morally imputed to X because the person of X is so transparently present in this fusion of doing and being.

Another sort of disrelationship between action and intention is introduced by 17 (for the sake of brevity we will concentrate on 17(b)). Here we observe the extension of an action beyond the limits intended by and directly influenced by the agent. We may suppose that X had no relatives or friends in the city other than his mother and brother; we may likewise suppose that neither the mother nor the brother had friends in the city; and finally, we may suppose that X put his mother on a train to a distant city on the very day the action took place. Now X's brother cannot be blamed for sharing with his mother a meal that he believed to be wholesome. He was neither purposive, knowing, reckless, nor negligent in feeding her the poisoned eggs. But what shall we say about X?

We may assume that X was intensely (though quite properly and non-Freudianly) fond of his mother; we may even trace part of X's hostility toward his brother to their competition for her affection. Under these quite reasonable suppositions we see that X is as free from moral blame for the death of his mother as his brother is—if we hold to the view that moral offenses are voluntary. X did not intend to kill his mother any more than his brother did. X did not know that his mother was in even the slightest danger of being killed. Far from being negligent or reckless, he took the precaution of recalling that he had put her on the train to another city and watched the train pull out only a couple of hours before his brother arrived. X was not purposive, knowing, reckless, or negligent in so far as the poisoning of his mother was concerned. It makes no sense to say that killing his mother was his voluntary act.

At this point we must be clear about two facts: first, we must know that X is guilty of crime in 17(b); second, we know that he is morally blameworthy in 17(b). These facts are not in doubt. The problem is: what are the essential characteristics of a theory of moral responsibility that can account for these facts?

In law and morals the problem has usually been solved on the basis of a patently inappropriate application of the theory of voluntary responsibility. In this case, for instance, it may be said that X intentionally and voluntarily (with *mens rea*) served poisoned eggs to a human being in order to kill him. On the basis of this voluntary action—but by the use of a theory of status responsibility—X will be held responsible for the consequences of his illegal and immoral voluntary act, even though these consequences run counter to X's intentions and desires. Sometimes, of course, the law limits the criminal's responsibility to the foreseeable consequences of his act or to those consequences that a reasonable man in his position would have foreseen. (The law is not particularly troubled by the fact that a reasonable man would not be in the criminal's position or, if he were, would no longer be reasonable.) But I feel sure that most lawyers, jurymen, and moralists would hold X morally and criminally responsible for the extension of his action in 17(b), despite the fact that X did not intend what happened, nor could he nor any reasonable man have foreseen these consequences. X would be blamed despite the fact that it would be morally objectionable to blame him on the basis of a reasonable and consistent application of the view that moral offenses must be voluntary.[40]

I firmly believe that X is responsible and blameworthy for what happened in 17. But the justification for holding X responsible must be on grounds of his status or ontological responsibility. X, like all persons, is dependent in action upon a matrix which may truncate, fulfill, or extend his action in such a way that his action is concretized so that it may coincide with or be in disrelation to his plan or intention. But the action—as it comes to be, whether in or out of accord with his intention and voli-

40. In law one might apply the fiction of comparable intent; such a move is, of course, patently inadequate. Legal fictions are simply *ad hoc* corrections to defective legal theories.

tion—is his action. There is no basis for crediting him with his virtuous actions in perfect relation to his intention, unless his person and responsibility are enlarged to include elements of the ontological matrix over which he has at best limited control. Indeed, the ontological matrix is a part of his own person, no matter how narrowly he defines it. His volition is never independent of the limiting conditions of his intelligence, knowledge, imagination, emotionality, and energy. Limit the person to what is under his voluntary control, and he disappears without trace along with his volition. If we acknowledge a sufficient number of ontological conditions, over which X has no voluntary control, to account for the existence of X and his capacity to act voluntarily, we have already acknowledged to a significant degree his moral responsibility for what he is no less than for what he does.

We extend this basic point only to a minor degree in recognizing the moral blameworthiness of X for *being* the man who voluntarily contributed to the situation in 13 that was transformed *without* his knowledge, intention, recklessness, or negligence— that is, *without* his voluntary participation—into the situation at 17(b). In 17(b) his voluntary act of killing his brother has been cut short prior to fulfillment. But in 17(b), X has the being or status of a murderer. He is the man who bears the volitional guilt of his brother's murder without the ontological guilt, and he is the man who bears the ontological guilt of his mother's death without the volitional guilt.[41]

I think the line of reasoning used by the court in *Suvada vs. White Motor Company et al.* contains the elements of status responsibility infused with a trace of prior but not present voluntary responsibility and *mens rea* that I have in mind. X created the risk of poisoning someone other than his brother—however slight, non-negligent, and non-reckless that risk might be—in

---

41. By recognizing X's mixed responsibility, we can assess the full quality of his mother's death, despite the fact that we lack the precise noun, adjective, or adverb to articulate its quality. Her death was not quite a murder, but neither was it mere manslaughter; certainly it was not accidental homicide.

order to reap the benefits of his brother's death, just as the defendants in *Suvada* built, advertised, and sold for profit machinery which created an inadvertent risk. X would have gladly accepted moral praise for the philanthropic use of his brother's estate had he inherited it; being rich would have given him the ontological basis for certain moral virtues which might be lacking without the estate. The defendants in *Suvada* may be well respected for the philanthropy which rests on the ontological basis of their risk-creating manufacturing and selling.

The consequences of X's action in 13 are outlined in 17. X is responsible for 17. Number 17 describes his action, not because of anything he did at 17 but because he *is* at 17 the man who *did* what 13 describes. We find the person of X in 17 only because in 17 he *is* the same man whose person was expressed in 13. Status responsibility rather than voluntary responsibility justifies our blaming him for 17. But his status responsibility in 17 derives from his mixed responsibility in 13.

Before considering a serious objection which Hart might raise to this line of reasoning, let us consider the subtle responsibility of X's brother in 17(b). He is the man who gave the poison to his mother. His position is like that of the mother who takes thalidomide as a sleeping potion and gives birth to a deformed child, or of a man who kills the child that suddenly runs in front of his car. In thinking of his role in his mother's death, X's brother is not tortured, as the poor mother must be, with the thought that she bought her ease at the possible risk of harming her child. Nor is he bothered, as the unfortunate driver is, by the thought that, by participating in a vehicular civilization and doing little or nothing to improve the safety features of our streets or cars, he has run the risk of killing a child. There are no antecedents to X's brother's action which contain any traces of voluntary personal involvement—none that might have contributed to or colored his action in 17(b). His volitional innocence, and his good fortune perhaps, leave him in status innocence as well. It is a precarious innocence, however, that could be compromised by his having thought, "What a disgusting old lady," just before he handed her the eggs intended for him.

In offering my interpretation of the largely ontological basis rather than the voluntary basis of X's responsibility in 17, I have been troubled by an objection that Hart might reasonably raise. Suppose we were to ask X if he could establish the conditions which on Hart's view would excuse him from all moral blame in 17(b). X could certainly claim that 17(b) was completely unintentional in so far as he was concerned. But could X claim that he had taken every possible precaution? Would Hart say there was one obvious precaution X had deliberately ignored, namely the precaution of leaving the poison out of the eggs?

The objection looks formidable, but its plausibility actually rests on the details of 17 and not on the issues of responsibility. Suppose, for instance, that X's brother had been Adolf Hitler and that 17(b) took place in 1943. We might all agree that X was an unlucky hero, like Colonel Staufenberg, but could we fail to blame him, at least in some moderate degree, for his mother's death? When X takes upon himself the status of an assassin, as in 13 (assuming that the brother is Hitler), he establishes the ontological basis for his personal, moral involvement in what follows, even though it is not a voluntary or intentional or negligent consequent of his action in 13.

Perhaps the point can be seen with greater force if we consider a continuum in which the agent's immediate action is not morally or legally wrong or blameworthy. Following the conventional views of contemporary Americans and Europeans, let us suppose (a) that sexual intercourse between consenting adults of the opposite sexes is not morally offensive or blameworthy, and (b) that it is morally offensive and blameworthy to be the parent of a bastard child. If we take these moral suppositions for granted, let us consider the following alternative situations in which—unless otherwise noted—Y is a healthy, young unmarried woman:

1. Y is raped and becomes pregnant.

2. Y is so seriously ill that advanced pregnancy would be fatal; she takes every contraceptive precaution but becomes pregnant.

3. Y has no idea what causes babies, has intercourse without being aware of the possible consequences and becomes pregnant.

4. Y, with full knowledge of the cause of pregnancy, takes all contraceptive precautions, has intercourse, and becomes pregnant.

5. Y, with full knowledge, is negligent in the use of contraceptives and becomes pregnant.

6. Y, with full knowledge but in the ecstasy of love, uses no contraceptive and becomes pregnant.

7. Y, with full knowledge, uses no contraceptive because of religious scruples and becomes pregnant.

8. Y, with full knowledge, complete self-control, and no scruples against contraceptive methods, does not use them and becomes pregnant, not caring one way or the other.

This series is ordered on a continuum of undiminished or increasing volition as we move from involuntary to clearly voluntary action, without extending the continuum to include any actions which involve the intention to become pregnant.

Accordingly, Y never intends to become pregnant, and in situations 1 through 4 she is neither reckless nor negligent. Can she not claim then that, in so far as the first four situations are concerned, her action is morally blameless and unintentional, and that she took every possible precaution?

Suppose Hart were to reply that she is confused about the action which requires justification. She intentionally had intercourse in all but the first situation. But if she did not provoke the rapist, she is not to blame for anything in 1. And since she took every precaution to avoid becoming an unwed mother, she has done nothing wrong in 2, 3, and 4, for there is nothing mor-

ally blameworthy, *ex hypothesi,* about intercourse. At this point
Y will have to say, "But Professor Hart, I am pregnant. As things
stand now I shall become morally blameworthy for being the
mother of a bastard child."

How is Hart to cope with this situation on his theory of the
voluntary character of moral offenses? The intercourse is not
wrong, and on the voluntary theory of action and responsibility
there is no act of becoming pregnant or of growing a baby. One
does not become pregnant voluntarily or voluntarily develop a
child in the womb. Hence, on this theory there is no way one
can be morally blameworthy for becoming pregant or producing
a child except as a consequence of voluntary intercourse. But
since we hold that intercourse is not wrong, we must then
acknowledge the absence of any wrongdoing if pregnancy follows when all precautions have been taken. One cannot admit
that intercourse is morally right *per se* and then argue that in
order to take all precautions against pregnancy one must refrain
from intercourse. When one recognizes that intercourse is morally
acceptable, he is committed on the voluntary theory to withhold-
ing moral blame for pregnancy if all precautions short of sexual
abstinence have been taken. On Hart's theory we have the absurd
consequence that no moral blame can attach to having a baby
out of wedlock provided it was not planned and all precautions
short of abstinence were observed.

The absurdity is even more glaring with regard to the moral
blameworthiness of fathers who have children out of wedlock.
Impregnating, like being impregnated, may be a highly personal
act. But it can be so only on a view that takes seriously the notion
of an organic mode of personal action and organic intentionality.
Procreation cannot even be accomplished physically by the
father; so far as he is concerned, it is an act by proxy, and the
proxy is a germ cell completely detached from his body. If he
has any effective intent in procreation beyond intercourse, it is
by means of the organic intention of his proxy. To speak of his
procreating voluntarily makes sense on an enlarged view of
voluntarism which absorbs a considerable portion of Bergsonian

organistic intention. But this Bergsonian view is not compatible with Hart's metaphysical asceticism. On his view the man who has intercourse without intending to have a child, and who sees to it that proper contraception is used, must be free of all moral blame in fathering a bastard child.

Further evidence for the theory of responsibility I am urging is that it does not fall into this absurdity with regard either to Y or her male partner. On my view it is primarily the being of the father and the mother, not their voluntary act of intercourse, that provides the basis of their parental obligations and their blameworthiness for being parents out of wedlock. Like X in 13 and 17(b), the parent of a bastard child is responsible for being the person who set in motion factors that culminate in the development and birth of the child. There is a far greater degree of personal involvement in this situation, however, because of the organic expression of personality that is absent in the poisoned eggs. The personal agents of the voluntary act of intercourse are present in procreation, not as chemical or mechanical forces but as the living, organically intentional, fertilized egg with their personal genetic structure.

Both fathers and mothers must recognize and accept their responsibility for what they are, and for what they become as a consequence of what they are, even when there is no bond created either by intention or negligence that unifies what they are with what they become by reference to what they do.

Action broadly defined is that which binds past to present to future; it is the substance of personal duration. We destroy this bond or deny its existence by accepting a narrow, voluntaristic definition of action and responsibility, and we lose the continuity of the moral self. Kant's old problem of providing some basis for moral continuity in a self which is unqualified in volition, except as it qualifies itself through the voluntary action in every moment, will be our problem unless we accept the necessary minimum of status elements in our concept of moral obligation and responsibility.

The adherents of voluntary responsibility cannot evade these difficulties by holding that Y, after becoming pregnant, is responsible only for doing whatever is necessary to avoid having the child out of wedlock—by holding, that is, that Y is excused from all moral blame if she makes every effort either to have an abortion or get married. It would be difficult to justify abortion in any but the first or second instances, and even the first case poses some problems if one recognizes intrinsic value in human life.[42] Nor is the alternative of marriage universally satisfactory: it may be impossible for Y to marry, or any possible marriage might be morally more objectionable than the offense of having the child out of wedlock. The father may have died; Y may conclude after careful deliberation that the father or any man whom she could marry would exert a morally corrupting influence on the child; or Y or the father may conclude that to marry would be so destructive of career to which an obligation is also owed that it is morally better to accept the blame for having the child out of wedlock without compounding moral offense by an immoral marriage. However we turn the problem around, there is no way of establishing the moral responsibility of Y or her partner for the unintended consequences of their non-negligent intercourse, without supplementing the voluntary theory of responsibility by the introduction of status elements. Yet there is no way of denying their responsibility without abandoning our initial premise that it is morally wrong to have a bastard child.[43]

But suppose we take the argument one step further. Let us drop the supposition that it is wrong to be the parent of a bastard child—a dubious supposition despite its conventional support—

42. I suppose it can be argued that the neglect and abuse to which a bastard child is often subjected can be avoided by killing the child. The legitimacy of the argument might be more apparent, however, were it urged by the illegitimates. My experience is that natural-born bastards are just about as intent on living as self-made ones.

43. The degree of Y's status responsibility in having a child out of wedlock will vary in the situations from 5 to 8 according to the degree of voluntariness and the extent of negligence or recklessness in the use of contraceptive devices in her actions. These further considerations are left to the reader.

and hold instead merely that it is wrong to be voluntarily, recklessly, or negligently the parent of a child for which reasonably adequate care and provision has not been and cannot be made. With this revision, what shall we say of the expectant mother who has not been negligent or reckless in the use of contraceptives and who was reasonably confident of their adequacy? If moral offenses must be voluntary, she can be morally responsible only for future voluntary acts—for example, the neglect of her developing child. But our expectant mother may insist: "Since I am not voluntarily (or morally) responsible for being pregnant, I refuse to alter my life because of this fact. And if I am blamed because I refuse to care for myself or my child, those who blame me must blame me in violation of Hart's principle that moral offenses are essentially voluntary. Those who blame me must blame me for refusing to meet a standard which, though appropriate to voluntarily expectant mothers, is not appropriate to an involuntarily pregnant woman like me. On the voluntary conception of moral responsibility, I am no more obligated to care for my child than to care for a wart on my nose."

I assume that we agree that this pregnant woman has an obligation to care for the child she is carrying. But what reply can we make to her statement? If the thesis that moral offenses must be voluntary is sound, and if (having done her best to avoid pregnancy) she is not voluntarily pregnant, how can she be blamed morally for failing to meet a standard appropriate to her actual status (which she tried to avoid) but totally inappropriate to a non-pregnant status (which she voluntarily but ineffectually chose)? In terms of the status and conditions she voluntarily chose, she is not required to care for her developing child. But because of a change in her status—through no choice or fault of her own—she is now obligated to care for it. She can claim, on the basis of the voluntary thesis, that since she did not choose the condition on which the new obligation is based, she does not choose to violate that obligation. Admittedly, she chooses to *act* in violation of the obligation to care for the child. But since she did not choose the condition on which the obligation depends, she does not choose to *violate* the *obligation;* hence, she violates no moral rule binding on her under the voluntary thesis.

Here we confront an essential feature of moral obligation which the voluntary thesis does not adequately account for— namely, moral obligation may obtain whether or not it is chosen. Moral obligation obtains according to the nature and the situations of persons. While it is true that one's obligation may be changed by the degree to which he has voluntarily altered his nature or his situation (through education, recklessness, or contract, for examples), moral obligation normatively regulates his action whether his nature and condition are within his voluntary control or not.

In short, the context in which he is held to account for his voluntary actions (which are by no means purely voluntary but which, as I have shown, contain status elements) is an involuntary, necessary one. And if, in accordance with the voluntary thesis, one could excuse himself from an offending action by showing that he could not help it, it should be possible always to excuse oneself whenever he finds that he is of a nature or in a situation contrary to his voluntary control. For one can say, "I cannot help being in this situation, and if I were not in this situation, my offending conduct—even if voluntary—would not offend."

The fundamental basis of moral obligation is found in the nature and situation of the agent. These status elements are preconditions of the possibility of moral offense. And these preconditions are the consequences of prior voluntary actions only in some, but by no means in all, instances. The status elements, which define the agent's obligations, often arise without help from and despite the intentions of the agent; and they can never result merely from his voluntary choice. Hence, either we must abandon moral obligation as meaningless or we must abandon the voluntary thesis. Accepting the latter alternative, we hold (returning to our example) that the expectant mother is liable to judgment by an involuntarily imposed standard because she is in an involuntarily contracted condition of pregnancy. And we hold that her offense, if she violates the duty to care for herself and her baby, is not an *essentially* voluntary offense, because it is defined by a standard which is involuntarily imposed on the basis of her involuntarily established condition.

The foundation of moral obligation (and therefore of moral offense) in facticity, or status, is fundamental. I may be privileged to argue that since I did not choose my skin color, I will alter it; or that since I do not voluntarily have a crooked nose, I will have it bobbed. But I cannot argue that since I did not choose my sex, I will have it changed; [44] or that since I did not choose to become a father, I will refuse to support my child. Moral obligations impose restrictions on my conduct because of my nature and my situation, even if neither is a product of my voluntary choice.

Hart says, at the conclusion of the quotation we have been examining, "in morals, 'I could not help it' is always an excuse, and moral obligation would be altogether different from what it is if the moral 'ought' did not in this sense imply 'can.'" We have already seen the confusion and artificiality involved in trying to show that "I could not help it," and I have argued that there are many situations in which "I could not help it" is not an excuse. Consequently, I have just argued that Hart's thesis of the volun-

44. See *Anonymous vs. Weiner*, 50 Misc. 2d 380, 270 N.Y.S. 2d 319 (Sup. Ct. 1966). In this case the petitioner brought suit to have the official record showing his sex altered to correspond with the results of a medical operation which changed it. See also Dr. Harry Benjamin's *The Transsexual Phenomenon* for a medical discussion and defense of the right to alter one's sex. But Dr. Benjamin supports surgical transformation of sex in only very unusual situations where there is a serious psychological disturbance in gender role and gender orientation. See also H. Benjamin, "Clinical Aspects of Transsexualism in Male and Female," *American Journal of Psychotherapy*, XVIII, No. 3 (July 1964), 458-469, and "Nature and Management of Transsexualism: With a Report from Thirty-One Operated Cases," *Western Journal of Surgery, Obstetrics, and Gynecology*, LXXII (March-April 1964), 105-111.

tary character of moral offenses itself distorts the meaning of moral obligation. But the question remains whether, in rejecting the claim that "I could not help it" is always an excuse, we have transformed moral obligation into something altogether different from what it is.

Two things must be said. First, even if we radically change the view of obligation defended by Hart, it does not follow that we shall alter the character of moral obligation—we may merely articulate its nature more precisely. This is not necessarily a logical issue about the meanings of words, despite the fact that Hart, and linguistic philosophers generally, so regard it. Second, in any case I have not altogether transformed the character of moral obligation, for I have tried to present and defend the view that "I could not help it"—though not always an excuse—would in many circumstances excuse one from the most severe degree of moral blame. One is excused from the degree of moral blame appropriate in cases of consciously voluntary wrongdoing, provided one can show that what he did was not fully voluntary. On this point the traditional voluntaristic position on moral obligation is not altered.

But I have also argued that the application of ethical rules and principles in the absence of a theory of ethics containing (1) a concept of responsibility which provides for a continuum of increasing and decreasing status and voluntary elements, and (2) a system of substantive values to overcome the abstractness of formalism, will never sustain a notion of moral obligation or responsibility adequate to account for the subtle but extensive range of guilt and innocence, virtue and vice, praise and blame in personal action. Without these factors no notion of moral obligation or responsibility can be adequate to account for the fundamental moral virtue of accepting one's being or the fundamental moral offense of refusing to do so. And it is important to note that a part of the virtue of accepting one's being lies in the acceptance of one's partial blameworthiness for what he is.

Theories like Hart's or Kant's, which restrict responsibility to voluntary conscious acts and limit moral offenses to consciously intended or reckless acts in violation of principles or rules, can never give content or substance to moral action or to the moral person. Human choice is not something isolated from the choosing person. Rather, it is a thoroughly organic mode of self-expression and self-discovery. There are gradations of choice and degrees of voluntariness; but at every instant, even in those acts of purest, freest, most voluntary choice, choice depends upon the being of the person and the matrix of his action, both of which contribute to the moral quality of the person and his action, even though neither is to any great extent subject to his voluntary control. We shall never find a person in his action unless his doing is his being, or at least a part of it. We have neither understanding of man nor a basis for moral and legal judgment of him unless we recognize the human person as a unity of being and doing. This cannot be done without partially reshaping the concepts of moral obligation and responsibility in order to free them of the limitations of simplistic voluntarism. We must reshape the concept of responsibility and the notions of intention, awareness, and choice so that they apply in varying degrees over the entire range of personal existence. When this reshaping is done, we shall have a better understanding of moral obligation and moral and criminal responsibility.

The voluntary conception of moral obligation and responsibility appropriately characterizes maximally personal actions. But an adequate conception must appropriately characterize *all* degrees and kinds of personal action from the most voluntary to the least voluntary. For this a theory of responsibility is required in which there is a fusion of status or ontological and voluntary elements, and in which moral obligation is understood as applying not merely to the volition but to the being of each person.

Such a theory, when fully developed, will make necessary the reformulation of the judge's instructions to jurors in criminal cases. Jurors will no longer be asked to say "Guilty" or "Not guilty." Rather, they will be asked to find from among four to eight clearly formulated types of personal action, the type most nearly descriptive of the behavior of the accused. And on the basis of the jury's finding of the being-and-doing of the accused, a revised criminal code will prescribe punishment, treatment, or release. Throughout, however, a defendant in a criminal case will enjoy full protection of legal counsel and the procedural guarantees of the criminal law. For the recognition, in such a theory, of an attenuated element of *mens rea* and *actus reus* in the so-called status crimes of drug addiction, chronic alcoholism, and so on, will preclude the withering away of the criminal law and the abandonment of those accused of such crimes to the less carefully controlled and perhaps less just procedures of medical boards.

When this theory is fully developed, it will account for the moral virtue of accepting one's being and the moral blameworthiness of one's refusal to do so. It will make clear, moreover, that part of the virtue of accepting one's being lies in the acceptance of one's blameworthiness for what he is. We may even be able to understand the doctrine of original sin ("In Adam's fall we sinned all"), as well as Oedipus' ultimate self-condemnation expressed in Sophocles' play by his act of blinding himself.

Maurice Natanson

ALIENATION AND SOCIAL ROLE

When illustration is taken as problematic, illustrations become fugitive to discourse. My present concern is with certain structural features underlying role-taking and not with examples of roles or the empirics of role-taking. Part of the difficulty in getting at structure in this context is that formal sociological features of actual roles and role-taking may divert the attention of the investigator from their phenomenological counterparts. To avoid a confusion of levels of analysis, I would like to set forth, as directly as I can, what I take to be the problem at issue here and the line of attack I propose to follow.

Every social role taken presupposes role-taking on the part of the actor. But role-taking transcends its own exemplifications, for the specific acts that comprise the role-taking on any given occasion may be seen as manifestations of a more primordial activity which we may refer to as the intentionality of role-taking. I propose to term this last "role-action." We have, then, social role as a complex of societally formed requirements for undertaking and performing patterned action in the social world; role-taking as the dynamics for effecting and carrying out such roles in actual practice; and role-action as the intentional dimen-

sion underlying role-taking. Illustrations for roles and role-taking
are manifest in experience as well as in sociological literature but
are, in principle, recalcitrant to the domain of role-action. Illumi-
nation here must be accomplished by indirect lighting. The problem at issue is to understand something of the nature of role-action, to display at least some of its essential features, and to
establish some of the lines of relationship between role-action
and role-taking. What helps to cut this task down to possibly
manageable proportions is the particular aspect of role theory
that interests us here: its connection with the problem of social
alienation. Again some delimitation is necessary.

There are at least four distinctively different though related
aspects of the general theme of alienation: first, the sense, feeling, or disposition of the individual's estrangement, with psychological variants of the loss of identity or authentic being,
depersonalization, and existential fragmentation; second, the
Marxian theme of the divorce between the worker and the meaning of his work, with the resultant loss of the object created in
work by the creating subject, and the subject in turn reified into
a thing-like commodity; third, the sense of historical dislocation
in terms of which societal purposiveness and the meaning of
community are abortive and crippled remainders or fractions of
their past fulfillments or essential possibilities; fourth, a fissure
in religious consciousness, marked by claims and announcements
of our living in a post-Christian age, in a world in which religion,
if not God, is dead. Urgent and vibrant as all of these dimensions
of alienation are, none of them concerns us here. Rather, we must
turn to a fifth thematic meaning: alienation as a structural deformation of sociality. We shall be interested not in the feeling
or awareness of being alienated but in a grounding condition of
social order. The moment of social structure at which we shall
locate alienation in this sense is in the general theory of social
role and, more specifically, in the aspect of social role we have
already indicated: the intentionality of role-taking. That feature
of sociality exhibiting the danger of structural deformation (and,

hopefully, enabling us to explain more fully the meaning of that deformation) is, then, role-action. Conjoined in this way, alienation and intentionality are noetic correlates which undergird and constitute roles and role-taking. They point to the possibility rather than the instantiation of social action.

Since our problems are this side of a sociology or social psychology of alienation and roles, it is fitting to approach them by way of a reconstruction of their elements. I am going to display some of these architectonic features of role-action and consider the nature of their alteration, transformation, and possible decomposition. The projected reconstruction is conceived as a map of structural conditions for the possibility of the happening of social action; accordingly, it may be taken as an exercise in subjunctive cartography. I am searching for a segment or slice of the intentionality of role-taking which may serve as a model for constitutive development, which would reveal a history of the sedimentation of meaning packed into social action. The starting point for such an *Aufbau* will be a characterization of some of the elements comprising role-action.

Five intentional *a prioris* present themselves for consideration: first, an openness or sheer capacity for role-taking, which we may term the "assumption of power"; second, the possibility of returning to role-taking, which we shall call the "assumption of recourse"; third, the regaining of role-taking in normalized or essentially familiar form, and we may call this the "assumption of uniformity"; fourth, the expectation that role-taking will operate in a texture or ambience characteristic to the individual, which may be termed the "assumption of recognition"; and fifth, the anticipation of a falling back from role-taking, which we shall call the "assumption of release." Each of these requires further explanation.

1. The Assumption of Power: An openness for role-taking may be understood as intending the routine flow of experience in mundane reality as having bounds or limits which curtail or suspend a given aspect of awareness and permit the "taking up" of

a new and different activity whose commencement, flow, and terminus lie within the general domain of naive awareness. A given act of role-taking then presupposes the "letting-be" or willingness of the agent to demarcate a segment of his field of social action as role-involved or role-committed. Within a spread of action, then, the assumption of power stakes out a claim that so much of what is available be given to role-taking. Since we are not starting with role-taking as already given but with the structural conditions for such givenness—with role-action—we may say that intending role-taking constitutes the very establishment of periods or pauses in the course of naive experience which permit the agent to assume roles. Further, the originary character of naive experience bears the impress of such periodic organization: naive experience is already segmented into intervals available for role-taking.

2. The Assumption of Recourse: Moving along the same line of analysis, we may say that not only is it possible to have role-taking but the role-taker can return to his role-taking. The period available for the assumption of the role is matched by a hypothetical reservation: role-taking is not only possible, it is repeatable, and the role-taker may return to it. The intending of role-taking as structuring social action includes the intending of essential repeatability. The assumption of power then points to the assumption of recourse, for the very availability of role-taking is intended as free of the occasions of its operation. Repeatability is not understood here in a temporal sense. It is not that later in a role-taking career role-taking will again arise. Rather, role-taking itself, in its operative character, intends an "againness," a continuity which protends repetitiveness. The sedimentation of the meaning of assumption of power begins to show itself in the element of recourse: for there to be an openness to role-taking is for there to be an openness to re-performance.

3. The Assumption of Uniformity: Openness and againness point to the essential sameness of the role-taking thematically at issue. The uniformity of the action is intended as regainable in

familiar form, i.e., the sameness is not a formal identity but a recognizable style built out of acts which in effect establish a claim: the role-taking done is continuous in character with the role-taking which may later be done. Re-performance is then more than an instancing of role-taking; it is a renewal of the *kind* of action intended, a sustaining of the intentional signification originally involved in this root of social action. Again, a sedimentation of meaning informs this element of role-action. Recourse, essential againness in role-taking, qualifies the intending of the role-taking to be regained as familiar. Because familiarity is not already presupposed at this stage of reconstruction, it may be suggested that the *a priori* of familiarity is constituted in the intentionality of recourse: the againness of re-performability includes the taking of the "again" as essentially recognizable. This leads to the fourth element.

4. The Assumption of Recognition: Uniformity translates into generalized terms. Sameness and againness are available for any role-taking activity. But there is the problem of the connection or relationship between the role-taking the actor expresses in his action and *his* role-taking, i.e., the particular or peculiar way in which role-taking is familiar to him as *his*. The assumption of recognition is that element of role-action that establishes the possibility of the actor becoming acclimatized to the idiosyncratic texture of his action. Intending role-taking as recognizable by the actor means acknowledging the possibility of such recognition as a constitutive feature of role-action. The moment of intention already includes what is intended as possibly peculiar in style to the actor. Sedimented in the structure of recognition is the assumption of recourse as well as uniformity as bound to the structural perseverance of the actor in role-taking, the subject for whom againness and sameness are themselves repeatables in the mode of familiarity and the integrity of an individual ambience.

5. The Assumption of Release: Role-taking is an activity built on demarcations. The naive course of experience implicitly splits

itself into segments, times, periods, stretches, intervals, and spans through which social action enunciates itself as a coherent enterprise. Role-taking presupposes an *a priori* of deliverance from any unit in the career of role-performance. The playing of a role, in these terms, is rendered possible by virtue of concluding the role performance and returning to the flow of socially "neutral" awareness. Coeval with the intending of role-taking is the intending of release from such activity in the form of a falling back from or a withdrawal from its routine. Role-taking, then, is an affair of intervals, a surging up of activity within limits announced by a "to-be-ended" or a "to-be-completed," or at least a "to-be-halted" for some time being. Our final element bears the sedimentation of meaning intended in the rest. A release from role-taking means acceptance of its starting point in the assumption of power, for that original acknowledgment of the limitation of activity can only be understood as protending a return of the role-taker from his social engagement.

Taken together, the elements show the intentional contours of role-action. In their unity they reveal the stages of the reconstruction of role-taking. A statement of that unity is now possible, but I would like to try it in language that does more than repeat the terminology already employed or extends the distinctions already drawn. Here then is a summary history of the elements.

Social action has a periodic cast. The routine of mundane existence is built up out of portions of experience which have discernible termini. Start and end are labels for the reaches of the periods into which existence is divided. Role-taking is possible because social action is constituted as open to the initiation of limits. And the process of limitation makes possible a continual return to the limitation effected—a return, furthermore, to the same mode of determination. That mode, in turn, shows itself as intimately known by the actor and promises, finally, that the terminus of action will be reached. Transposed into the language of the role-taker, role-taking presupposes that there is a determinate role to be taken, that the role once taken can be taken again, that taking it again yields the same role, that the same role is performable in the role-taker's own way, and finally, that the role-taker will, at last, be relieved from the duties of the role. This simpler form of statement is, unfortunately, at the expense of a fundamental change from the perspective of role-action to that of role-taking. A more lucid account of role-taking can indeed be given than of role-action, precisely because examples of the former can easily be exploited, whereas the intentionality underlying those examples cannot itself be exemplified. At best a parallel of sorts is possible. Let us say that the language of the role-taker and of role-taking may serve as a clue to the intentional correlates they presuppose. Thus the assumption of power establishes the signification of "role-to-be-taken" and the assumption of release grounds the meaning of "role-completed." The sedimentation of meaning characteristic of the career of role-action is that of the carrying forward of intentions, each of which washes up against the shores of the others, carrying back some surface matter while leaving its own characteristic deposit.

Now it is possible to reverse the direction and line of our inquiry and ask whether the elements of our reconstruction of role-action can suffer fundamental alteration or decomposition. The *a prioris* of role-taking are not presented here as static eternals; they are rather to be understood as subject to transformation and, indeed, as immanently confronted with the threat of decay. At this point we meet with the problem of alienation, interpreted as a fundamental deformation of sociality. In sum, alienation is the danger of breakdown of role-action. We term it noetic destruction. It is now possible to see it at work in connection with the elements we have presented. The major consideration is the wrenching or failure of the intentional structure of role-action by limitation of the abstractive capacity essential to and definitive of role-taking. The weakening or disruption of the abstractive power can be seen in each of the elements of the reconstruction, once the question is raised of what would be involved in role-taking if any one of the elements of role-action were negated. A quick glance in this pathological direction is possible.

A denial of the assumption of power would mean the loss of the capacity to enter into roles at all. "Entering-into" would emerge as a damaged notion, for the segments or places we ordinarily take for granted as the loci of role-taking would be sealed off into a seamless, interval-less flux. A denial of the assumption of recourse would wreck the building up of projects by way of role-taking, for a role once taken would be lost to a progressive building up of interpretive possibilities in the life of the role-taker. With the root cancellation of recourse, any role-taking would be an innovation stamped as unique, underivative, and without significance for future undertakings. Similarly, the loss of uniformity would mean an incapacity to "do-again-in-the-same-way." Even if repetition in role-taking were possible, that which was repeated could not be grasped in its integral form. Furthermore, the failure of recognition would follow quickly, for to intend an instance of role-taking as *mine*, as peculiar to my way of doing things, presupposes the unity of role-action yielding again and again the same exemplary role-taking intimately bound to the same exemplary role-taker. To sever the intentionality of recognition is to make the self a stranger to its role-world. Finally, the impairment of release would result in what might be called role-flight, an acceleration of intentionality in which role-taking merged with a general release of consciousness from responsibility to arrive at judgments or conclusions. Though the apparent character of role-flight is a continuous stream of multivalent possibilities, none of which is attended to in a coherent and stabilized manner, the opposite diagnosis is in fact possible: the negation of release results in the stasis of consciousness, an immobilization of role-taking in which the elements are rendered so starkly unitary as to lose their very identity. A contrast of role-flight with the psychiatric description of "flight of ideas" is pertinent despite the obvious differences in levels of analysis. According to one account of the manic patient:

The *stream of thought* is more rapid than normal or is at least so experienced by the patient. The output of talk is incessant and shows the characteristic "flight of ideas," i.e., talk and thought are controlled less by sequence of meaning than by casual associations: similarity of sounds and words, rhyming, punning, and all sorts of word-play, as well as by associations from every sort of object in the environment, which readily engage the patient's distractible attention. The superficial impression of a great range of ideas is fallacious; their range is really very limited. . . . The patient is unable to keep to any topic, to finsh any task, even, in the more severe states, to finish a sentence; every object in the environment is no sooner perceived than it exerts, as it were, a forced response, which drives the patient on his headlong path.[1]

What we are calling noetic destruction is a correlate of such flight: the apparent rush it generates is in reality an inversion of identity created out of the incapacity of consciousness to sustain and integrate its intentional forces. When the order of elements comprising the structure of role-action suffers such immobilization, there results the deformation of sociality which can properly be called alienation.

What is deformed, basically, is the abstractive capacity involved in each of the elements of role-action no less than in the unity of their synthetic operation. Failure to abstract reflects a disorganization of the capacity to abstract, and it is that capacity I have been trying to locate and examine through the dynamics of role-action. Following the motif of mental pathology, I am tempted to refer to the noetic failure of role-taking as "social aphasia." It is unnecessary to apologize for the vulgarization of a technical term. In any case, there are some insults for which apology is out of the question. If the phrase has any justification, it is as a sign pointing to the phenomenon under study. To lose or to compromise the abstractive capacity underlying role-taking is to render the role-taker strange to his environs. That strangeness might be considered in terms of two questions: First, is the refusal to take up role-taking a choice open to the role-taker?

1. W. Mayer-Gross, Eliot Slater, and Martin Roth, *Clinical Psychiatry,* London, 1960, p. 213.

Second, is the failure to take up role-taking an automatic consequence of the damage done to the abstractive capacity presupposed in role-taking? It might be suggested that role-taking is still possible to the faulted role-taker as a device or artifice which he can manipulate. A mechanical playing out of roles can then reflect a mechanics of role-taking. To "choose" to fulfill the requirements of social roles when the actor is "role-injured" is to fluctuate in the strata of role-action. The positive failure of role-taking altogether is less one of the permutations of mental pathology than a root threat constantly underlying normal awareness in mundane existence. It is not the actualization of abstractive loss which measures the breakdown of role-action but the possibility of such failure. In these terms, role-taking is an achievement constantly given over and against the fundamental option of intentional refusal.

Understood in this way, role-action takes on a voluntative force and character. Yet will is granted to intentionality rather than to the individual role-taker. Setting aside the question of whether the voluntative dimension is then to be located in a transcendental ego as the matrix of intentional activity, it is possible to say that the role-taker in his role-taking inadvertently fulfills or may fail to fulfill the possibilities available to role-action. The role-taker and his role-taking become the screen through which the intentional correlates of role-action are filtered. Each manifestation or instancing of role-taking carries with it a transcendental signification pointing back to its appropriate source. Alienation then becomes the eruption of a transcendental failure in the midst of the mundane world. We find it as threat and circumstantial possibility rather than as actualized worldly resultant. Its most sinister form, perhaps, is the paralysis of the voluntative force which binds the elements of role-action together and gives them operative strength. Such paralysis must be thought of as the danger of loss rather than an existent disease. Following Erwin Straus, we may say that

"Dis-ease, the experience of being not at ease, leads to the discovery of the 'diseases,' "[2] but we may carry this line a step further and suggest that the possibility of "dis-ease" is an *a priori* which renders the actualization of sickness and suffering meaningful to the sufferer. Not paralysis but the threat of paralysis, not loss but the threat of loss is the gravamen of the charge of alienation. Roles, role-takers, and role-taking are the actualizations of the correlative possibilities grounded in the intentionality of role-action. Alienation affects the empiric surface of role-activity by virtue of its compelling threat to the *a prioris* of role-action. Whereas social accommodation is possible for the role-taker confronted with dangers to his role-taking, no such accommodation is possible, in principle, for role-action threatened internally. This claim requires substantiation.

In the sociology of roles and role-taking there is the phenomenon of "role distance," admirably presented by Erving Goffman [3] and defined as a separation between the individual and his role effected by the individual for handling a variety of situations in which, for a variety of reasons, he may not wish to be identified with his role. Thus, as Goffman shows, older children or adults on a merry-go-round exhibit role distance by either mocking their action (pretending that they are in great danger of falling off their horses) or ignoring the context of the action (the parent attending only to the small child he is watching over on the ride). Other illustrations involve the realm of the surgeon, his assistants, nurses, and so on, in the social setting of the operating room or the clinic, where establishing role-distance has a number of functions, including the maintenance of equilibrium and medical efficiency in the course of complex situations in which minor errors may lead to a disruption of the proceedings

2. Erwin W. Straus, *The Primary World of Senses: A Vindication of Sensory Experience,* trans. Jacob Needleman, New York, 1963, p. 291.
3. Erving Goffman, *Encounters: Two Studies in the Sociology of Interaction,* Indianapolis, 1961.

and trivial irritations to major blow-ups. Taking ineptitude by an intern as the occasion for a joke may be the chief surgeon's way of maintaining his own balance in the operation, just as self-derision for some fumbling of his own may be a way of heading off panic in his assistants. The establishment of role-distance is a means of manipulating role-taking for more or less specified and directed purposes. In the medical domain it is often a technique for the preservation of a sane self in the midst of otherwise unbearable suffering or incredible awkwardness. As a final example of role-distance I shall give my own rather than one of Goffman's descriptions: Imagine a scene in the orthopedic wing of a hospital in which a patient is being placed in a plaster cast which covers her body from neck to hips. Masses of plaster of Paris are being prepared by the assistants and applied to the patient, while the surgeon unwinds endless rolls of gauze and applies them to the partially dried parts of the cast. The patient cannot move, an enormous amount of plaster is being stuck onto her body, the assistants are like aproned fantasts from an old-time pie-throwing movie, and as the patient looks ahead to five months of encampment beneath this sticky monstrosity, the orthopedic surgeon does perhaps all he can do: as he winds the long gauze stripping onto the plastered body of the patient he sings: "Merrily We Roll Along."

Manipulation of role-taking is then not only possible but seemingly a human necessity in daily life, and, most important, it *can* be effected. When the role threatens to overrun the role-taker, when his role-taking becomes perilous in some way, he can accommodate by the establishment of role-distance. And of course there are other techniques for manipulating the form of role-taking. Overtly making the role-taking an articulate piece of social reality is a means of accommodation that has come to be called, appropriately enough, "the 'bit' technique." It has been described tersely:

> The "bit" technique goes like this: At all cost one must avoid the stigma of being too serious; to do so, you stick a self-mocking

label on any scene in which you might be caught displaying deep emotion. Thus: "I don't want to do the 'engaged-couple bit,' but . . ."; or "I don't want to do the 'expectant-father bit,' but . . ." If one further masks the scene with a heavy dose of banter, it finally becomes permissible to express feeling. Doing "bits" with people is the "in" way of establishing fellowship. They allow one to show affection while ridiculing it, to be sentimental while appearing tough.[4]

Accommodation by the role-taker in role-taking is not matched, however, by an equivalent strategy in role-action. I have suggested that in principle it cannot be. The reasons, most simply, are these: accommodation requires a delineation of the units to be separated or held off from each other, yet granting those units presupposes the intentionality of role-action; the establishment of a neutral zone or buffer between the role-taker and his role must involve the elements of uniformity and recognition in order to effect such zoning from one time to another in the career of role-taking—otherwise the utilization of these devices would be restricted to a unique event; and without recourse and release the role-taking could not achieve the generality and periodicity requisite to activity which itself forms part of the structure of the social world. In the end, role-distance is possible to role-taking because role-takers and their roles are epistemic facets of a mundane reality in which social action is presupposed as given to its participants as well as to its sociological observers, whereas distance from role-action is ruled out by virtue of the grounding function it has in establishing the meaningful unities of role, role-taker, and role-taking on whose structural shoulders sociality is carried. Role-distance assumes the self which chooses to deploy its social field in a particular manner; role-action constitutes and sustains the very meaning of field and the possibility of a choosing agent. It cannot divorce itself from itself, but it can suffer the phenomenon of deformation and so be confronted with the threat of alienation. Granting the very possibility of alienation

4. Martin Duberman, in a review in the *New York Times Book Review,* September 19, 1965, pp. 60-61.

in this sense is tantamount to acknowledging its legitimacy as a phenomenological problem.

In suggesting that alienation and social role have noetic relevance for and grounding in the intentionality of role-action, I have recommended a volitional conception of consciousness which expresses itself in the positive constitution of sociality over against the immanent threat of disruption and decomposition. Sociality, on this rather Manichean account, requires a victory or at least a favorable balance of power of the force of order over the force of decay.

John M. Anderson

THE SOURCE OF TRAGEDY

I. *Intuition of the Hero*

In a comedy or in a comic situation the world brings fortune, and man as a protagonist or as an appreciator accepts capricious events; he goes along with them come what may. We recall of a comedy a sense of the participation of the protagonists in the flow of events, that they were carried along in the rush; and, in consequence, we recall our own appreciative identification with the turns of the wheel of fortune. In comedy we are caught up by the other and we accept it; our awareness is not brought to focus upon the individuality of the protagonists or ourselves.

In the tragic sense of life or in a tragedy, by contrast, it is man who holds our attention as he brings himself to stand before the other. So much so, indeed, that we recall tragic art by the name of the hero who becomes the symbol for it. It is as if the fool, the simpleton, of a comedy were irradiated and transfigured so as to take the center of the tragic stage. It is as if man, having identified himself with and been engulfed by the rush of circumstance, had emerged from this baptism in the alien with a new and more significant character. We sense in tragedy the emergence of the hero, and, indeed, this emergence has been portrayed often as a kind of epiphany. In consequence, we commonly think of the tragic hero as a person of great stature, as one whose character develops sharply and violently. The understanding of man's character as heroic in this sense can lead to the heart of tragedy; but, as we shall see, the tragic hero may be presented in terms of almost pure misery and suffering, as he often is in modern works. Still, whatever he is, it is the hero who defines tragedy.

Let us begin our consideration of tragedy with some simple situations which are called tragic. Through an examination of these we may hope to fix an intuition of the tragic, to elicit some essential elements which may serve as a base line for a survey of more complex and more profound structures within tragedy. If we hear about a man diving into a raging torrent to try to rescue a drowning child and dying in the attempt, we commonly call the situation tragic. We say this in part, no doubt, because we see the terrible forces of nature conquering man. But we say it not only on this account but also because the man in this situation has acted so as to defy these forces. We see man as agent certain to be engulfed by insuperable natural odds, but plunging into them nonetheless. Thus we envision the agent as a hero who stands forth in the midst of a terrifying and hopeless situation.

In some situations, mildly tragic, the protagonist himself develops so as to stand forth, so that we see the situation as tragic through his eyes. This may happen, for example, when an old man, nearing the end of his life, looks back upon its course and reviews its turmoil and conflict, the hates and passions that filled it, its successes and failures. Of course this review may plunge him back into memories and a kind of vicarious reliving of his life, but it need not. At this time his will is quiet, he has little to live for, and in a sense his life is over. This may help him to see himself as having lived the terror of a human history, to see himself as having been caught up in the course of the world. He

may sum up his life, may manage to take an impartial and comprehensive view of the past, and to emerge through this a kind
of heroic figure.

In negative circumstances, in circumstances which entail his
destruction, the agent in a tragic situation stands forth refusing
to be conquered. He responds to negative circumstances by opposing them in a special way. His response is quite different
from that suggested by Whitman when he says:

> I make the poem of evil also—I commemorate that part also
> I am myself as much evil as good, and my nation is—
> And I say there is in fact no evil.

The ego in this poem is presented as identifying with the negative, as participating in the whole which includes it. This ego is
no tragic hero, for such a hero responds in a way suggested by
Herman Melville, when he says in *Moby Dick*:

> Delight is to him . . . a far, far upward and inward delight—
> who against the proud gods and commodores of this earth, ever
> stands forth, his own inexorable self.

Evidently part of what we commonly mean when we speak of a
tragic situation includes a hero who faces the hopelessness and
terror of the circumstances in which he finds himself. Indeed, our
sense of the stature of the hero is so deep that we may make too
much of it and take his greatness as the key to tragedy. We may
be led to conceive of the hero as transcending the circumstances
that destroy him. Yet this is hardly his significance.

To understand the significance of the hero in tragedy we must
note that his emergence takes place within the context of artistic
activity. Thus it is our artistic, selective response to the circumstance of a man's death in the effort to save a drowning child
which develops the tragic. The situation becomes a tragic one
as we interpret it to include negative elements, and as our comprehension of the agent's character develops so that we see him
standing forth. Thus not all old men, indeed only a few of them,
come at the end of their lives to stand in a tragic situation. For

to achieve this, they must come to see the course of their lives as taking place in the matrix of negative circumstances, as leading to inevitable death; and they must come to see themselves as emerging in this context as confronting life rather than participating in it. Their life achieves the dignity of tragedy, that is, in and through their interpretive responses to its literal events and circumstances. Thus it is a kind of artistic response to circumstances by a participant (or on the part of an observer) which develops or selects the patterns of a context having a tragic structure, and it is a mistake to suppose that any element in this structure—for example, the hero—can be understood apart from it. When we come to view a courageous man's attempt at rescue as the act of a hero, we also come to see those circumstances which destroy him as contributing to the development of the artistic patterns of tragedy. Similarly, the old man who sums up his life in a certain way enters, as he does so, a developing artistic context in which those circumstances that will destroy him are seen as contributing to this structure.

What is meant here may be seen more clearly, perhaps, where art is present in an explicit sense. Let us consider the autobiography of Henry Adams, a *book* which we read and to which we respond. Adams tells us he began his adult life with faith in human nature and faith in science. He believed that power could be harnessed for the benefit of man. As his life developed he found his illusions slipping away, his hopes for a political career and accomplishment disappearing, his aspirations to achieve the social expression of human values frustrated. He says he found the human mind stripped naked, vibrating in a void of shapeless energies and wasted and destroyed by them. He came to feel, he says, that in the nineteenth century there was nothing real but the expression of power without an aim. In a word, he came to view modern culture as opposing man, as the embodiment of forces and powers that contributed nothing to man and would end by destroying him. In the face of what he regarded as inevitable doom for mankind, Adams raises his voice to describe the situation as he sees it. He states and dwells upon this situation in an expression of despair; but it is an expression in which Adams emerges as the voice of this despair; it is an expression by the human voice echoing against blind power and chaos, brought to being in response to them.

The human voice he raises is the voice of the artist, and the artwork which his autobiography makes available to us comes to be out of this echo reflected from blind power and chaos. It is an artwork, that is, which Adams' tragic despair reveals as developing from its source in what is alien and opposed to man. We enter a different artwork because Adams depicts shapeless powers wasting man, and because the voice he raises in the face of them is the voice of an artist. In this way Adams opens the path into an artwork which clearly has its roots in the alien, which clearly develops in relation to this.

The point concerning the place of the artwork just made is exemplified in a much different way in the Chinese poet Bo Chui's "Last Poem." The translation by Arthur Waley reads:

> They have put my bed beside the unpainted screen;
> They have shifted my stove in front of the blue curtain.
> I listen to my grandchildren reading me a book;
> I watch the servants heating up my soup.
> With rapid pencil I answer the poems of friends,
> I feel in my pockets and pull out medicine-money.
> When this superintendence of trifling affairs is done,
> I lie back on my pillows and sleep with my face to the South.

The circumstances which oppose man are introduced into the account which the poem gives very obliquely and very indirectly. They are hinted at, suggested, by the activities of and circumstances surrounding an old man. But we hardly become aware of the significance of these activities and this situation until the last line of the poem tells us that Bo Chui faces death. Then the fact that a man has been brought to the end of his life, and that this end is unavoidable, is presented to us. And this fact confronts Bo Chui as well. It is to this fact that Bo Chui, as a figure in the poem, responds with human dignity: he composes himself and awaits his fate. But this is not quite all, for we know that Bo Chui responded to the circumstances confronting him in another way as well; he wrote his "Last Poem," as he calls it. The poem itself reflects the same sense of human dignity in the face of death as do the acts the poet depicts within the poem. The poem itself portrays the fact of human mortality with restraint, and it affords a mode of response to this fact which states man's dignity in the face of it. The poem, however, is a mode of response which has its source in those facts which condemn man; and it is a mode of response which incorporates them, which builds with them something in which man *may* participate.

In Adams' autobiography and in Bo Chui's final poem, the fact that the artist is depicting himself introduces an ambiguity which aids in developing the structure of the artwork as tragic. Thus the hero of the poem is depicted as confronting those unavoidable circumstances which will destroy him, and he takes his stand before them. At this level there is no resolution. But the hero is also the poet, and the poem develops in response to those circumstances which destroy the poet. He and we enter a different artwork, this poem, because Bo Chui raises his voice in the face of these circumstances, and his voice is the voice of an artist. Thus the poet opens a path into an artwork which has a source in what is alien to, what is other than man; an artwork which is sustained and developed in the terms of this alien source.

Before developing an analysis of the tragic, let us recapitulate. In the first place, in a tragedy negative elements are presented directly and with emphasis. They are depicted as so powerful as to engulf and destroy the protagonists. But, in the second place, there is a hero—that is, a man who develops in such a way as to stand forth confronting the negative circumstances, but whose development nonetheless reflects the sustaining contribution of these circumstances to the artwork. Thus, third, the

hero moves as a figure in an artwork which the negative circumstances support and sustain.

II. *Man's Fate*

Evidently, the protagonists in a tragedy find themselves caught
up in the coursing of events which destroy them. But if this is
an essential part of a tragedy, it is so because of a complex pattern which gives to the destruction its peculiarly tragic meaning.
As evidently as the negative circumstances in a tragedy destroy
the hero, there is art in which the destruction of the protagonists
takes place without raising the action to the level of tragedy.
Flaubert's *Madame Bovary* is a pivotal work in respect to this
point. In this novel Madame Bovary's circumstances and her
character produce her downfall; indeed, because of them her
end is inevitable. The circumstances are those of a mean pro-
vincial society, her character is no worse than that of many
middle-class people in that society; yet because of both she becomes a victim of circumstances, for she can neither escape them
nor change her own nature. The novel is impressive, but is it a
tragedy? Does the account of Madame Bovary's destruction have
the complex pattern that is found in tragedy? No doubt she is
destroyed because of what she is, but can we say that what she
is is different from the events that destroy her? Is her destruction
an inevitable accident, a mere consequence of the character
which she happens (accidentally) to have? In a word, is
Madame Bovary the heroine of a tragedy?

Madame Bovary is an instance of a trend in the style of modern and contemporary tragedies—if they are to be called that. It
seems possible to call Madame Bovary miserable and to recapitulate the pattern of her life by calling it pathetic. This is possible
in Hemingway's *A Farewell to Arms*, too, where the chief protagonist announces the intent of his story at the beginning of
his account of the retreat from Caporetto:

> I was always embarrassed by the words sacred, glorious, and sacrifice and the expression in vain. . . . We had heard them, . . . and had read them . . . now for a long time, and I had seen nothing sacred, and the things that were glorious had no glory and the sacrifices were like the stockyards at Chicago if nothing was done with the meat except to bury it.

Catherine's description of her own imminent death expresses the same tone:

> "I'm going to die," she said, then waited and said, "I hate it." . . . Then a little later, "I'm not afraid. I just hate it." . . . "Don't worry, darling, . . . I'm not a bit afraid. . . . It's just a dirty trick."

Painful and pitiful death, certainly. An account of misery and death, of course; but could this be an instance of the death of a tragic hero? And could the intent of the book be consistent with tragedy?

Madame Bovary, A Farewell to Arms, Ibsen's *Ghosts* are examples of modern and contemporary art which is often termed tragic art, but which seems to differ in structure from earlier tragedies. The evident difference between this art and earlier tragedies like *Oedipus the King* or *Hamlet* lies in the contrast between the character of the heroes. There is some justice in observing that earlier tragedies depict their heroes as great-souled, as splendid, as standing out amid the forces that destroy them, transcending them. By contrast, modern works are accounts of despair, of misery, even of human distress; accounts, moreover, which are not alleviated by the nobility of their heroes. Modern critics have noted that ancient tragedy deals almost exclusively with kings and courts, and they are wont to recall that Aristotle said, ". . . Tragedy is an imitation of persons who are above the common level. . . ." And they are led to conclude that only such works are tragedies; whereas modern works, although similar in structure, fail to be tragedies just because they fail to ennoble, fail to accord to their heroes that stature which somehow places them beyond the reach of those circumstances that destroy them.

Yet if one quotes Aristotle one must add to his comments about the character of the protagonists his statement that character is subsidiary in tragedy. He says, ". . . without action there cannot be a tragedy; there may be without character." And one should recall that the definition of tragedy which he gives does not refer to character. "Tragedy, then, is an imitation of an action that is serious, complete, and of a certain magnitude. . . . Tragedy is an imitation, not of men, but of an action and of life. . . ." Evidently, Aristotle found the core of tragedy elsewhere than in the grandeur of human character. And, indeed, while it is true that the nobility of many classical heroes has something to tell us about tragedy, it is also true that the misery and the pitiful deaths of ordinary men in modern works do not, of themselves, prevent them from *acting* in a tragedy nor from being the hero of it.

The heroes of modern tragedies may serve as the occasion for reconsidering the nature of tragedy and the place of the hero in it. Those modern heroes whose fate is syphilis, like Oswald Alving in *Ghosts* or the hero of Thomas Mann's *Dr. Faustus;* those modern heroes whose misery overcomes them so that they die without grandeur, or whose death is symbolic, a death of the soul and a kind of extermination of hope—these heroes may serve to reveal something of the structure of tragedy which we might otherwise miss or underemphasize. Very likely, the insight of the creators of modern tragedy is just this: they see the need of a different hero, because by emphasizing misery and suffering they may focus our attention upon a significance of tragedy which might otherwise be lost to us through the attraction of those splendid figures who are the heroes of older tragedies. But that to which they would recall us is to be found in the older tragedies as well. The essential movement of a tragedy is not the development of the character of a man so that we exult and glory in the greatness of his soul even at the moment of death. We may feel passionate admiration for the hero of a tragedy, of course; this may enhance the art, but it is not peculiar to tragedy. The essence of a tragic hero lies in the depiction of those activi-

ties through which man comes, as essentially human, to confront
what is alien to him, and in which he stands under the necessity
of accepting the contribution of the other in the face of his
human demands, though it destroy him.

A part of the significance of this distinction may be seen in the
ways in which the artist introduces negative elements into the
pattern of the artwork. First, he does this as forcibly as he can.
He never attenuates the horror and terror of the circumstances
he depicts in their effects on man. Thus, Sophocles in *Oedipus
the King* dwells upon parricide and incest, the two horrors which
engulf his hero. In *Hamlet* Shakespeare depicts the impact upon
a son of the fact that the murderer of his father is married to his
mother. In O'Neill's *Desire Under the Elms* the desire of the son
for his father's wife is consummated and leads to the wife's murder of their child. One result of such compounding of horror is
to force us to consider such acts as monstrous, to force us to
comprehend them as having been brought about by forces outside man. Certainly the evils resulting from lust or greed or other
vices may be grasped as humanly motivated; but there are actions which can have no such motivation, which if they occur
can be accounted for only in terms of man's domination by un-
charted currents and unknown levels of existence. The man who
commits incest and the woman who murders her child are be-
side themselves; they act from sources which do not fall within
the horizons of humanity. Through the horror of such acts we
realize that such people must be torn and twisted by external
currents, that they must be moved by what to them is as alien
and overpowering as their acts seem to us. By the depiction of
what is morally inconceivable, the artist presents his protagonists
as having been wrenched out of their human context and nature
and buffeted by an alien sea in which everything human floats
precariously.

Emphasis in a tragedy upon the most terrible moral transgressions helps the artist to set the protagonists in the context of
what lies beyond man. But this emphasis also serves to bring to

explicit awareness what is peculiarly human; it focuses attention upon what man is. A tragedy written in the terms of incest, or of parricide, or of the murder of children reflects not only the fact that man fails to maintain his standards; it reflects, too, the fact that as a moral agent man has no recourse but to hold to these standards. These humanly impossible transgressions are just those terrible distortions into which man's action falls because he will not yield, cannot forgo the standards which define his humanity. We see in the distortion of such actions the very edge of humanity; and because we see the edge, we see the internal structure of man's nature all the more clearly. We see, that is, man's nature as demands made upon the alien circumstances which he confronts.

In this sense, the movement of the hero in a tragedy is a movement to the limits that define humanity itself. And this bounding of his nature has the significance of a flaw or defect. In Goethe's portrayal of Faust, Faust comes to be defined in terms of man's desire for knowledge; his nature develops to become that of man. Faust becomes a symbol expressing the unavoidable human demand that the world fall within finite human comprehension. In Faust's desire for knowledge we see him as man, the lines defining human nature drawn; and through this lens we see beyond him as well, to what opposes and destroys him. What was Othello's defect? He tells us himself:

> Speak of me as I am; nothing extenuate,
> Nor set down ought in malice; then must you speak
> Of one that loved, not wisely, but too well . . .

Yet is it a defect to love? Certainly not when viewed from within the human horizon, for it is man's nature to focus upon the particular and to become passionately attached to it. But loving person or place or idea too well is to push to the bounds of human eros, to reveal this as it is, as limited, and so as set within what is alien to it and opposes it. It is not, however, to deny that love characterizes man.

In Sophocles' *Oedipus the King* it is Creon who tells Oedipus, as all is lost:

> Crave not mastery in all,
> For the mastery that raised thee was thy bane
> and wrought thy fall.

Mastery of this or that, of course; but to desire mastery of all is to commit the sin of pride. Yet without mastery what is man? The limning of man's nature as a mastering develops from particular occurrences in Oedipus' history which are referred to in the action of the play. Thus we come to know that before Oedipus' birth an oracle foretold that he would kill his father and marry his mother. When Oedipus is born, his father, the King Laius, acts to forestall the predicted event; he has the child's legs bound and orders him to be exposed. Acting within the limits of human competence, what else could he do? Yet Oedipus escapes this death. And Oedipus himself, when he later learns that he is to kill his father and marry his mother, leaves his foster parents in order to avoid this fate. The play, at this level, is a history of human action, competent and effective action, through which Oedipus eventually becomes king of Thebes and solves the riddle of the Sphinx. He becomes, that is, just that paradigm of human competence, who, seeking to deal with the plague threatening his city, is capable of finding the man who is responsible for it. But as Oedipus rises to the task of discovering the man responsible for the plague—that is, himself—he begins to loom as larger than a particular individual engaged upon specific tasks. He emerges as an archetype of *human* action; he discovers not only himself, but man.

We come to see the King as a person whose movements are not accidental but autonomous and necessary. His motivation to mastery emerges as the very nature of man *and* as a movement which cannot be set aside or altered. Oedipus himself suggests the justifiable character of this movement when he compares himself with Apollo, the god of light. It is Oedipus who tells Tiresias, when the seer refers to his crimes:

> Offspring of endless Night, thou has no power
> O'er me or any man who sees the sun.

In this relation to Apollo, Oedipus claims for his nature a legitimacy which cannot be denied. Yet as the outlines of his nature become clear in Oedipus' actions, the limits of human competence are revealed in its results, parricide and incest. As Oedipus moves to the very limits of his nature he is engulfed by the impossible darkness which surrounds it. But at this moment, as he drives the pins of his wife-mother's brooches through his eyeballs, he reaffirms his nature, man's nature, as it condemns him to the darkness engulfing it.

Sophocles presents Oedipus as a man of light, as exacting clarity, as a demander of explicitness. He presents him, that is, not as an ordinary personality but as an archetype. He presents him as required by the legitimacy of his demand to develop to his limits as a man and so to stand open to the alien circumstances which underlie him. In this encounter with what is to be found beyond the horizon of his awareness, he falls into the distorting power of the inscrutable forces of the Titans, for he extends his actions beyond recognizable form. And having come to this encounter, he affirms the development which led him to this bound, this death. The moment of tragedy is the moment when Oedipus, having moved beyond his ordinary personality to stand as a legitimate demander of light, confronts the impossible darkness he would penetrate, and affirms both his need and his right to stand there. Strictly speaking, the hero of a tragedy is this pattern of action; whatever else he may be is an elaboration upon this movement.

Shakespeare's *Hamlet*, too, is the story of an individual who is placed in circumstances that force him to realize to the fullest what his nature is—and to find it lacking. The situation which

forces Hamlet to begin to limn his own nature is, of course, the
revelation (by the ghost) that the murderer of Hamlet's father
is now married to his mother. Hamlet is presented with an incredible situation, one which—if he ever comes to believe it—
can be described only by saying that the course of life has been
wrenched from its normal channel. Yet this circumstance requires
a response, as Hamlet recognizes when he says:

> The time is out of joint: O cursed spite,
> That ever I was born to set it right!

In his first attempts to respond he tries to deal with the cataclysm
as if it were a normal event in ordinary life. He seeks to deal with
it in terms of his acquired personality, the terms which have ac-
crued to him through his education and the building of his character. In consequence, he cannot believe it; he seeks to find out
if it is true. He thinks about it, exercises his ingenuity to find out
more about it, strives to come to some conclusion about it. Evi-
dencing great ingenuity, he stages the play within the play; but
even after this has established the truth that Claudius did kill
his father, Hamlet still cannot act in terms appropriate to this
fact. At the crucial moment calling for violence, he says:

> Now might I do it pat, now he is praying;
> And now I'll do't: and so he goes to heaven . . .
> A villain kills my father; and for that,
> I, his sole son, do this same villain send
> To heaven.

Here the required violence is stopped by thought, and Hamlet
does nothing, can do nothing at the level of action required.
Thus we are brought gradually to see that no matter how Hamlet
exercises the ordinary resources of his personality so that he may
respond to the extraordinary deflection of history which has occurred, his response will be inadequate. The forces which have
set the time out of joint, which have wrenched history from its
course, cannot be set right through any development of the ordinary responses of which Hamlet is capable.

Yet if Hamlet cannot deal with the situation that confronts him, neither can Claudius any longer deal with Hamlet. Claudius' attempts to cope with Hamlet culminate in his banishment to England; but Hamlet miraculously escapes death and returns. How? At this point Hamlet is not to be overcome by the ordinary powers of other individuals. If he has not transcended the bounds of his own personality and so come to act in a truly extraordinary way, he has defined these bounds, come to be aware of his limits, to be able to stand upon these limits, and to some extent to see beyond them. Through this he has made himself safe from the plotting of Claudius, preserved himself for his fate.

This definition of his bounds reveals something which is not merely accidental, not merely contingent, but his humanity itself. As Hamlet plumbs the depths of his personality, pushes toward its boundaries and defines its limits, he limns not his acquired personality but the nature of man, a transcendental nature which stands beyond the reach of Claudius or of any of the accidents of an ordinary human life. Thus, if Hamlet is still powerless before the horrors that confront him, *this* limitation, *this* flaw, is not to be understood as an inability to cope with ordinary circumstance; this flaw must be understood as a characteristic of man, a fundamental inability to deal with the primordial forces that wrench history from its course and control his destiny.

Returning from England, Hamlet comes upon an open grave. We know it to be Ophelia's, but he does not know this. He is thus forced to meditate upon death, and because of his ignorance upon death in general, as a human fate, rather than upon a particular death and its specific circumstances. He sees in the open grave the destruction of Caesar and of all men. At this moment, having moved already to the very edge of his nature, Hamlet begins to see beyond this limit, begins a different kind of encounter with the alien, which up to now he has tried to deal with only in *his* terms. Learning that this is Ophelia's grave, he is pulled into it. He thus re-enacts an age-old myth that man is

led to cross the threshold into the extraordinary realm by means
of love; and he emerges from the grave as having done this, as
a different being, for he says:

> . . . This is I, Hamlet the Dane.
> . . . have I in me something dangerous,
> which let thy wisdom fear,
> Hold off thy hand.

Hamlet has buried in the grave of Ophelia his ordinary personality. He emerges, he feels, as an agent whose acts flow from his
participation in the ground of history. As such an agent he acts
with confidence, as if the terror and horror with which he must
deal could be set right.

For a moment we seem to see Hamlet as a new and kinglike
figure, in the words of Horatio:

> Why, what a king is this!

Yet he is no such king. Indeed, as we are told, this Hamlet never
appears on the level of the action of the story at all. It is Fortin-
bras who observes of the dead Hamlet:

> Let four captains bear Hamlet, like a soldier, to the
> stage; for he was likely, had he been put on, to have
> proved most royally . . .

The Hamlet who wrenched history back upon its course did not
come to exist as a kinglike man; that is, he acted only through
the forces that had set the time out of joint in the first place.

Hamlet died willingly. For pursuing the hope that he could find
within his personality the means for dealing with the terrible
situation confronting him, he was led to break this personality in
the course of this impossible, self-appointed task. His death, in
this sense, is the death of his personality, a sacrifice of this in order
to participate in those forces which could transmute his acts into
the violent and alien movements required by the circumstances
that confronted him. But Hamlet's death is also the death of man
as such, for in his efforts to extend the bounds of his nature he

reveals what man is and so inscribes him. He sets man's limits and so shows both what man's nature is and that man's nature needs to stand in relation to what is alien to and will destroy him. In this sense, Hamlet's death is that of a hero, for it points to the possibility of man's participation in another realm. What might happen in this participation the hero does not know; but that something might happen he does know; and that he must open to, must put himself at the disposal of the forces which could bring this realm to be he knows also—even though if he does this, he dies for it. The long struggle of his development as a hero brings Hamlet to stand as a man, destined to set right the movement of those forces which have wrenched history from its course, in acts which require his participation in the alien ground of history, in acts which move toward the sacrifice of his human nature to demonstrate the continuous significance of what is alien to man.

III. *The Heroic Movement*

The hero is an essential part of a tragedy, yet who is he? How are we to conceive of that Oedipus who willingly moved into exile, of that Hamlet who might have taken the stage? To put the question in this way is to make it difficult, if not impossible, to answer; for this question assumes that the hero has come into being as a great soul, as a personality of noble stature. And, of course, the artist may have suggested this.

Thus the artist may present the hero as standing at the point which connects the realm of human history and a realm beyond this, the point which connects time and the timeless. Many tragedies contain somewhat obscure references to a transcendent realm which the hero seems to represent, and in which the hero may seem to take a place upon his death. In *Oedipus at Colonnus* we find the hero living in the wood of the Furies and refusing to depart from his rest in this sacred land. When he moves, in this drama, toward his death, he seems to die transfigured. And in

Milton's *Samson Agonistes* there is a suggestion that Samson is the representative of God among His enemies. T. S. Eliot in *Murder in the Cathedral* permits Becket to say at the end of Part I:

> I know
> What yet remains to show you of my history
> Will seem to most of you at best futility,
> Senseless self-slaughter of a lunatic,
> Arrogant passion of a fanatic.

Yet the play is affirmative, and the implication of the chorus is that Becket is a saint.

In tragedies such as these there is the suggestion that the futility, the misery and suffering, the destruction of the hero comes about because he represents the oracle or some transcendent order whose patterns are beyond ordinary understanding. That is, a hero who acts in terms of such an order must be destroyed by the patterns of the ordinary world. But even in such affirmative tragedies, the suggestion of the relation of the hero to a transcendent order is not unambiguous. If the suggestion of the chorus in *Murder in the Cathedral* is that Becket is a saint, this will not be found in any single comment but only in the cumulative impact of the whole. This point is well put by Stephen Dedalus' dictum on tragedy in James Joyce's *Portrait of the Artist:*

> Aristotle has not defined pity and terror. I have. Pity is the feeling which arrests the mind in the presence of whatsoever is grave and constant in human sufferings and unites it with the human sufferer. Terror is the feeling which arrests the mind in the presence of whatsoever is grave and constant in human sufferings and unites it with the secret cause.

If, in a tragedy, there is an implication that the hero represents an ultimate order, this order remains inscrutable; it is not really comprehended. Joyce's observation that the cause of tragedy is secret is of the essence, for if the drama were to be given a setting in the transcendent order, if the hero were to be a figure moving clearly at that level, there could be no tragedy. Yet if this setting is unclear, the nobility and stature of the hero remain unclear as well.

The suggestion that the hero is a representative of a higher order evidently emphasizes the significance of the hero; but since it is and must be a veiled suggestion, one must accept such an account as elliptical. The artist may use another device for enhancing our sense of the significance of the hero. Thus he may depict the hero as coming to recognize the fate he approaches. The hero may be shown as developing through his own efforts and powers to this final awareness. When this development culminates, the consciousness of his fate seems to comprise a unity which defines and ennobles the hero. The paradigm of such a figure is Oedipus. Certainly in his case we see how a series of acts directed toward the discovery of the source of the plague comes to be bathed with the significance and horror of his discovery that *he* is this source. We do see this awareness as a culmination and regard Oedipus' achievement as a sign of his great stature.

The unity of the self-knowledge Oedipus achieves ennobles him. Yet a similar moment of awareness cannot be found in most tragedies. Even though Hamlet announces a new identity when he emerges from Ophelia's grave as a hero, the identity is not that attained through self-knowledge—for Hamlet is aware of his predicament almost from the first moments of the play. And Racine's heroine, Phèdre, develops no sense of her position; she is well aware of it as the play opens. Ahab in *Moby Dick* seems to go down quite blindly. Evidently the moment of recognition can serve to emphasize the significance of the hero, but it does not define the hero.

Yet if neither the nobility of an individual having a place in a transcendent order nor the consciousness of fate is the determining property of a hero, how is he to be recognized? How can we as appreciators know, or the artist as creator outline, the hero?

Underlying any suggestions of the hero's noble character, and present even where these do not occur, is a complex movement which carries the chief protagonist willingly (perhaps with growing awareness) to the limits of his distinctively human nature, a movement which leaves him at this limit at the mercy of but open to the alien circumstances that surround him. We may say that the hero of a tragedy is just *this* movement, that by the hero we mean this kind of action. That is, the hero becomes a symbol for these actions, and it becomes clearer that to grasp the nature of the heroic we must examine the way the artist portrays such action.

It is characteristic of heroic action that it leads to destruction and that this is the fate of the hero. But the movement of the hero toward his fate is not presented as an act of his will. On the contrary, it is portrayed as a course of events affording no choice; the hero is depicted as acting from grounds of his nature which are so fundamental as to be beyond changing. Oedipus' drive toward mastery or Phèdre's consuming passion cannot admit of change; they must develop and so seal their fates. But there is also a quality of affirmation in heroic action, something the artist suggests and re-enforces by veiled reference to the hero's nobility or to his great stature.

In tragedy this suggestion is veiled and does not permit a resolution of the paradox of affirming an action that leads to destruction. At least no resolution seems possible at the level of the hero's action and in terms of that context in which he acts. But the paradox may be resolved if the heroic movement is understood as a form of the tragic drama rather than as characterizing an individual. Thus, from the point of view of the artist who writes a tragedy, there is no paradox in the fact that *he* depicts the hero as moving along a course leading to destruction, and that in developing this form, in writing the tragedy, this action is affirmed. Histrionically, within the tragedy, the action of the hero leads inevitably to destruction; but the delineation of the heroic movement by the artist is an affirmation of this movement, and through it there is an affirmation by any appreciator of the drama as well.

When the artist attributes nobility to the hero, when he implies that the hero may be a representative of a transcendent realm, he reflects within the symbolism of the story the significance of his telling it. Such devices may lead to confusion; but they need not if they retain sufficient ambiguity of reference so that they cannot be taken literally. If this is present, the quality of affirmation conveyed cannot be located *within* the drama but adheres to the drama as a developing artwork. When these devices are used in this way, they convey the same significance as does the incorporation of historical materials into a tragedy. Many tragedies have a history, that is, they retell an old story, or repeat a myth, or are an artistic interpretation of events which have occurred in the past. The many versions of Faust's story are an evident instance of this; Shakespeare's *Julius Caesar* is another. But there is also a variety of tragic dramas where different characters, locales, and historical periods obscure common heroic movements: apparently different tragedies may have in common a theme of consuming passion, or a desire for mastery, or a symbolic human weakness. In such cases the repetition of a theme, whether this repetition is explicit or not, becomes significant in the art. Such repetition underlines the fact that the heroic action presented is being affirmed in the art, for the artist, certainly, and the appreciator, most likely, are aware that an ancient theme has been selected for restatement. This kind of repetition is unambiguous, for it locates the affirmation of the destruction of the hero in the artistic enterprise. It makes clear the fact that the heroic movement is a part of the forming movement of the artwork, that dynamic realm in which the artist (and appreciator) may come to live and move and have his aesthetic being.

If this distinction resolves the paradox, it leaves open the further question as to the function of the heroic movement as a forming movement leading to disclosure of content in the artwork.

Although the heroic movement is a relatively abstract form, we may come to see its function by recalling the function of much simpler and more specific forms in art. Underlying this complex pattern of a tragedy are the intrinsic rhythm and stress patterns of the prose or poetry which marshals the words for our review, so that they appear with an uncommon aura and intensity which they could never have without these forms. The use of rhyme, rhythm, and stress, of alliteration, image, and ambiguity in the writing of a tragedy serves to reveal an immediate content of sense material and myth, of memory and imagination. In such revelation this content emerges as held within form, as intuitive and absolute. It is the function of these elementary forms to achieve this disclosure of immediacy. But more complex form not only reveals content; it catches and holds an initially fugitive content. The function of such form, of which tragedy is an example, thus may be thought of as the function of a path—a path which begins with the disclosure of immediate content and is followed to make this content continuously accessible.

This movement along a path into the artwork allows content to emerge through the forming activities of the artist or appreciator, to be articulated by form, to be a given part of an ultimate made up of sustained formed content. In this sense, this movement is a movement from the opaque immediacy of the given toward an articulated content, and a return to immediacy in immanent form. It is a movement of disclosure and reaffirmation of immediacy, a movement forth and back. But more than this, such an evocation of content through the forming movements in tragedy suggests the possibility of a continuing contribution to art by what is given. And it is just here that we may see the birth of tragedy, for what the form of tragedy does is to make the expression of this possibility of continuing contribution by the given an explicit part of the artwork.

There are always non-human, given elements contributing to the development of any artwork. Thus the givenness of sensuous materials or the uncanny figures and episodes in myth occur in

art as yielding to forming of the elementary kinds we have discussed, and so as taking a place within the artwork. In developing the form of tragedy, however, the artist introduces such given
elements by emphasizing ways in which they evoke terror and
horror. He presents the non-human as what opposes man, as
alien. By doing this he places the chief protagonist in a threatened position. The hero must move in response to what is negative, and in his response he inevitably penetrates to the limits of
his nature; for the terrible circumstances which confront him
allow no specific resolution. Through the development of this
movement the artist depicts a confrontation by what is other than
man. In order to express the absoluteness of this confrontation,
the artist shows it as determined by man's bounded nature;
that is, the hero not only cannot transcend his human limits and
avoid destruction, but his fundamental nature requires him to
face destruction. As developed in art, heroic action expresses
both man's need to be related to what is other than he, and his
right to be human in this relation.

The movement which forms a tragedy takes the other which
has been caught momentarily in the elementary forming of the
artwork—as, for example, sense material and myth—and recasts
it to set it apart again as negative, as opposed to man. The tension introduced in this way is resolved by the heroic movement;
but it is resolved only to express the possibility that the yielding
to forming by the other, which has occurred in the case of sense
material and myth, may be continued; that the other can be a
continuing source of the artwork, a contributor to its becoming.
The forming which builds a tragedy destroys the image of man
for the sake of expressing the possibility of the becoming of an
artwork through its source in what is other than man. Yet, since
man participates in an artwork which has such a source—as the
forming of the given through the elementary patterning of words
and rhythms, for example, attests—we may believe still that it is
only man's image which is destroyed and that he is in reality
open. Phèdre's love become all-consuming passion destroys her

individuality but returns in the creation of the drama, her elemental need, her striving, to the flow of that process which is the becoming of the artwork. The hero symbolizes man's participation in a process dominated by what is alien to him; and tragedy as art captures and presents a sense of what it means for man to accept the contribution of what is other than he to support a process of coming into being which is essential to him.

In tragedy, what is other than man is seen as a continuing contributor to the coming into being which is the artwork; the other is understood as supporting the continuing possibility of this becoming. Those modern artists who emphasize misery and suffering in the heroic movement need not miss this insight, whatever their ultimate achievements. It is possible for an artist to miss the tragic insight through emphasis upon misery and suffering; but it is equally possible for an artist to miss this insight through a portrayal of the hero as noble. When the artist presents the hero as unequivocally a representative of a transcendent realm, his destruction loses its tragic quality. And if the artist presents the hero as merely a pathetic specimen of ordinary humanity, living his life and dying within the natural and social world, the sense of tragedy also vanishes.

The reason for an artist's failure to achieve tragedy in these two quite different ways seems the same. In both cases the significance of the heroic movement is located within the drama, that is, in the one case in an account of a noble creature dwelling in a transcendent realm, and in the other case in an account of a pitiable personality in the environmental circumstances that determine him. But neither the portrayal of the hero as glorious nor as pathetic will do. Either portrayal requires a response from us which carries us out of the developing artwork. The point is not that glorious figures and pathetic figures have no place in art; they may have. The point is that such figures, expressive as they are of human meanings and value, cannot stand as the culmination of the heroic movement. That movement begins in a conflict between man and what is alien to him, it develops this opposition, and its significance as an essential form in tragedy depends upon this. To resolve the opposition in the heroic movement by presenting the hero at the last as a figure having predominantly human meaning, whether of pathos or of glory, changes the structure of the drama.

Thus those modern artists who emphasize misery and suffering in the development of the heroic movement fail to achieve tragedy if they allow the sufferings of the hero to deny his expression of his right to be human, his right to stand in opposition to the alien he needs and that he seeks to confront. This right is lost if the hero becomes a pathetic and merely pitiable object; but it is not lost just because the heroic movement is outlined in terms of unrelieved suffering or of the destruction of a soul. Even in *A Farewell to Arms*, after the pathetic death of Catherine, after the hero has told us . . .

> But after I had got them out and shut the door and turned off the light it wasn't any good. It was like saying good-by to a statue. After a while I went out and left the hospital and walked back to the hotel in the rain.

and after such a restatement of the theme of the novel as:

> The world . . . kills the very good and the very gentle and the very brave impartially. If you are none of these you can be sure it will kill you too but there will be no special hurry . . .

. . . we still know that this explicit destruction is not the full story, for the very structure of the novel implies that after the narrator walked back to his hotel in the rain he wrote this novel. By this means he returned his own humanity, his love, and Catherine's love to an artwork in which what is other than man is a source of a coming into being. The use of the first person narration here makes sure that however pitiable the end, we must see this end as the beginning of art.

Depiction of unrelieved suffering need not undermine the

hero's right to stand opposed to the alien so long as the artist
depicts the hero's movement as a path into an artwork. How this
is done and how well it is done is a problem for the artist's inventive genius; but when it is done we see beyond our pity for the
human sufferer, beyond our terror of the alien circumstances
that destroy him, and into the possibility of a continuing coming
into being for which what is other than man is a source.

John E. Smith

THE EXPERIENCE OF THE HOLY
AND THE IDEA OF GOD

The phenomenological approach to any philosophical problem means an approach through the analysis of primary experience and the reflective grasp of what we actually encounter. This view, though positive, implies the negation of certain other views. First, it means that experience is not to be understood either as a way of transforming reality into mere phenomena devoid of power and otherness, or of reducing reality to the data of sense; second, it means that experience is not to be identified with an exclusively private or "mental" content confined to an individual mind; third, it means that ingredient in experience is a real world of things, events, and selves transcending the encounter had by any one individual or any finite collection of individuals. The general assumption behind these negations is that experience is neither a substitute for reality nor a veil that falls between us and what there is, but rather a *reliable medium of disclosure* through which the real world is made manifest and comes to be apprehended by us.

Our task here is to seek an understanding of the experience of the Holy, to mark out distinctive features of the situations in which the presence of the Holy is felt, and then to express the relation of these features to the idea of God as the supremely worshipful being of religion. Rudolf Otto, in his well-known study *The Idea of the Holy*, began with the record of certain experiences or encounters with God which played a special role in the foundation of the Hebraic-Christian religion. The question might be raised, however, whether instead of beginning with the special experiences that are recorded and interpreted in the biblical, especially the Old Testament, literature, it would be more in accord with a phenomenological approach to start from a broader base and consider certain recurrent situations that are to be found universally in experience. In this way we can face more directly the difficult problem of passing from the experience of the Holy to an historically specific idea of God.

Let us approach the Holy by the method of contrast. A distinction to be found in some form in every culture known to us is the distinction between those persons, objects, events, and places that are said to be "Holy" and those that are called "profane." The most distinctive and yet most abstract characteristic of the Holy is that it is *set apart* from what is ordinary in human life, because of the sense that the Holy is powerful, awe-inspiring, dangerous, important, precious, and to be approached only with fitting seriousness and gravity. The Holy stands over against the profane, which is, by contrast, open, manifest, obvious, ordinary, and devoid of any special power to evoke awe and reverence. The profane belongs to the ordinary or customary course of events and harbors no mysterious depth within itself. Whereas the Holy can be approached only with due preparation, profane existence is readily available and is taken for granted without evoking much thought or concern.

The initial contrast that enables us to make the fundamental identification of the Holy is a distinction—not a separation or total disconnection. The Holy is "other than" the profane but not "wholly other." In order to avoid separating the two spheres so that they are severed of all intelligible connections, it is important to notice the dual nature of their relations. On the one hand, the Holy is set apart from the profane, but on the other hand, its disconnection from the profane is not the final fact about its being. Otto tended to emphasize their separation and the "wholly other" character of the Holy because he was trying to present it as an ultimate and irreducible feature of reality, and also to avoid the reduction of the Holy as a religious reality to the sphere of morality. But the Holy must impinge upon and become ingredient in life, including the activities of profane or ordinary existence; it cannot be merely set apart. The Holy is not to break through life or destroy it as if life were of no account, but rather to consecrate and sustain human existence. In addition, therefore, to the awe and reverence expressing our sense that there is a *gulf* between the Holy and our ordinary life, there is also the concern on our part to have communion with the Holy, to partake of its power and thereby elevate profane existence to a new level of importance.

In the course of experience we discover that the situations we encounter divide themselves into two basically different sorts. On the one hand, there are situations such as traveling to work, purchasing a book or an umbrella, meeting friends for luncheon, calling for information about train schedules, and so forth, which reduce to routine, which do not challenge or arrest us in any way, and which we do more or less habitually, regarding them as "normal" or "regular" parts of the business of living. On the other hand, there is another type of situation running through experience, and it calls for a different description. This type of situation has an insistence that arrests us and leads us to reflect on the seriousness and import of life as a whole. Such arresting situations are encountered in their most insistent form at the two boundaries of natural life—birth and death—but they are also to be encountered during the course of life in the form of certain "crucial" times that mark what may be called the "turning points" or times of decision, judgment, and risk in the life both of individuals and nations. In addition to birth and death, there is the time of marriage, the time of attaining adulthood, the time of serious illness and recovery, the time of war and of the concluding peace, the time of choosing a vocation and of launching a career, the time of setting out upon a long journey. Each of these times is marked off from the "ordinary" course of events, and in every case we frequently describe it as a time of "life and death," by which we mean to express our sense both of the power manifest and of its special bearing or import for our life as a whole. We are vaguely aware in such situations of something that is powerful and important, and our most universal response is that of "celebration." Such times, we feel, must not be allowed to sink to the level of ordinary routine; in some way they must be kept apart from all that is usual or taken for granted. On one side, these times set themselves apart from the ordinary because of their own arresting character; on the other side, there is our response or sense that these times must not be allowed to pass away unnoticed or to be reduced to the sphere of the ordinary. Celebration or ceremony is the attempt to preserve and intensify the importance of the crucial junctures of life.

The various forms of celebration which take place on these occasions are evidence both of their arresting character in themselves and of our human capacity to be arrested by them and to acknowledge their power. Everyone, even the most completely rationalistic person who regards himself as committed only to the pursuit of truth and objectivity without ceremony, experiences the seriousness and arresting character of weddings and funerals and the anxiety attaching inevitably to the birth of a new being. The philosophical task posed by such situations is to discover what there is about these events that evokes our response so that we come to identify them as times when the Holy is present. Assuming, as we may, that the cycle of human life contains such special and arresting times as we have indicated, we must attempt to discover wherein their special power resides and ultimately how they are related to the idea of God.

The most basic fact about the special events is their temporal position in life; most of them occur once and do not recur. Birth and death have an obvious "once-for-allness" about them, as do the attainment of manhood and the time of marriage. The latter, at the very least, is *meant* to be the establishment of a permanent relationship. What happens but once in life cannot be placed on the same level of importance with the endlessly repeated and repeatable events of the daily round. The unique temporal position of these events harbors in itself a special capacity, a capacity for calling attention to the being of the self and to life as a *whole*. This feature is, of course, most evident in the two boundary events of life. In birth and death we have to do with absolute beginnings and endings, with the coming into being or the passing away of an individual being who is unique. In both cases it is the total being who comes before us, the person as an indissoluble unit. The focus of attention on the person as such helps to direct attention to the *being* of the person and away from the parts and details of life.

In the case of the crucial events falling between the boundaries of life and death, attention is also directed to the *course* of life viewed in its total quality or worth. Life as such and the purpose of living come into view at points where decision affects the direction and destiny of life in its entire cycle and not just in one aspect or part. We experience awe in the face of the crucial events because we see in them, at one extreme, the possibility of death and the destruction of our hopes or, in less serious situations, the possibility of a failure so basic that the purpose of living may seem to be destroyed. Conversely, the crucial events may prove to be occasions of creative self-realization and the laying of foundations for lasting achievement. A crucial event is said to be a time of "crisis" because it means a judgment upon life in the sense that a time of decision reveals the quality of a life and opens the possibility for success or failure with respect to that life as a whole.

The use of the term "crisis" to describe the crucial event ex-

presses the dual sense of *choice* and of *judgment* appropriate to
such situations. From the standpoint of the agent who contem-
plates marriage, for example, there is the responsibility of choice,
commitment, and the attendant risk that comes with realizing
freedom at a specific point in life; an unwise or ill-considered
choice at this point affects the course and quality of life as a
whole and not only in some part or limited aspect. Choice in a
crisis situation is "momentous" just because of the holistic nature of the consequences. In a trivial situation concerning a part
of life, one can "experiment" and, through a process of trial and
error, gradually arrive at the best method for achieving success
without at the same time involving one's entire being in the process. But trivial situations are very different from the times of
crisis; the latter involve our entire being, and the idea of "ex-
perimenting" with a marriage, for example, as if one could enter
that relationship casually and sporadically, is inappropriate and
severely damages the personal relations that must exist if the
union is to be a success. The notion of experiment and trial is
inappropriate at those points where the being of the person as a
whole is in question.

On the other hand, a crisis situation brings with it more than
the demand for decision on the part of the agent; a crisis brings
us to a juncture where the direction and quality of life are
judged or tested by the nature of the situation itself. The attempt
to lead the quiet or sheltered life is generally the attempt to
avoid becoming involved in situations that call for, i.e., demand
or exact from us, a response that at once reveals the nature of
our persons, our most intimate desires and values, our ultimate
beliefs and commitments. The situation by itself, of course, exercises no "judgment," but its nature forces us to reveal ourselves,
even if we try to avoid meeting the demands it makes upon us.
In this sense the special events in life are literally the "times that
try men's souls." The time of "crisis," as the Greek term from
which the word is derived means, is a time of "judgment."

The crucial times, moreover, reveal the precariousness of our existence and underline the truth that in existence no realization is absolutely guaranteed in advance. Precariousness is seen as affecting not only the details of life but life in its entire being. The crucial times make clear that we confront not only problems *in* life, but a fundamental problem *of* life, namely, the problem of finding the power upon which we depend for our being and our purpose. The arresting character of the special times consists largely in their shocking us and thus forcing us out of the routine established within the framework of ordinary clock time into an awareness of our being and its purpose in a total scheme of things. Concern for details and the partial interests that make up so large a part of ordinary existence gradually deadens our sensitivity not only to our problematic being as selves in a precarious world but also to the ultimate questions about the world itself. Where all is "ordinary," open, manifest, and devoid of either depth or mystery, awe and reverence disappear and are replaced by boredom and indifference. But life has a structure of its own that works against the reduction of everything to the level of the profane. Life has its critical junctures, and these exert power over us, so that however completely the affairs described as the "ordinary business of living" prevent us from attending to what Socrates called the "care of the soul," the crucial times serve to bring us back to this concern and to a grasp of the problematic nature of our individual existence.

Thus far, the experience of the Holy through the crucial junctures of life has been understood entirely in terms of the *temporal* pattern of life, and we have referred exclusively to crucial *times* and *events*. But the whole of life is not exhausted in its temporal features; we are creatures of space as well as of time, and the question naturally arises: are there special or crucial *spaces* that have an arresting function, driving us out of the uniformity and the habitual routine of ordinary life and leading us to respond in awe to the Holy, to become aware of our own being and of the need to find a pattern and a purpose in life as a whole? Since space has its quality in itself and contemporaneously—a holy space does not possess its holy character in virtue of any *summing* of its parts, but immediately and at once—it will not intrude itself upon us as the temporal event does, but rather we shall have first to seek such a space and place ourselves in it in order to experience its power. When we are actually *in* such a space, it will have its own insistence and arresting force, but its effect can take place only when we have opened ourselves by going to the appropriate place. Here space differs from time and crucial events in that the latter descend upon us whether we will or not, whereas we must go to a special space or structure one for ourselves in order to realize its Holiness.

The best-known form of holy space is the sanctuary or physical enclosure clearly marked off from profane space and consecrated as a special place where the Holy is present in the form of the divine to be sought and worshiped. Once again, it is well to consider whether, instead of beginning with a readily acknowledged holy space, we can find features belonging to the spatial environment of life that would help to explain how it can be the mediator of the Holy in and through its own character. We may begin with the distinction evident in experience between the open, public, and neutral space in which the activities of ordinary life take place and shape, and those spaces where it is possible to break through routine and habitual responses in order to find ourselves confronted with the fact of existence and with the question of the purpose of our life as a whole. For example, a stadium filled with people waiting to see a football game is a singularly inappropriate space for discussing a matter of theological concern or for expressing thoughts most intimately expressive of our being and purpose. The space is too completely open and public; it has no arresting power to drive us back to a consideration of what is highest in importance or ultimate in being. On the contrary, such space is entirely extroverted and calls for self-forgetful expressions of enjoyment; the space of the stadium harbors no mystery within itself. Moreover, in such a space we are not elevated in either reverence or awe, and indeed it seems to prevent our withdrawal from the scene and makes it impossible for us to contemplate our being or the ultimate nature of things. For the consideration of what involves our lives as a whole and concerns us most intimately, we need a different kind of space.

We must have a space that is not public in the sense that it is a scene where ordinary business is generally conducted, or where anyone may enter without warning or preparation. We must have a space different from one we normally pass through in the course of going to another place. A space that is able to express the sense of the Holy has three characteristics: first, it is set apart from ordinary or routine experience and thus cannot be universally accessible; second, it must have historic associations which remind us of the experiences of the Holy had by others in the past, as in the biblical example of Moses turning aside to see the burning bush, where a previously open and profane space became a holy space in virtue of the arresting experience associated with it; third, the holy space must be so structured as to direct our thoughts to ourselves and our own being and at the same time away from ourselves to an awareness of the Holy power upon which all existence depends.

The crucial times and the holy spaces may arrest us and bring us to a realization of the problematic character of our existence, of our dependence upon a power not ourselves, and of the need to find an object of supreme devotion. But by themselves these events and spaces do not solve our problem. The most they can do is arrest us and impel us to consider the question and the possibility of a form of Holy Life upon which our existence depends. There is no necessary, logical transition from an experience of the Holy, in encountering the crucial events and places, to the reality of God as understood in a specific, historical tradition such as the Judeo-Christian understanding of God represents. On the other hand, the experience of the Holy belongs to the structure of life and the world; it is not dependent on the assumption of certain traditional religious ideas, as if there were no experiential content in the crucial events themselves but only a "religious interpretation" in the form of a tissue of ideas. There is therefore a clear distinction to be drawn between the idea of God, specifically and historically understood, and the experience of the Holy. On the other hand, the two need not remain unrelated to each other. There is an ultimate connection between the experience of the Holy as a pervasive fact of human life and some idea of God or other, but there is no necessary transition from the experience to an historically specific conception of God. There is a missing link that remains to be supplied. The idea of God as the holy power in existence arises in our consciousness on occasions when we are arrested, taken out of our daily routine, and led to contemplate our being only if we have the belief that the power we sense is one upon which our ultimate destiny depends and is a reality that demands our worship and the devotion of our entire being. The sense of the Holy, with the awe we feel on the occasions when the Holy becomes manifest to us, is connected with the idea of God *only* if we identify that Holy with the controller of destiny and the supremely worshipful being.

It is, however, an error to identify the experience of the Holy, as it is open to any human being, with the apprehension of a definite Being as such, as if the approach to God through the Holy was a form of empirical confirmation of the divine existence so understood. Here there are too many possibilities for interpretation. We may hold that the structure of human life remains universal in character despite the undeniable differences that exist in the staggering variety of cultural forms and practices in religion, art, and morality. But just because there is such a plurality of religious traditions and cultural forms, we are not justified in identifying the experience of the Holy, taken as a phenomenon of universal scope, with the intuition of God as understood from the standpoint of any one religious tradition.

On the other hand, it is an error to suppose, as contemporary non-philosophical theologians do, that because there is no neces-

sary logical transition from the experience of the Holy as a pervasive ingredient in experience to the God who is called "the
God of Abraham, Isaac, and Jacob," there is no logical relation
at all obtaining between the two. Unless we are prepared to
show that, for example, the sort of experience in which Abraham
participated is absolutely discontinuous with human experience
as known to us, there is no ground for denying an intelligible
connection between our contemporary experience of the Holy
and the God of the Judeo-Christian tradition. The way is left
open for *interpreting* the power present in the crucial events and
places encountered in living experience, in terms of the doctrine
of God to be found in that tradition. Insofar as the power encountered in the experience of the Holy is regarded as that upon
which our being, the purpose of our life as a whole, and our
destiny depend, it is legitimate to introduce the idea of the
biblical God at this point. That there is no logical necessity in
the transition from the Holy to the God described in the Bible,
such as might be based on an intuition of the individual Being
of the Judeo-Christian tradition, does not preclude our interpreting the Holy in that sense.

The transition from the Holy to God, while not logically necessary, is nevertheless not without some ground; it is rooted in a
mediating concept which we may call the general *concept* of
God derived from reflective analysis of recurrent experience and
presupposed as part of the meaning of every specific religious
doctrine of God. The topic calls for more extended treatment,
but one essential point can be elucidated. The term "God" need
not be restricted to use as a name (although there are contexts
in which it so functions) but stands as well for a concept that
finds its basis in philosophical reflection on the world and ourselves. This concept embraces the idea of a supremely worshipful reality which gives being to and controls the final destiny of
all finite realities. If the term "God" were merely a name, significant exclusively within the confines of a special religious tradition, there could be no intelligible connection between the ex-

perience of the Holy and God. But because there is a concept of God available for our use, it is possible to connect the concept of God with the experience of the Holy in which we become aware of the dependence of our being on a power that is at once the supremely worshipful being, and that upon which we depend for our final purpose and destiny.

The general concept of God as the object of supreme devotion, derived from reflective analysis of experience, including encounter with the environment and ourselves, mediates between the pervasive experience of the Holy and the specific idea of God existing within an historical religious community. The latter idea is itself dependent on experiences of the Holy, but those experiences are selected, historically specific encounters which have served as the foundation for an identifiable religious community. Thus the Hebraic community finds its unifying and identifying reference point in the historic encounters of the Patriarchs, Moses, and the prophetic figures with the Holy; likewise, the New Testament communities were rooted in the historic encounters of Jesus, Paul, and the disciples with the Holy, this time mediated through an historic personage. The historic encounters with the Holy, however, demanded in each instance an interpreter whose task was to set forth the specifically religious meaning of these encounters. At that point the generic concept of God comes into play. The experiences of the Holy come to be understood as encounters with God through the identification of these experiences as religion, i.e., as encounters with that reality which alone is worthy of absolute devotion. Once the transition from the Holy to God has been made via the generic concept of the supremely worshipful reality, the specific character of the historic encounters supplies the concrete content. For the Judeo-Christian tradition, for example, God is understood as Will and Righteousness, as Love and Mercy, because of the nature of the encounters had by Moses, the prophets, and Jesus with the Holy.

A NOTE ON THE CONTRIBUTORS

JAMES M. EDIE studied at the University of Louvain and the University of Paris, and now teaches philosophy at Northwestern University. He was instrumental in organizing the Society for Existential Philosophy and Phenomenology in this country. He has edited *What Is Phenomenology?* (Pierre Thévenaz's essays) and *An Invitation to Phenomenology*, and was co-editor of the three-volume *Russian Philosophy*.

HUBERT L. DREYFUS was born in Terre Haute, Indiana, in 1929 and received his Ph.D. from Harvard University. He is the translator of Merleau-Ponty's *Sense and Non-Sense* and the author of "The Three Worlds of Merleau-Ponty" and "Wild on Heidegger." He is at present Associate Professor of Philosophy at Massachusetts Institute of Technology.

ZYGMUNT ADAMCZEWSKI was born in Poland in 1921 and has studied at the Universities of Innsbruck, London, Columbia, and Harvard. He is the author of *The Tragic Protest* and is at present Associate Professor of Philosophy at the University of Waterloo.

WILLIAM EARLE was born in Saginaw, Michigan, in 1919 and studied at the Universities of Chicago and Aix-Marseilles. He is the author of *Objectivity* and the translator of Karl Jaspers' *Reason and Existence*. He is at present Professor of Philosophy at Northwestern University.

JOHN J. COMPTON was born in Chicago in 1928 and has studied at Yale University and the Universities of Louvain and Paris. He is the author of "On Understanding Science" and "Hare, Husserl, and Philosophic Discovery." He is at present Associate Professor of Philosophy at Vanderbilt University.

J. N. FINDLAY was born in Pretoria, South Africa, in 1903 and studied at the Universities of Oxford and Graz. He is the author of *Meinong's Theory of Objects and Values; Hegel: A Re-Examination; Values and Intentions;* and *The Discipline of the Cave.* He is at present Visiting Professor of Philosophy at the University of Texas.

THOMAS LANGAN was born in St. Louis in 1929 and studied at St. Louis University and the Institut Catholique de Paris. He is the author of *The Meaning of Heidegger* and *Merleau-Ponty's Critique of Reason.* He is at present chairman of the Department of Philosophy at Indiana University.

WILLIAM J. RICHARDSON, S.J., was born in Brooklyn in 1920 and received his Ph.D. from the University of Louvain. He is the author of *Heidegger: Through Phenomenology to Thought* and is at present Associate Professor of Philosophy at Fordham University.

GERALD E. MYERS was born in Nebraska in 1923 and studied at Brown University. He has edited *Self, Religion and Metaphysics* and is at present chairman of the Department of Philosophy at Long Island University.

FRANK A. TILLMAN was born in St. Louis in 1928. He studied at Columbia University and is the author of numerous articles on analytical philosophy, among them "Explication and Ordinary Language Analysis" and "Phenomenology and Philosophical Analysis." He is at present Associate Professor of Philosophy at Vassar College.

FERNANDO R. MOLINA was born in Miami, Florida, in 1930 and received his Ph.D. from Yale University. He is the author of *Existentialism as Philosophy* and contributed to *An Invitation to Phenomenology.* He is at present Associate Professor of Philosophy at Syracuse University.

FREDERICK J. CROSSON was born in Belmar, New Jersey, in 1926 and studied at the Universities of Notre Dame, Paris, and Louvain. He co-edited and contributed to *The Modeling of Mind* and *Philosophy and Cybernetics.* He is at present Associate Professor of Philosophy at the University of Notre Dame.

JOHN R. SILBER was born in San Antonio, Texas, in 1926 and studied at Yale University and the Universities of Oxford, London, and Bonn. He is the author of numerous studies on ethics and Kantian philosophy and is at present chairman of the Department of Philosophy at the University of Texas.

MAURICE NATANSON was born in New York City in 1924 and studied at the University of Nebraska and the New School for Social Research. He is the author of numerous books, among them *Literature, Philosophy and the*

Social Sciences and *Essays in Phenomenology.* He is at present Professor of Philosophy and Fellow of Cowell College at the University of California, Santa Cruz.

JOHN M. ANDERSON was born in Cedar Rapids, Iowa, in 1914. He studied at the University of California, Berkeley, and the University of Illinois. He is the author of *The Individual and the New World* and has translated Martin Heidegger's *Discourse on Thinking.* He is at present chairman of the Department of Philosophy at The Pennsylvania State University.

JOHN E. SMITH was born in Brooklyn in 1921 and studied at Columbia University and Union Theological Seminary. He is the author of *Reason and God, The Spirit of American Philosophy,* and *Royce's Social Infinite.* He is at present Professor of Philosophy at Yale University.